1

More Than Just a Wetback

By Maria Isabel Arbelaez Muñoz

ISBN 978-1-387-27175-7

This is a memoir. Characters, corporations, institutions, and organizations in this novel derive from real-life experiences. All characters have given their consent to be featured in this story.

Many thanks to Steven Bergano of *Creative Compositions* in Oyster Bay, New York, for his skillful portraiture used on the cover and to Dr. Joan Digby who guided me through many editorial and illustrative refinements, including the cover.

Published in the United States by Lulu.com

I dedicate this book to my mother, Marleny M. Muñoz Murillo, whose courage, compassion, and joy has taught me to embrace the past with remembrance and the future with eager anticipation; and to my son, German Felipe Arbelaez Muñoz, my sweet inspiration, my love.

More Than Just a Wetback

By Maria Isabel Arbelaez Muñoz

Contents

INTRODUCTION

I would like to introduce you to a book I wrote based on my experiences entitled, *More Than Just a Wetback.* The book vividly describes the circumstances of the household I grew up in in Colombia and how my family learned to adapt to adverse living conditions time after time. It's not a tale of tragedy. It is, in fact, an inspirational story about people willing to risk everything to pursue a dream.

Our dream was always to make a better life for ourselves. My siblings and I went on breathtaking adventures that took us far away from our home to many exciting, and sometimes dangerous, places. Regardless of where the journey took us, we learned many invaluable lessons about life, love, hardships, and family.

Eventually, most of us, one way or another, made it to the land in which we could truly follow our dreams: the United States. As you will find out, getting to the United States was a long and difficult journey, overflowing with hardships. The book recounts what it was like traversing through Central America and Mexico, facing danger every step of the way. In the end, every hurdle was well worth the efforts and risks we endured.

This is an immigrant's story, a true account of a family dedicated to each other and faithful that we would somehow beat the odds. Readers love stories that tell the tale of people who win in the end by facing challenges bravely. *More Than Just A Wetback* is precisely that type of book. Since the theme is immigration, I'm sure that you will find the work to be timely and a subject of interest to a broad range of readers.

My name is Maria Isabel Arbelaez Muñoz. I was born in Colombia and have resided in the United States since 1987. I went to Nassau Community College and study surgical technology. Did not graduate. I graduated from Queens College with a major in Anthropology and a minor in Psychology. I have a Master's degree in Gerontology from Hofstra University. I was trained by the well-renowned hypnotist Gerald (Jerry) Kein in Hypnosis at the OMNI Hypnosis Training Center in DeLand, Florida, and I'm a Reiki Master. This is my story, and that of my entire family.

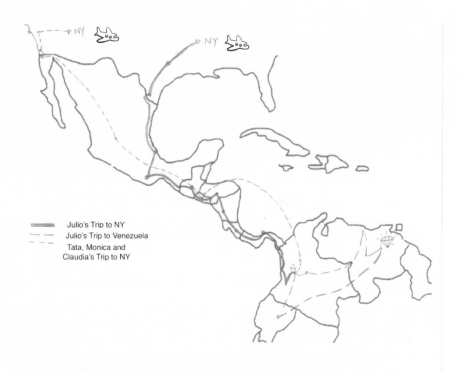

This map demonstrates the travel routes of Julio Cesar and my sisters. The map was drawn by my son German Felipe.

CHAPTER 1: A Growing Family

Once a week my mother mixed an egg with some oil, put it on my dry hair, and left it for an hour. As a result, my hair was blonde, healthy, and beautiful. It was seven-thirty in the morning, and I was getting ready to go to school. Because my hair was long and down to my waist, I could not take care of it myself so Mama had to help me by combing and braiding it every day.

Mama pulled my hair back a little too hard and when I told her that she was hurting me, she pulled even harder. It could be that she was still angry at me because of the argument that took place the day before with my father. During that argument, my father sided with me instead of her. He did not realize that Mama's anger toward me was his fault. Every time he sided with me in an argument, he separated himself more and more from Mama. At the same time, his lack of recognition towards her caused this breakdown in my relationship with Mama.

Papa has always been overly protective of us. He would make sure that no one was hurt physically or emotionally. But, had he ever considered the emotional hurt he unconsciously inflicted on Mama? She was not receiving the love from her husband that she wanted. The only thing Mama knew for sure was that when she awoke in the morning, she had seven little humans to take care of and many things to accomplish no matter how she felt.

Regardless, this time in Mama's eyes, I was a twelve-year-old female who had driven a wedge between a husband and wife, even though I was her daughter. And so, I left the house feeling responsible for Mama and Papa's arguments.

When I got to school, I went straight to the private church, which was used only by nuns and students. Before class began, I took the opportunity to cry and pray in the church. I asked God for forgiveness, hoping that at home the argument would not escalate. As always, I knew that by the time I got home, everything would be back to normal.

The family was growing. My oldest brother, Julio Cesar, was born on November 5, 1955. He is adventurous and likes living life close to the edge. Jesus Fernando, whose nickname is Chiqui, was born on October 18, 1958. He earned that nickname when he was a little kid because Julio Cesar could not say the word *chiquito*, which means "small little thing." Therefore, he shortened the word to Chiqui, and called his brother that. Jesus Fernando is one of the most fearless persons I know. He has a generous heart. My other brother, Jose Carlos Augusto, is nicknamed Carlitos. He was born on December 24, 1959. He is an honest and well-balanced individual who is always responsible and devoted to the family.

Maria del Pilar was born on January 14, 1961. Nicknamed Pilly, she is the fifth child. Without her emotional and financial support, the family would never have been able to make it; or, at least, it would have been more difficult. Maria Claudia Mercedes, La Negra, was born on January 18, 1964. She got that nickname because she is the darkest one of all of us. She has a very happy outlook on life and wishes every day to be a holiday. Maria Luisa Fernanda is the sixth child. She is a kind and humble person who is always willing to help. She was born on September 22, 1962.

The next child did not have a name yet because Mama was pregnant at the time. All of us were born only one year apart. My father resigned from the seminary when he was fourteen years old. He was young and vulnerable, and unfortunately brought home brainwashed beliefs of the seminary.

Mama could not take birth control pills because it was a sin in my father's eyes. Poor Mama, young, uneducated, and in love with Papa did not dare go against his will. So, she was becoming pregnant left and right. Now, I thank him, because that is why all of us have the gift of life.

I was twelve years old with the innocence of an eight-year-old. Cursing, conversations about sex, and listening to adult conversations at home were taboo. Most of the information we had about life was obtained at school or through friends, which in our case were very limited. Pilly, being younger than I, had no friends and always asked me to allow her to be part of my group. To me, she was too young to join us. I would blackmail her into helping me with house chores on the weekends in exchange to hang out with "the grown-ups."

We lived in Popayan, a beautiful colonial city that is well known in Colombia for its magnificent churches. It is also where the proper last names and existing aristocracy are respected. Mama decorated our house in the colonial style, with furniture made of intricately carved wood and brass and bronze decorations. Besides the family, there was a hen, a few baby birds, and a rabbit, all free to roam the house and grounds. While we would have breakfast before school, the baby birds would hop on the table and open their beaks, begging for food. We dunked the bread in hot chocolate and once soft, put it in their beaks. The house was always impeccable with the help of Julia, the maid. She was a heavyset black woman in her fifties. She ruled the house in the old fashion way and did not allowed us to act up. She was tough and loving at the same time.

We also had a street dog named Jalisco. Every time Mama was getting ready to discipline one of us with a belt, Jalisco would hold on tight to the belt with his teeth and stop my mother from swinging it. Jalisco was everybody's dog. The entire neighborhood knew him, and if the old lonely lady from across the street was going to church, which she did every day, Jalisco would follow her. He listened to the entire Mass while lying at her feet. Once the Mass was finished, they walked back to the house together. He knew he would be rewarded with some leftovers just because he was a good Catholic dog.

One day in the late afternoon, Jalisco came back to the house after doing his neighborhood wandering. He went directly under the dining table and laid there, looking at us with a sad expression. He whimpered in pain. We huddled around him, worried that something was wrong. He began to throw up and could not stop. Unable to do anything, we sat on the floor and just stared at him. I was pretty sure it made things more difficult for him, because I could feel in my heart that he perceived our pain towards him.

One of my brothers concluded that somebody who did not agree with his street behavior decided to poison him. Even though friendly to people who loved him, Jalisco could be unfriendly to those he perceived as not being good and honest.

He agonized for three long hours. We took turns petting him, bringing him water, and wrapping blankets around him. That night, he died. We took him to a peaceful place and buried him during the darkest hours. With him, I buried a piece of my childhood. It made me very sad to learn at that early age the lack of compassion that can exist in certain human beings. Jalisco was poisoned because someone did not agree with who he was.

My siblings and I moped down the street, back to our home. The space under the dining table seemed empty and uncomfortable without Jalisco there. Mama was standing in the kitchen, watching us staring at where Jalisco had been alive only hours ago. The vomit was gone. Mama must have cleaned it up while we were burying him. Mama did not say anything to console us. She just left us to our sorrow and returned to her cooking.

We nicknamed my grandfather Pipa. He remarried after the death of my grandmother Maria. His new wife was Matilde, and she was thirty years younger than he. She was only twenty-two years old when she married my grandfather. To me, she was too young and beautiful to be called a grandmother. Also, Matilde was so gentle and humble that you could not help but love her.

They lived in Cali, a city two-and-a-half hours north from Popayan. Every weekend, Pipa and Matilde stopped at our house and slept over before they went to their ranches that were two hours south from Popayan, in the Patia Valley. Whenever they arrived, we rushed to the street to welcome them.

"PIPA! PIPA! PIPA!" we hollered in unison. The chorus grew stronger and stronger as more babies were born into this family. Our hen also became familiar with my grandfather and Matilde. In the morning before they got up, the hen climbed into their bed, and in the space between their bodies, laid an egg.

One day, Mama told us we were having chicken for dinner. She usually went to the market and bought the youngest and fattest hen available. The poor hen for this meal must have gone through a ritual before being cooked. Mama turned its head three times and pulled hard to break the neck. She had done it so many times that she was an expert in chicken killing. A pot of water was placed on the stove, brought to a boil, and the hen was put in for a few minutes. Then it was taken out so the feathers could be removed more easily.

This time, however, Mama put the hen that laid the egg between Pipa and Matilde into the hot water, thinking she was dead. The hen jumped out of the pot screeching in pain, splashing water everywhere and flying around the kitchen. Mama could no longer be called an expert chicken killer.

When Mama said we were having chicken for dinner, we did not think much of the statement until we realized that dinner was going to be our egg-laying hen. We went on strike and did not eat that night. My brother, Julio Cesar, looked at the yellow, skinny lifeless feet and said, "I can't believe Mama is trying to feed us with the family hen!"

The following week, the hen was replaced with a new, younger, and fatter one. We made it very clear to Mama that we did not want to eat this hen for dinner either.

Mama was running out of time to give birth to the new baby and going to the hospital was the last thing on her mind. It was already dark in the early evening and, coincidentally, I heard through a friend of mine many months before that there was a midwife who lived in the neighborhood. I did not tell Mama about her, because we children were not allowed to participate in adult events; but as soon as I realized the urgency of the situation, I ran to my friend's house and asked her to help me find this woman.

We ran to the end of the street and when I got to the woman's front door, I knock hesitantly. An older woman with graying hair opened the door. She looked down at my friend and I, and raised an eyebrow at our sweaty faces.

"My Mama is going to have a baby! But she would not go to the hospital," I said between breaths.

"Wait here, let me grab my equipment," was all she said before disappearing back into the dark house. I looked at my friend and she shrugged. I waited on the doorstep, trying to catch my breath. My heart was beating rapidly. What was taking this woman so long? I was not sure how much longer Mama had. The older woman returned to the door with a bag. She locked the door behind her and then looked at me.

"Bring me to your Mama." I walked fast in the direction of the house with the older woman quick on my heels. My friend said goodbye to me and wished us luck as she broke off from us to return to her family. When we got back to the house, the midwife asked me for some warm water. She rushed into Mama's room where she was waiting in pain.

"Who is this woman?!" Mama hollered from her room. I ran to her side carrying a bucket of warm water, sloshing carelessly all over the place.

"Mama, everything is going to be alright. This is a midwife. She is going to help you with the baby," I said hastily. She looked at me, crossed her arms over her massive stomach, and scowled.

"What did I tell you about getting involved in adult business?" she scolded me. I did not respond. Instead, I left the bucket at the midwife's feet.

"You can leave me alone with your Mama now. Go see your father, and I will let you know when everything is okay." I looked once more to my mother before running out of the room. Papa and I waited patiently in another room. Five minutes passed and we did not hear a sound from my mother, just a loud scream from the baby when she was born. That was when we knew everything was alright. The date was May 29, 1969. I had yet another sibling.

Life made Mama a very strong and stoic woman. She had acquired a lot of experience from having so many babies. This was the eighth one. Being able to find the midwife who helped bring Maria Alejandra into this world gave me a sense of importance and participation to her entrance into this world. What I did not know at this early age was that Mama married Papa when she was fourteen years old, only two years older than I. Everything she knew about being a mother and wife had to be learned on her own. She just followed her maternal instincts and trusted them. And that is what made my mother so strong.

CHAPTER 2: My Mother's Family

My mother, Marleny Muñoz Murillo, was born April 27, 1939 in Tebaida, a small town in the state of Quindio. My grandmother, Camila Murillo Gomez, was born in Armenia, the capital of Quindio, on February 11, 1914. She was five feet two inches and weighed one hundred seventy pounds. Her hair was gray and short and easily kept so as not to slow her down. What made my grandmother beautiful was her adventurous spirit and constant readiness for a social happening.

Camila married Rafael Muñoz Ospina, a very distinguished and tall gentleman six feet, lean, with short brown hair and big dark eyes. He made his living operating a tailor shop and a dry goods store, selling fine and expensive fabrics to make clothing for men in Ceilan, a small town in the state of Quindio. Rafael and Camila had five children. From the oldest to the youngest were: Maria Belisa, Ligia, Marleny Margarita (my mother), Zuri Jhon, and Maria Teresa. Zuri John was the only boy in the family. He died when he was five months old.

My aunt Ligia was seven years old when this tragedy occurred. She was eating a ripe mango, and as it is normal for little kids, Zuri John wanted to have some. Ligia gave the baby the seed of the mango to suck on, with her best intention. Unfortunately, the baby got sick with diarrhea and the doctor could not do anything to stop the dehydration that followed. A couple of days later, Zury John died. Little kids sometimes do not realize the damage they can do with the things they say. Ligia was blamed by one of her sisters for the tragedy. This feeling of guilt led her to have terrible nightmares. She became depressed and wished she were dead. This was a painful tragedy for the entire family, because Zuri John was not only the youngest in the family, but the only male to continue the last name. No matter how hard her father tried to convince her that it was not her fault, the damage was already done. Ligia carries this emotional tragedy today.

Soon after this tragedy, the political violence in the country intensified. On April 9, 1948, there was a confrontation between the liberal and the conservative parties. The trigger of the conflict was the murder of Jorge Eliecer Gaitan. He was a popular leader of the Liberal Party and was running for president. There was destruction of private property, assaults, and murders of people allied with the wrong party. Many people, including Rafael and Camila, were forced to abandon their properties. They decided to take the girls from Ceilan to Armenia, where Camila's parents, Ricardo Murillo Vera and Elisa Gomez Arrubla lived.

Elisa was from a wealthy family in Colombia that came from Manizales and Santa Rosa de Osos. Her sin was to fall in love with Ricardo, a carpenter whose skin was a little too dark for her parents liking. As a result, her parents deemed her an outcast and disinherited her from the family. Ricardo worked twice as hard to achieve his goals and it paid off. He ended up owning an entire block of rental homes in Armenia. The city block was approximately 500 feet long by 500 feet wide, with houses attached to each other and streets on all four sides.

One day, a friend came to him in need of a cosigner for a loan at the bank. His friend did not make the payments on time, and Ricardo suffered the consequences, losing all he worked for. He was able to keep one of the houses in the middle of the block. It was unique because it had eight bedrooms and a hallway that ran from the front street across the block to the back street. In the backyard, Ricardo built a little house which he called "El Castillo," or "the castle." During the week, while the girls were living in Armenia with their grandparents, Camila stayed with her husband in Ceilan. On the weekends, the two would go to Armenia and visit her parents and their children. They slept in the castle.

The castle was ten feet wide by twenty feet long. There were two doors on the long side. One led to the bedroom and the other led to the kitchen. There was also a window on each side of the door with shutters and a flower box. The terracotta roof gave the castle a beautiful character, and it was surrounded by a nice garden and tall trees.

When Camila got pregnant with Maria Teresa, the youngest, Rafael was beginning to feel the symptoms of tuberculosis. He was tired most of the time, had no appetite, and a persistent cough. When they visited during the weekends, the castle, which was nothing more than a garden shed, became a perfect place of isolation from the family, his daughters, and the main house. As the disease progressed, Rafael started experiencing a shortness of breath. He had no energy to do the simplest of things, was coughing up blood, and had a terrible pain in the upper part of his body. He did not want his girls to get sick and so was forced to spend all his time in Ceilan. The reaching out to hug and kiss his daughters was never to happen again.

Rafael knew that his daughters were in safe hands. They were going to private schools in Armenia and had the unconditional love of their grandparents. The disease had significant social repercussions and was considered a stigma. For this reason, Camila and Rafael did not want family and friends to know of his condition. A month passed and the family became concerned when they did not hear from Camila. Ricardo decided to go to Ceilan to check on his daughter. When he got to Tulua, a city where he was supposed to make a transfer, somebody stole his luggage. All of his clothing and money was gone. He was delayed, and arrived in Ceilan around noon, empty-handed and poor. He knocked on the door of Camila's house. The woman who answered sounded very sad, as if something was terribly wrong.

"What do you want?" she asked very heavily, as if the world were resting on her shoulders.

"I need to speak with my daughter," Ricardo replied hastily.

"Wait here." The woman left Ricardo on the doorstep and disappeared into the house. Ricardo waited for what felt like a lifetime. Finally, the door creaked open and his daughter Camila came rushing out into his arms. He embraced her as she cried into his shoulder. They did not speak to each other. It took a minute or so for Ricardo to realize what was going on. He let his daughter cry into his shoulder, calling out Rafael's name. When she calmed down, she began to explain what happened. Ricardo wrapped an arm around his daughter, ignoring the fact that he had been robbed and had no money to get home that evening. He feared that he would have to ask his daughter to pay for a taxi.

"Rafael just died," she began. "A priest was with him, helping him go to the other side." She stuttered on her breath and continued to cry. Ricardo rubbed circles into her upper back. "Shhh, he is in a better place now because he is no longer suffering."

"Papa," she cried. "He was only forty-two years old."

"I know, my daughter. But everything is going to be all right." Camila nodded her head and brought her father into the house. She curled up into a ball on the sofa before telling Ricardo everything. That morning, Rafael had woken up with his feet very swollen. He had called for Camila, and said, "When your feet get swollen like this, it is usually because the place where you are going to be buried is calling for you. It is waiting for you."

"Hush now, you don't need to be talking like that," she replied, brushing off his comment. She wanted to believe that he was speaking with the fever's mind, not his own. But then, when Camila was taking a shower, one of Rafael's employees

26

came storming into the house, screaming for help. At that moment, Camila knew her husband's life had come to an end. She did not know how she was supposed to process the next moments in her life. Ricardo watched his daughter cry after telling him the story. After a while, he said, "Let me help you with the funeral arrangements." She objected, but he reminded her that this was important to do.

"And I want you to pack your things. I am bringing you back to Armenia with me. There is no reason for you to be here, alone." Camila had been saving some money to buy a piece of land in Armenia, with the intention of building a house. However, because of her husband's death, Camila burned *everything*.

Ricardo asked, "Sweetie, are you ready to go?" It was at that moment that she realized she had burned not only his clothing and the mattress, but also the money that was saved to buy the piece of land in Armenia. The money that was hidden in the mattress was gone, and so was the dream she had worked so hard to attain. It meant that economic and emotional independence from her family was gone, and it took Camila only a couple of minutes to burn that beautiful possibility. She continued to cry as her father consoled her.

"Everything is going to be okay," he said quietly and repeatedly into her ear but she knew that he was just saying these words to make her feel better because the truth was that nothing was going to be the same anymore.

My grandfather Rafael died in April 1952. Four months later, his daughter Maria Belisa, married Fabio Gutierrez, whom she had been dating for a year. A year after they married, their first child, Fabito, was born. It was around this time that Ligia, Maria Belisa's younger sister, got pregnant. The family agreed at the beginning that because of the circumstances, the baby should be given up for adoption. When Ligia was ready to give birth, Fabio, her brother-in-law, took her to Sircasia, a small town near Armenia. This way, nobody knew them and they could easily avoid relatives and friends from finding out about her pregnancy. As soon as the baby was born, he was removed from Ligia, as previously agreed upon. She left the town almost immediately, trying not to think about the child she had just birthed and given up so quickly. The baby remained at the house of the family that Ligia gave birth in. They were going to take care of him temporarily.

Ligia left that house with her head held high, but her chin down low. She was feeling alone, not realizing, because of her young age, that many others had gone through the same situation before her. When Ligia walked away from that house and her child, she did not realize she was never going to be free from the face she had created and of the consequences of her actions. Ligia had a way of putting the situation aside with a smile, although the pain was underneath. From that moment, she was going to live a double life.

Fabio started immediately looking for a family who had no children and were interested in adopting the baby. A few days after the search began, Fabio stumbled upon a couple: Camilo Isaza and Gilma. They were unable to conceive a child. They hastily promised to love the baby as their own. My aunt Maria Belisa and her husband Fabio registered the baby with their name before giving him up for adoption. He was baptized Carlos Alberto Gutierrez.

CHAPTER 3: My Father's Family

My father's father, Antonio Arbelaez Giraldo, was born on March 21, 1901 in a little town in Colombia called El Alto de las Coles. It is in Pacora, a place well known in the state of Caldas. His formal education ended at elementary school because of the death of his father when he was twelve. This forced he and his brother, Eduardo, to find jobs to support the entire family.

My grandfather's first job was working in the town plaza. He began every morning at four o'clock, erecting tables and canapés for the local merchants to display their food and other items. At the end of the day, he had to disassemble the tables and canapés, put them away, and repeat this job the next day. The rest of his education was self-taught and he displayed a talent for mathematics. Ironically, he eventually found employment working as a policeman. However, because of his compassion for people, the job only lasted two months. He was fired for turning loose a criminal that he felt sorry for.

His next endeavor was to become a butcher. And so, he went to work learning all there was to know about beef, from judging quality to cutting it properly. He was much more successful at this work than at any of his previous jobs, and he also seemed to enjoy it. He especially felt a level of pride in choosing and telling another butcher exactly what he wanted when he was out shopping with his family. As much as he enjoyed being a butcher, he wanted to find better ways to earn a substantial living. So he chose bootlegging, and sold untaxed alcohol and cigars. This was the beginning of his entrepreneurial life.

My grandmother, Maria Gomez Arbelaez, was born in 1901 in the city of Armenia in Caldas state. It was there that my grandmother grew up and married my grandfather Antonio, when he and his family arrived from Pacora. They had fourteen children, of which only seven survived. Those who did were: Rosalba, Luz Mila, Fabiola, Olga, Jose Arnulfo my father, Manuel, and Merceditas. We got the Arbelaez last name from both my grandmother and grandfather.

My grandmother was of regular height and light skin. She did not laugh much and was careful to not show her true emotions. Maybe her bad temper was more than justified due to the overwhelming responsibility and work she had to endure every day. Maria was a dedicated wife and mother who had to take care not only of her seven children but also of her sister and brother, who had no place to live. She used to smoke more than a rich prisoner to keep her sanity. It was normal for her to go through two packs of cigarettes a day. This habit was shared by her brother and sister who left butts all over the house.

It is impossible to write about my grandmother, whom I never met, without mentioning her sister. She never played an important role in our lives, but was always around like a ghost. Her name was Dolores, which means "pain" in English. Dolores was tall and skinny; in fact, so skinny that if she took her shoes off, we believed she would fall through a groove in the floor. Her eyes were green and she had blonde hair, a big nose, and that constant cigar dangling precariously from her plump lips. What was unique was that she liked to smoke the cigar from the wrong end.

Her nickname was La Mona, "The Blonde." She was lazy, messy, and did not dress well; but she was intelligent, and had an opinion about the divine and human worlds. Dolores enjoyed reading and frequently used to talk about "Quo Vadis." She recited by memory, "La Gran Miseria Humana" (The Great Human Misery) by Gregorio Escorcia Gravini. It went like this:

> *Dime humana calavera*
> *Que se hizo la carne aquella,*
> *Que te dio hermosura bella*

Que se hizo tu cabellera
Cual lirio de primavera...

Tell me human skull
What happened to the flesh
That gave you such beauty
What happened to your hair
Like a flower in spring...

Once she finished this long poem, the cigar went back to her mouth. Dolores rarely helped my grandmother in the kitchen, but was always around snooping for coffee or food. She also had a knack for creating problems over nothing. She was born in San Vicente, in the state of Antioquia, in 1880, and probably was good looking once in her lifetime because she almost got married when she was fifteen. But years passed, and with them, so did her attractiveness. She ended up becoming a full-time maiden. When her parents died, my grandfather invited Dolores to live with him for the rest of her life. She was already fifty-five years old when she arrived in the small town of Andinapolis.

Her arrival was unforgettable. Because there was no radio, newspaper, or television, Dolores's arrival created a big commotion. None of the nieces or nephews had met her before. Since early morning, they were standing outside looking to a point in the distance among the mountains that surrounded this small town. Dolores did not show up until late in the afternoon and she did it in an original way. She was riding a horse, backwards, with her face watching the tail. It was the first time in her life that she had ever ridden a horse, and no matter how hard her neighbors tried to help her rectify her awkward position before she left, she did not do it because she was afraid of falling off. Her arrival was a real surprise, and half of the people in the town were having a break from their daily routine.

My grandmother, who was waiting for her sister patiently, looked out from the balcony of the house and could not believe Dolores strange way of riding the horse. My grandfather, who had a wonderful sense of humor, had to sit down on the stoop of the house, laughing and drying the tears pouring down his cheeks with a handkerchief.

"My oh my, what does she think is on the other side of the horse?" my grandfather said between bursts of laughter. The nieces and nephews were also doubled over with laughter.

"Children, find your aunt a stool so she can get off the horse," my grandmother told the young ones, with a hand over her mouth to stifle the laughs. One of the nephews ran into the house in search of something for his aunt to rest her feet on. He returned moments later with a wooden stool with weak legs. He placed the stool next to the horse and watched as his aunt stumbled, none too gracefully, down. The horse whinnied and flicked his tail, its hairs catching Dolores in the face.

"Welcome home my sister," Antonio greeted her with open arms. The children huddled around too, captivated by this new family member's grand entrance into their small town.

"Please," she said, addressing all the children. "Do not call me Aunt. Just call me Dolores." Again, the children giggled, because they knew all too well that the name Dolores translated, "pain." This name, however, was perfect for her, because she was a hypochondriac who always complained of pain in her liver and a bitter taste in her mouth.

Something that made Dolores proud of her existence was her last name, Gomez Arbelaez. With a last name like that, she was convinced that she came from royalty. She liked to investigate the last names of the people she met, with the hope of finding blue blood relatives. If there was a Gomez or an Arbelaez with dark skin, Dolores used to say that they probably were slaves who inherited the last name from their owner. What made her most proud was to be a cousin of the bishop, Juan

Manuel Gonzalez Arbelaez. The best part was her proven anecdotes of his family to whomever would take the time to listen.

She used to go to bed at the same time as the hens, at six in the afternoon, but only after praying the rosary. For my grandfather, no matter how strange a woman she was, Dolores was a member of the family whom he always treated with love and respect.

In fact, my grandfather's generosity, combined with his good looks and charisma, got him in a lot of trouble with beautiful women on more than one occasion. My uncle, Manuel, remembers a radio program broadcasting music that people could call in and dedicate to a friend or a lover. A dedication happened to come to my grandfather from a woman who was his secret admirer and a so-called friend of my grandmother. The broadcaster announced her name for all to hear. A love song played immediately after. It was called, "Mi destino fue quererte," or *My destiny was to love you*.

Whenever my uncle Manuel retells this story, he chuckles to himself and says, "I will never forget that moment and those minutes when we heard the song. It would go, *Ay que suerte tan negra y Tirana es la mia, al haberte encontrado a mi paso una vez, tan feliz y contenta que sin ti vivia...How black and tyrant is my luck since I found you along the way. How happy and tranquil was my life without you...."*

Manuel reminisced, "What happened between my mother and father, when he came back from Andianapolis the day of the broadcast, I do not know. I just know that I was a witness to the scene when my mother's so-called friend came to visit her. She was beautiful, of that I am sure. She had thick, luscious curls and a voluptuous body. That day when she visited, my mother was furious. When the woman walked towards her to give her a hug, my mother said, 'Get out of my house, you husband stealer.' In utter shock, the woman had no difficulty finding the exit. And they never saw her again. I always thought that my father had a good taste in women."

My grandfather had a terrible addiction to gambling. His behavior when he was caught up in the gambling fever brought terrible suffering and pain to the family. Gambling changed his personality. When he was involved in cock fighting, he screamed, his face became totally red, his voice cracked, and his eyes bulged from their sockets while he was exhorting his roosters to win the battle. It was a frightening scene to behold. He raised fighting roosters at his home and at five in the morning, the roosters crowed waking the whole house from sleep with their kikiriquis. My grandfather took Manuel to many little towns to see cock fights. Manuel was horrified at the sight of these animals fighting to the death; and no matter how my grandfather tried to teach him about the sport, Manuel was never interested.

When Manuel felt obligated to go around the country with his father to various cockfights, he became so upset at the sight and sound of the fighting that he slipped away to avoid it. When he heard the screaming of the fans subside, he returned to be with his father. Finally, when he reached the age of fourteen, Manuel found the courage to stand up to his father and refused to go to any more cock fights.

The behavior of a human being is contradictory by nature, and this behavior was an enigma and a contradiction to the basic convictions of our family's own beliefs. My grandfather happened to be a compassionate man, full of love for life and gentleness toward people and animals. How then can we explain his passion for cock fighting? This sport is barbaric and cruel, and Manuel viewed the participation in it as something he wished to have no part of. He was ashamed.

My grandfather was a man of unlimited energy; a man who, by today's standards, would have been considered a pioneer. He enjoyed each day of his life, and any difficulty only served as an incentive to accomplish his plans: acquiring farms, cultivating areas where no one had gone before, and growing coffee and other agricultural products. While he was starting to experience economic success, my grandmother took ill with cancer. She never went to the doctor, and unfortunately at that time, regular visits to the gynecologist did not exist. When she started experiencing pain caused by uterine cancer, my grandfather dedicated all his time to taking care of her, even abandoning his farms to be at her bedside. He paid the best doctors, best clinics, and treatments that existed in Bogotá to save her from something that has no compassion for anyone: death.

She died on May 21, 1952. Upon my grandmother's death, my grandfather decided to distribute the seven farms he acquired to his children. In 1953, he moved from Armenia to Pereira, a city that was forty-five minutes away. He bought a farm that he called "El Marne" in the region of Combia. This farm was beautiful and filled with coffee plants and trees bearing many fruits. Three homes were situated on this massive plot of land. The greatest luxury of this farm was that it had electricity, which furnished the houses with light. During that time in Colombia, this was a rarity to have on a farm. My grandfather would spend much of his time at El Marne, as it became an escape from reality.

CHAPTER 4: A Family Dividing As Knots Are Tied

My father, Jose Arnulfo Arbelaez Gomez, was born in August 2, 1931 in the city of Armenia. Since his early years, my father displayed a fondness for Catholicism and in 1943, at the age of twelve, he joined the seminary in Cali. When my father returned from the seminary for a visit, dressed in his seminary cloak, everyone in the family was eager for him to bestow upon them blessings. Sometimes while having dinner, my father would lapse into using Latin words and expressions, playing games with the words to describe the family meal. He would make them laugh by saying, "Lunchorum, Lentlerum, Plantainrum!"

A close family friend, Don Alfonso Velasquez, was invited one day for dinner. When the meal was over, Don Alfonso was rewarded with a blessing from my father. He sat with his mouth slightly open, gazing at my father as if he were in a dream.

"This young man is a saint," Don Alfonso whispered, over and over.

My father was humble. He accepted the praise, but wouldn't say anything in response.

After two years at the seminary, my father came home to visit the family once again. He discarded the seminary garb and went to the local cantina where he succeeded in getting drunk. When he staggered home that evening, he announced that he was not going back to the seminary. To add insult to injury, he threw up the massive piece of steak he ate just a little bit earlier.

At the end, the idea of the seminary became just smoke and he returned to the school, El Saleciano. He was not only a good student, but brilliant. His notebooks were clean with beautiful writing. Manuel, his younger brother, remembers to this day a drawing that Papa made of Policarpa Salavarrieta, who was a heroine of the independence of Colombia in the early nineteenth century. The heroine was wrapped in the tricolor flag at the moment she was shot. It brought tears to Manuel's eyes as he reminisced.

When my father finished high school, he made the decision to hire a manager to run the farm he inherited from his mother, and became a manager to his father's farm, El Marne. It was around this time that my father met my mother.

One Sunday, my grandfather took all his children to a restaurant. On his way back home he met an old friend in the street who told him, "There is a very distinguished family who has just arrived from Armenia and are renting one of my houses. Why don't you come over tomorrow? I would like to introduce them to you."

The next day, my grandfather went to meet this new family and took with him his son, Jose Arnulfo. Living in the house was Ricardo, with his wife Elisa, their daughter Camila, Maria Teresa (who was Camila's younger daughter) and a young and beautiful fourteen-year-old. She had long, luscious curls and big brown eyes. Her name was Marleny Margarita. For six months, my father gave my mother serenades every eight days. There was a cantina on the corner of the house where my mother lived and it was there where Papa met the musicians on Saturday afternoons. It gave Papa the opportunity to choose the most romantic songs with the musicians. At eleven at night, when everyone was sleeping, they stood at the foot of her window and sang five songs.

Papa sent flowers to my mother every day, and after six months, he asked her to marry him. They got married on June 7, 1954 in Pereira, capital of the department of Risaralda. My grandmother, Camila, being a widow and living at her parents' home with two girls, did not disagree when my father asked to marry her daughter. This marriage was an opportunity to give my mother's life a new direction and gain economic stability. After the wedding, they went to live at El Marne.

The following year, my grandfather Antonio Arbelaez saw, by coincidence, an old friend he met when he was living in Andinapolis. Her name was Francisca Londoño. She was born in Calarca, state of Quindio, on June 4, 1906. Doña Francisca had been a rural teacher, and one of her biggest accomplishments in life was to teach my Aunt Rosalba how to read. Many teachers failed in this endeavor.

One day, Doña Francisca invited my grandfather to her house. There, he met her daughter, Matilde, who was only twenty-two years old. At my grandfather's house, there was a general rejection at the possibility of him remarrying. When Matilde was introduced to the family, there was a standoffish reception. Her kindness towards her future stepsons, Manuel and Jose Arnulfo, was to no avail. Deep in her heart she knew they were going to be the most difficult ones to win over.

She was a beautiful, young, educated woman with exotic Oriental features. In 1955, my grandfather Antonio lived across the street from La Comunidad de las Adoratrices, and one block away from the cemetery where my grandmother Maria had been buried in Pereira. This was a big house consisting of one floor with a basement where everybody thought there was a ghost.

Days before my grandfather's wedding, he bought the house next door to where he was planning to live with Matilde. A wall was torn down between the old house's living room and a bedroom in the new one. That way, the children were free to come and go as they pleased without feeling that he was abandoning them by marrying this new, younger woman.

Antonio Arbelaez and Matilde Giraldo Londoño were married on May 30, 1955 in the Cathedral La Pobreza de Pereira. Manuel continued with his hostile attitude towards Matilde and spoke to her only when it was absolutely necessary. Meanwhile, the girls were more welcoming. One afternoon when Manuel came back from school, he found himself with a surprise. His closet that was always a big mess was very neat with his clothing folded, his shirts ironed, and everything in his room in the right place. Whereas Manuel demonstrated open hostility, Matilde reacted with noble love and affection. Upon seeing that Matilde only meant to do good, Manuel started valuing her more. It took him a while, but soon he could appreciate how happy she made his father.

Manuel says today, *"If there is an exact word to describe Matilde, it would be **real**. She was a woman who never faked or calculated anything in her involvement with others, especially those who became part of her family. She was spontaneous, and someone you could always trust.*

*And to all these qualities, we should add another word to describe her, which is **tolerant**. She was tolerant with this new family of grown-ups. She came into a family of five women, with two difficult men almost her age. It was very difficult to say that she was a stepmother, because most of the time, words of cruelty and selfishness are associated with it. She became a mother, but she also became a sister and the best of all. If her purpose was to win our hearts, she really did."*

Matilde was born August 18, 1932 in Calarca, Colombia. She was a student graduating with honors. Her mother, Doña Francisca was a dominant woman. In fact, my grandfather had to put his foot down numerous times in the beginning because he was worried that her influence over Matilde would ruin their married life. Fortunately, Doña Francisca became my grandfather's ally and never again made important decisions in her life without consulting my grandfather first.

Doña Francisca was married to Pablo Emilio Giraldo Marin. He was tall, lean, with light eyes, fair skin, and white hair. I remember he would walk around wearing an apron and a hammer in his hand fixing things around the house. Stubborn and with little imagination to provide for the family, he found a wife who was his salvation. He said to himself, "Francisca has a sewing machine, we will never starve."

Doña Francisca was a strong and hardworking woman who never knew the phrase: *to be hungry.*

CHAPTER 5: A Life on The Move

Now that my grandfather Antonio was married, my parents left El Marne and moved back to Pereira to live with my mother's grandparents, Ricardo and Elisa. They were living in a house big enough to accommodate everybody.

When it was time for my mother to give birth to her first son, she started experiencing the normal pain during contractions. Being only fifteen years old, she thought the symptoms were from a mere stomach ache. She took Alka-Seltzer the entire day for the pain, and the following day at eleven in the morning, Julio Cesar was born.

Every night Ricardo approached Julio Cesar's cradle and sang until the child fell asleep. Julio Cesar was Ricardo's favorite great-grandchild. The child was four months old when Ricardo became ill. He felt so sick that he went to bed to wait for death to come to him. He had a high fever and was delirious. However, when everyone thought that he had died, Ricardo got out of bed more alive than ever. They all looked at him in surprise, unable to understand what had just happened.

He said, "I died and I saw God. He has granted me a few more days to live." Three days later, in the morning he asked my mother, "Sweetie, what time is it?"

"It's ten o'clock," she responded. Elisa put a large pot of water filled with medicinal plants on the stove and when the water cool enough, she gave Ricardo a bath. When she finished he said to Elisa, "I would like to have lunch outside in the backyard and I want everyone to be with me."

Elisa knew this was going to be the last meal in Ricardo's life. So, she cooked him his favorite dish, a Colombian stew, *sancocho.* At lunch, no one spoke. It was very difficult for Elisa to accept the fact that the man with whom she shared most of her life would leave forever. Before three in the afternoon, Ricardo asked to be brought in from the backyard and said to everybody, "My time is approaching." He lay down and waited for the inevitable. At three o'clock, Ricardo exhaled his last breath.

With the family getting smaller, my parents decided to move to a smaller house that was shared by Elisa, my mother's mother Camila, her only single daughter left, Maria Teresa, and without a question, Dolores. I was born in this house. My father baptized me as Maria Isabel, after a beautiful song he liked very much, "Muñeca de Loza" (Doll of Earthenware) by Pepe Aguirre. He would sing it in his beautiful, melodic voice:

Maria Isabel...
Divina mujer,
Tus caricias y tus besos
Nunca los podre olvidar.
Oh! Cruel mujer...
Sin Corazon,
Eres muñeca de loza
Con el cuerpo de asserrin.

Maria Isabel...
Divine woman,
Your touch and your kisses
I will never forget.
Oh! Cruel woman...
Without a heart,
You are a doll of earthenware
With the body of sawdust.

A year later, Jesus Fernando was born and two years after, Jose Carlos Augusto. We were all born in Pereira. That year, my grandfather Pipa heard of a region in the state of Cauca called, El Valle del Patia. It was rich in soil and inhabited by people of color. These people were descendants from Africans and obtained their freedom by General Jose Hilario Lopez on May 21, 1851 during the Colonial period. They inherited with these poor lands temperatures that could reach forty degrees centigrade and the last names of their former owners. These names included Mosquera, Valencia, Caicedo, etc. Pipa bought a ranch called El Manzanillo, which was crossed by a road that only had one car passing by every hour. Years later, it became known as the Pan-American Highway. He then moved to Popayan, a city only three hours from the ranch. It was convenient for him since it was here that he brought the cows to be sold for beef and milk. Papa was Pipa's favorite child and that favoritism made him dependent both emotionally and economically. Papa would not make a business deal without consulting his father first. Because of this connection, we moved to Popayan as well.

My father sold the farm he inherited from his mother and bought a cattle ranch forty-five minutes away by horse from my grandfather's. He named it "El Carmen" because of his devotion to the Virgin, La Virgen del Carmen.

It was in Popayan that my sister, Maria del Pilar was born. We did not live in this city for too long because Pipa decided to move to Cali, a larger city with more opportunities for business and social life. We had no choice but to follow him. Fortunately, my mother, by nature, is a person who likes adventure and looks for opportunities to change her life. Therefore, moving from one city to another with five children was never an inconvenience. The constant packing and unpacking did not bother her, neither did the experiences that came with a new place. This is what she always looked forward to.

One morning, when I was a little girl, she woke me up earlier than usual. "Mary," she whispered my nickname persistently. I groaned and rolled over, covering my head with the bedsheet. "Mary, get up. It is time to pack again."

I remember I felt like I was going to cry when I heard those words. I was tired of moving. I did not like the packing and unpacking. I was just starting to make friends and enjoy the new city when my father was ready to pack up and go again.

"Mama," I asked. "Where are we going now?" Mama shrugged, folding some clothing and packing them tightly between the blankets in one of the trunks. "Don't worry. It will be another adventure."

"I am tired of moving. I don't want to leave my friends again!" I whined. My mother had stood up to her full height then, and looked me right in the eyes. "There is no reason for you to complain, Mary. Here is another opportunity to learn, to explore, to get fresh beginnings. You should feel blessed to be living as we do." That had kept me quiet for a while. As we finished packing up our belongings in the house, I pondered over the words of my mother, and how she was the strongest woman I knew. And so, since that day, I took a different approach to the constant moving. It began to instill a sense of adventure in me, which made me relate more to my mother than I imagined it would. I was no longer afraid of new beginnings in life, and I would look forward to the moment when circumstances would force my parents to make another move.

My sister Maria Luisa Fernanda was born on September 22, 1962, and I don't have any recollection of when or how it happened. I just remember my mother having another baby girl. Maria Claudia Mercedes was then born on January 18, 1964, and Julio Cesar and I being the oldest, were chosen to be her godfather and godmother. Mama made me a beautiful violet dress for that special occasion.

There was a big fight between Julio Cesar and I. We were two spoiled brats fighting for who was going to hold the body and who was going to hold the head. I ended up winning. In the family pictures, you can see a happy Maria Isabel winning her first big fight and Julio Cesar with an unhappy smile on his face, holding Maria Claudia Mercedes' little head.

Around the same time, Papa's cattle ranch was providing us with a substantial income, so he decided to open a factory to manufacture men's pants. The brand was labeled "Arlon Industries." One of the treats was when Papa took me across the street from his factory and bought me snacks from a little shop.

Nelson, the manager of the factory, used to come over to the house and talk with my father about business. I was only seven years old at the time, and he was my first experience at being flirtatious. At that early age, I saw him as a very handsome man. One way I would try to draw attention to myself was by "painting" my fingernails. I would rub my bare fingernails against the brick on the inside walls of our house. The red of the brick would stick to my nails, giving the illusion that I was wearing red nail polish. Then, I would walk into the room where my father and Nelson were sitting, and put my hand on the sides of my face, pretending to be a grown woman. Nelson would chuckle and watch me, but he did not flirt back.

Maria Claudia was four months old when my mother's grandmother, Elisa, died in Pereira. It meant not only the end of her life, but also the end of a family house for my grandmother Camila and her youngest daughter Maria Teresa.

This situation forced Camila to go to her daughters for economic support. She started spending some months with her older daughters, Maria Belisa and Ligia, in Bogota. When she felt she was becoming a burden to them, she packed her things and lived with our family in Cali.

We adored her. She was a very energetic person who loved to do things all the time with us. She encouraged activities not only with her grandchildren, but with her nephews and nieces as well. Camila was ready to go wherever there was action, and if there was none, she would make it happen. Maybe

45

it was because of her that my mother inherited such an adventurous spirit.

When Mama was not around, Camila would play the role of mother. She was concerned when we got scratched up, which she tried to hide as best as she could from Papa and Mama. She was well aware of how overprotecting and overbearing Papa could become with us. We were not permitted to ride a bicycle because he was afraid we would get hurt. He even called the doctor to the house when we had normal childhood ailments, like a fever.

Meanwhile, my mother's youngest sister, Maria Teresa, went to live with her uncle, Gerardo, in Pereira. One day, Maria Teresa had a serious argument with her fiancé and decided to go to Bogota to visit her older sister, Maria Belisa.

Maria Belisa and Fabio had put together a small restaurant that allowed them to remain afloat with their five children. Eight days after Maria Teresa had been in Bogota with her sister Maria Belisa, a frequent customer confessed his love to Maria Teresa. His name was Octavio Echeverry. He was leaving that month for the United States. At that time, visas were issued without a question. Octavio was going to the United States in search for better opportunities. The American Embassy had even offered him a green card before he left Colombia.

Fifteen days after he met my Aunt Maria Teresa and fell in love with her, Octavio proposed marriage. For Octavio, knowing who Maria Belisa was as a mother and wife, he knew he could trust that she was the right person for him. They married twenty days later, just before he left for the United States, with a promise that he was going to send for her as soon as he could. Octavio wrote letters, sent money, and telephoned Maria Teresa, but nobody believed that he was going to keep his commitment.

Maria Teresa was three months pregnant when Octavio sent the paperwork for her to be reunited with him in New York. This surprised the whole family. She became the first to make the journey to the United States.

CHAPTER 6: Maria Belisa

Camila, my grandmother, spent most of her time living with us in Cali, and when she felt that her presence began to smell like fish, she went to Bogota to live with her older daughter Belisa. Camila used to repeat this Colombian saying when people over-stayed their visit. It was: "fish and guests smell after three days."

Since her husband's death, Camila had been forced to live with her daughters. The money she saved all her life to buy a house became ashes when she burned the mattress in which her husband slept in while he was dying from tuberculosis. It was in the mattress where she kept the money and realized it was gone when it was too late.

At that time of the year in Bogota, the weather was cool. It rained every day. That is one of the reasons Camila thought that Cali, with warmer weather, was going to sit better for her bones. When Belisa's husband Fabio took her to the bus terminal, he noticed Camila was acting strange. Fabio leaned toward her and asked, "Camila, are you okay?"

Camila, without raising her head, began to move in silence and Fabio realized she was shuffling. He became concerned and decided to cancel the trip to Cali so he took her to the hospital. Camila had a stroke. Belisa realized the seriousness of her health and immediately called my mother. She said, "Marleny, our mother is dying. Come as soon as possible."

Mama went to the bus terminal in Cali with Julio Cesar. They traveled all night, and during the trip, Mama could not stop feeling a strong pain in her soul. It was a restless feeling. "God, grant me the grace to find my mother alive and be able to express to her how much I love her," she kept repeating to herself. Unfortunately, when they arrived at the hospital, it was too late. Camila had already lost consciousness and two hours later, she died.

It was Mama's birthday the day her mother passed, and she said, "What a sad way to celebrate one more year of life." It was April 26, 1966. Camila was only fifty-two years old.

Working in a clothing store, Belisa was able to save enough money to open a small restaurant that was only a block from the house they lived. Belisa got up at five in the morning, left her four boys and the girl asleep, and walked to the restaurant before dawn. Fabio took over during the afternoon and this arrangement allowed her to spend time with the children. Fabito was the oldest, followed by Ruben Dario, and Luis Fernando. Frustrated that she could not have a girl, Belisa told La Virgen del Perpetuo Socorro (The Virgin of the Perpetual Help), "If you give me a girl, I promise to give her your name; I will call her Maria del Socorro." Belisa prayed so much that the Virgin felt sorry for Belisa and gave her a little girl. Then came Jorge, the youngest.

Belisa was at the restaurant clearing the tables after people finished lunch when a woman no older than forty-five came in with two young girls. The older woman said to Belisa, "My name is Nancy and these are my two daughters." The younger one had white skin as if it was porcelain, her long hair reached the beginning of her buttocks, and her eyes were big and blue. Her beauty completely overshadowed her sister who had short dark hair and looked more like a boy. She was so used to having her younger sister get all the attention that she did not care anymore how she looked.

"We have not eaten in two days and we have nowhere to sleep. We left the town we lived in because I got tired of the blows my husband gave me when he came home drunk every day. If you give me work, I promise you will not regret it." Nancy was not asking, she was begging. Belisa went to the kitchen and told the cook, "Prepare three dishes with beans and rice. Oh, and fry some ripe plantain too. I think we got help."

When Fabio came to the restaurant that afternoon, Belisa introduced Nancy and her two daughters to him. Their house had three bedrooms and Belisa put her children in one room and gave Nancy and her daughters the other one. The next day, Belisa said to Nancy, "You and Elsy come with me to the restaurant and Clara Ines you stay here in the house helping me with the children."

Belisa could not believe three angels fell from the sky to make life so much easier for her. To Belisa, Clara Ines was the most special of the three. Many times during the evening, when she came home exhausted after a hard day of work, Clara Ines would be waiting for her with warm water to wash and massage her feet. She worked hard in the house and was a healthy girl, which is why it was a surprise to Belisa when Clara Ines told her she did not feel well. Belisa said compassionately, "Clara Ines, take this money and go to the doctor. I think you are working a little too much."

A week later, Clara Ines was serving dinner to Fabio and Belisa, and as she headed to the kitchen, Belisa said to Fabio, "I don't know why but I have the impression that Clara Ines is pregnant."

"Oh please for God's sake don't start talking nonsense." He got up from the table and said to Belisa, "I'm going out." He did not return until after midnight. Several weeks passed and when he was at home, he avoided any conversation with Belisa. Clara Ines began to gain weight and was no longer the same. She had changed so much and was not as happy and attentive as she had been before. One morning while they were in the restaurant, Belisa said to Nancy, "Go to the house and make sure everything is ok."

That afternoon while Belisa was at the restaurant, she sent Clara Ines a glass of milk and a piece of liver with slices of onion on top. Her son, Ruben Dario, delivered it to the house. Five minutes later, Ruben Dario came back and told his mother that Nancy did not allow him inside. Belisa went immediately to her house to see what was going on. She found Nancy at the laundry sink washing a blanket soaked in blood.

"Where is Clara Ines?" Belisa demanded when she saw the seriousness of the situation. Nancy nervously said, "She is in the bathroom." When Belisa went to the bathroom to see what happened, she could not believe her eyes. There was blood all over the bathroom and Clara Ines was against the wall, standing and very pale, as if she was going to faint.

"Clara Ines, go and lay down. I'm going to call an ambulance." Belisa followed her to the bedroom and on the bed was a newborn child wrapped in rags. Belisa said to her, "How were you able to hide your pregnancy all this time? Who is the father?"

Clara Ines fell on the ground and grabbed Belisa's feet. She cried more from shame than the physical pain of having given birth. The only words that came out of her mouth were, "Forgive me, please forgive me." Belisa did not question her any more.

The ambulance arrived to take Clara Ines to the hospital as Nancy stayed with the newborn child. The child cried all night and Nancy lulled him until he fell asleep. The following morning, Nancy left the house before anyone was up and took the child with her. In the afternoon, she came back without him. That night, Fabio was up after midnight and then went into the bedroom and undressed with the lights off while Belisa pretended to be asleep.

The following morning, Belisa opened the restaurant as usual. She was exhausted after not having slept the entire night. When there was nobody in the restaurant, she went to the kitchen and sat on a stool. She closed her eyes and said to herself, "Last week my life was so predictable." She stood up, came out of the kitchen, and looked around. She said, "I have worked so hard and for what? From now on my life will never be the same." She went home and packed three dresses, two pants, and four pairs of underwear in a suitcase. She left the house without ever looking back. Belisa went to temporarily live at her Aunt Concha's house without the children. Meanwhile, she prepared the necessary papers to obtain a visa to live with her youngest sister Maria Teresa and her husband Octavio in New York.

When the children returned from school, they learned that their mother had packed and left. The older one, Fabito, was ten, Luis Fernando eight, Ruben Dario seven, and Maria del Socorro (La Nena) six. They were confused because they did not know what happened. At the same time, they thought their mother was going to walk through the door at any moment. But Jorge was only four years old, and in his little head, nothing made any sense. He only knew his mother was gone and was not going to kiss him that night before he went to bed. He crouched at the door of the entrance, looking through the crack under the door hoping to see his mother show up. He was hugging the bear he slept with every night, which his mother gave him on his fourth birthday.

There was no human power to make him go to the bedroom and lay down. He wanted to be near the door in case his mother came back. He would not stop crying and screaming, "Mami, where are you? Mami please come home!

After many hours tired of crying, Jorge fell asleep. He repeated this every night. He would sit at the foot door, waiting for his mother. When Fabio realized Belisa was not going to return, he took the children to his mother's house. He could not take care of the kids and work in the restaurant at the same time. Fabito, the oldest, did not have to think for a minute where to go. My mother's sister Ligia adored him and he knew he would be safe with her.

Ligia was married to Alberto Bode. He was born in Chile and was very much involved in horse racing. He was a famous horse trainer in the country, owned the best racing horses, and he and Ligia were the owners of the only existing betting parlors in Ibague and Girardot. Ligia and Alberto had four boys: Alberto, Miguel Angel, Gerald and William Enrique. Maria Clara was the oldest and the only daughter in the family.

Belisa did not have difficulty getting a visa, so she moved to United States. Once there, she worked hard to send money back to her children. That was her best and only way to compensate for the terrible feeling of guilt she had for having abandoned them. She was not aware of the headache and loneliness she had just inflicted upon her own children.

She paid a great expense-perhaps the greatest-when she left behind her five children. Without knowing, she was destined to change the lives of many people, including the life of her youngest son Jorge and her only daughter La Nena. Belisa remarried in The United States to Ramiro, whose brother was married to Belisa's younger sister, Maria Teresa. They had a son, Kevin, and by the time Jorge and La Nena came to live in New York, she was able to offer them a stable home.

Belisa is responsible for changing the life, not of one, but of many generations to come in the Arbelaez family.

CHAPTER 7: Summers and Milk Baths

The high point of every year was when school ended and we packed up to go to the ranch. The three months we spent every summer at the ranch were filled with experiences which, if I close my eyes now, I can imagine as if I am there again. The smells, sights, and sounds come flooding back to me as if it was just yesterday. It was at the ranch that I learned appreciation for nature and the simple things in life, such as waking up at four in the morning and going to the milking stalls to collect the breakfast milk.

Before we left the house, Mama prepared a cup with two spoons of sugar and a few drops of whatever liquor she had available. The cups were held by one of the farm workers beneath the utter of a cow, and the rich warm milk would mix with the sugar and liquor, foaming on the surface. This became the best drink I would have in my adolescent life.

The farm was in the foothills and offered a picturesque view that stretched as far as the human eye could see. From the main road, approximately a quarter of a mile away, there was a brook. You would have to cross that brook to reach the dirt road leading to the house. Most of the time, the majordomo brought the horses all saddled to wait for us at the property's edge. We would then climb onto the horses that carried us across the brook and up the road to the house.

On both sides of the road were luscious green pastures filled with Holstein cows, those being black and white, and Cebu cows, the color of a stormy grey sky. We feared the Cebu because they were often dangerous and aggressive. I will never forget one afternoon when my brother Julio Cesar was playing in the pasture when he wasn't supposed to. We had a German Shepherd that liked to bark at the cows, thus infuriating them. We were standing outside the house, watching the Cebu cows ready to attack Julio Cesar. Since the dog would not stop barking, my father took out his revolver and killed the dog. He had no choice. It was my brother or the dog. Papa was in so much pain after this incident. He loved the dog, and what was most painful was having his children crying and screaming around him because he killed it in front of their eyes.

Next to the main house on the right was a large corral. This was where the cows remained when they were herded in from the pasture in the late afternoons. The calves were separated in a different corral because this was a dairy farm and they did not want the calves nursing at their mothers and consuming the milk we were supposed to collect.

This was the perfect time for us to play with the calves. In the morning after the cows were milked, the calves joined them, with us participating in the spectacle of the calves being reunited with their mothers after a whole night of loneliness. This was one of my favorite things to witness during the summers.

One of the family traditions at the farm was that whoever was the baby at the time was given a milk bath. The baby was placed underneath the cow's udder and my mother proceeded to bathe him or her in its milk. Mama believed that bathing in a milk bath would make us have beautiful skin. Since all of us were very close in age, there always seemed to be one of us who was the new baby for the season.

One year, Maria Luisa and Maria Claudia fought to be the baby at the time. It had been a beautifully sunny hot day. They were wearing identical shorts and tank tops when Mama announced it was time to bathe the baby in the milk. Maria Claudia jumped on the balls of her feet, raising her hands in the air, begging to be chosen.

"Mama, I'm the baby!" she cried out. Maria Luisa looked at Maria Claudia, raised her eyebrows, and then looked at Mama. She crossed her arms over her chest and said, "It's not fair, she was the baby last year!"

"No, I wasn't!" Maria Claudia screamed back at her. Mama just stood there watching them, trying to suppress laughter from spilling out of her pursed lips.

"Maria Luisa and Maria Claudia, *enough.*" They immediately closed their mouths and returned their hands to themselves. They looked up at Mama, the sun creating a slight halo around her head, making her hair glow around the edges. She looked like an angel, and at that moment, they gave up their fight. "The sun has already risen, and it is too late to bathe the baby in milk. We will do it another time." That was the first year that no one was bathed in the milk of the cows.

The main house had a center hall that went from the front of the house all the way to the back, ending in the kitchen. The workers' living area was on the left of the hallway and we lived on the right. In the kitchen, the majordomo's wife prepared the meals with my mother. Usually, the wife was supposed to oversee cooking; but my mother, knowing how many mouths there were to feed, never took advantage of the woman.

The kitchen had a large wooden stove which constantly had to be restocked with firewood. The concentration of heat was unbearable, especially since it was also scorching hot during the summers. Some days, it would reach over forty degrees centigrade. We had no electricity, and at night the house was illuminated by oil lamps and candles. The water was stored in large clay cisterns that helped it to remain cool for many hours. It was transported from a well that was built outside the house and had to be pumped by hand into buckets.

It was magic to wake up in the morning with the sounds of chickens running around, clucking for food. The majordomo's wife would walk back and forth, throwing corn to the hens. Some of them would follow her with their chicks as she called out, "Cutu, cutucutu cutu, cutucutu cutu!" We always had fresh eggs for breakfast, and the cheese and butter were made at the farm.

To do the laundry, Mama went to the river at the bottom of the hill, half a mile walking distance from the house. We swam in the river and played while she did the laundry. She would never ask us for help. Instead, she would smile and hum to herself as we giggled and splashed and swam around her. She would scrub away at the clothes, making sure they were as pristine white as possible.

One day when Mama was doing the laundry, she noticed a big snake slithering nearby. Without making much noise, she said, "Children, get out of the water immediately. Be quiet, and run back to the farm."

We looked at each other, confused as to why we had to end our playtime so abruptly. But Mama's white, stern face made us silent. We feared to object to her word. And so, we snuck out of the water and raced up the hill to the farm. We did not look back, nor did we know why Mama told us to leave in the first place. She did not return to the house until almost an hour later.

"Mama," I asked her when she entered the house with the basket of laundry under her arm. "Why did you make us leave?"

"There was a snake, Maria Isabel. I did not want it to hurt you." She offered me a warm smile before walking past me towards her bedroom. I followed in her footsteps.

"But it could have hurt you!" I called out at her back.

Mama did not respond until she was in her room. She placed the basket on the bed and turned to look at me. "Maria Isabel, my child," she said as she put her arms on my shoulders. I looked up into her soulful eyes and waited for the words to come from her lips. When they did, they sounded like the words of an angel. "Snakes do not attack pregnant women, ever since the Virgin stepped on one when she was pregnant and killed it

57

with her mere force." From that moment forward, I always believed Mama's words.

Sunday was the day we got to ride the horses to the village and church. It was only a thirty-minute ride by horseback, but it was one of my favorite things to do. Papa would always lead the way. The children who were old enough rode by themselves. The younger ones would partner up, two to a horse. We would ride in single file, with Mama bringing up the rear with the youngest child nestled in her lap.

As we entered the village, to the right of the main road, lived an old black woman in her eighties. She was Papa's favorite person in the village. It was a tradition to stop at her hut whenever entering the village. My father would dismount his horse and salute the old lady in a majestic way. He would raise his arms towards the sky and say, "The Queen of Cherries nobody loves!" She would giggle and extend her arms. My father would embrace her, and before leaving, he would gift her cigarettes and some money to spend during the week.

Most of the people in the village, on Sundays or weekly evenings, would sit outside to get a break from the heat. This was also the best opportunity to socialize with those passing by on the road. As we proceeded further into the village, we came upon houses better described as shacks, with grass roofs, dirt floors, and walls made from cow dung and painted a dirty white.

The villagers sat outside their shacks, quietly greeting the family, and at the same time, were curious from year to year to see the newest born in the family. They had a superstition they should not look upon the eyes of a newborn, for they believed that such a stare was very strong and would kill the baby. Being descendants of the Africans, the people in the village had learned from their ancestors to be superstitious. To ward off this evil eye, they slapped the baby and made the mark of a cross with saliva on the stomach and forehead.

Further in the village, as we came closer to the church, a large plaza appeared, and in the middle was a massive tree. It was so grandiose that it cast a shadow over the entire plaza. Everyone knew our family and we exchanged all our greetings by the time we reached this plaza. This familiarity always left me with a warm feeling. The friendly faces would continue into the church and during the Mass.

After Mass, Papa took us to the general store, across the square from the church. Papa and Mama did some food shopping for the week while we would be treated to candies and whatever our little hearts desired. All over the place were large sacks fashioned from burlap, full of rice, beans, and potatoes. Each one of us would pick a sack and sit on it to enjoy our treats.

Once the shopping was done, we walked outside to the hitching post, remounted our horses, and proceeded back to the farm. Unfortunately, Papa never allowed us to ride a horse any faster than a walk, and the only time we had the opportunity to gallop, was when we were out of his sight. We did not dare complain when we fell off the horse, especially those times that we would get hurt badly. That was a subject we discussed only amongst ourselves in private. Even Mama was not privy to our conversations. Julio Cesar was by far the best rider and the only one of us with his own horses. "La Castaña," which in Spanish means "brown," and "El Moro" were both names chosen to describe his horses, based on their coloring. He never fell off his horses.

Like all good things in life, summer vacation always came to an end, and we had to pack up our things and memories to head back to Cali.

In 1962, the political conditions were not going well and President Guillermo Leon Valencia ordered the devaluation of the peso. What was once my father's good fortune was starting

59

to crumble like the shacks that many of the summer villagers lived in. Papa lost the factory and was forced to declare bankruptcy.

I learned that when things go wrong, they *really* go wrong. During the process of closing down the factory, Papa moved some machinery and finished goods to a rented warehouse for safe keeping, intending to at least try to recoup some of his fortune. That same night, the warehouse was broken into and everything was stolen. Papa continued to run the ranch, and the family still appeared to live quite well.

CHAPTER 8: The Christmas Bull Fight

During Christmas, Mama made a large Nativity scene with statues, models of towns, rivers, and whatever creative addition anyone had in mind. Starting on the sixteenth of December, we prayed the novena every night until Christmas Eve. Every night, kids from the neighborhood came to the house and after the prayers and Christmas songs, Papa handed out candies and snacks to everyone.

Praying every night was boring to us, but the incentive of candy always helped us get through it. When Christmas was spent in Cali at Pipa's house, the family gathering consisted of my Uncle Manuel and my father's sisters: Luz Mila with her seven children, Olga with five, Mama with seven, Fabiola, Rosalba, Merceditas and, of course, painful Dolores.

Most of the time, we were easily thirty people. Pipa's house was big and beautiful on the corner of a large park, right next to the church. This proximity was important to such a Catholic family, especially during Christmas. Traditionally, the family would arrive fifteen days before Christmas Eve, and would leave the second week in January. My aunt Merceditas, who had been at the convent for five years, and finally decided to return to earthly life, would play the guitar and sang Christmas songs with us.

Christmas Eve, Mama and Matilde would spend many hours in the kitchen preparing a feast. During this time of year, the house was always filled with all kinds of delicious, mouth-savoring scents. At eleven that night, everyone left the house to go to church while Mama and Matilde stayed back to place the gifts under the tree. After listening to the Mass, it would be midnight, and we would return to the house to eat and exchange gifts. At thirteen, I still did not know that Santa Claus wasn't real. My parents always made sure their kids would have Santa Claus fantasies for as long as possible. However, on my thirteenth Christmas, before going to Mass, I went to Pipa's bedroom and discovered, to my surprise, all the gifts wrapped and waiting to be placed under the tree. I was disillusioned, but at the same time, I felt that now I had become a part of the adults' lives and the secret was kept for the smallest ones.

Another tradition we had during Christmas was to see bull fighting. Pipa had to purchase tickets six months in advance for the annual January event. Cali is recognized as one of the best plazas in the country, with the finest bulls and toreros coming from all over the world. It was always exciting to hear the trumpets introducing of the performers against a backdrop of fans dressed in fancy clothes. The matadors were always the most distinguished with their costly "suits of lights," custom-made and embroidered with golden threads. They wore plain white shirts, short black jackets, pants that reached mid-calf, and knee-high stockings that were pink. The shoes were flat leather slippers secured with intricate bows.

No matter how many times I saw a bull fight, I could not understand how we were supposed to enjoy watching a beautiful and brave bull being killed. The bull is usually at least four years old and weighs from 1100-1600 pounds or more. What impressed me the most was when the picador entered the arena on horseback with a long pole and sharpened point on the end.

"What is he going to do?" I remember asking Papa one time. His eyes were fixated on the scene. When he spoke to me, it sounded as if he were in a trance.

"They are going to weaken the bull. It will also make him angry."

"But why?" I asked, confused as to why they would make the animal suffer in the first place.

"This is a show, Maria Isabelita" he responded. This time, he looked at me and saw the worried expression on my face. He cupped my cheeks with his thick, roughened fingers and smiled. "Do not worry my beautiful doll, the bull will die quickly once the show is over."

"I don't want to see him hurt!" My lower lip trembled. I was barely holding back the tears from streaking down my cheeks.

"Then you do not have to watch. I will tell you when it is over." He turned back to the arena and watched with grave intent. I had bitten down on my lip and turned back towards the disgruntled bull. I vowed to myself that I would watch from start to finish. It might have been a show, but I felt that I owed it to the bull.

The picador would stab the mounds of muscle on the bull's neck in order to make the animal angry. The bull would bleed which weakened it and made it less dangerous. Then, with sharp sticks, the banderilleros planted the banderillas into the bull's shoulders. At the end, the matador used a small red cape and a sword to attract the bull in a series of passes. At the end of the faena, the matador stabbed the bull between the shoulder blades and through the heart.

When I saw the sword entering the chest of the bull, I gasped. The tears spilled from the corners of my eyes, but I did not cry out. The people surrounding me roared with excitement, beating the air with their fists and shouting at the death of the bull. I covered my mouth with my hands, afraid that I was going to scream or say something that was not appropriate for the end of the show. The bull toppled over, and the people went even crazier.

That was the first bull fight I watched from start to finish, and I was petrified. I made sure to watch every bull fight after, always hoping for the survival of the bull. Unfortunately, my prayers never came true. Sometimes, if the bull had put on a good performance, people would ask the organizers of the event to spare his life. In other cases, if the one with a good performance was the torero, he would get one ear, two ears, or two ears and a tail. The prize changed depending on the event.

This event generally brought our Christmas holiday to a close. After, the families would return to their respective homes. We had become to Matilde not only her children, but also her grandchildren. Nothing would have made Matilde happier than conceiving her own children.

Some say that Pipa suffered of swollen glands when he was old, and that was why he was sterile. Other people say that he underwent prostate surgery. The truth is that nobody ever saw him in a hospital. And Matilde never grew with a baby bump. We would forever be the children she could never have, and she cherished each moment we spent together as if it was the last.

CHAPTER 9: The Burdens Mama Carried

I was fourteen when my father decided to move the family to Puerto Rico in search of better economic opportunities. We immediately started the paperwork necessary to obtain visas and Mama sold most of our furniture. Papa was supposed to go to Puerto Rico without us for at least three months to get established. The thought of leaving the family for that length of time forced him to change his mind. So, he decided not to go.

After Papa sold the farm and lost his business, we started to experience difficult financial times. Mama and Papa were left with eight children, no furniture, and no place to live. My Aunt Ligia offered my mother the house she had in Girardot and jobs at the betting parlor for my father and brothers. We, the children, were not really affected by the situation, because Ligia and Alberto had money. This allowed us to enjoy private schools, a country club, and all the opportunities that money could furnish. The transition from rich to poor had not hit the older children yet, and my disregard for reality was evident when it came to schooling. I had attended private schools all my life in every city we lived in. At that time, it was possible because my parents could afford it. But now, under the present circumstances, I was forced to adapt to a new lifestyle. What I did not know yet was that I still had a lot to learn about life. For me to go to a private school in Girardot, I was supposed to show the papers from previous years at other schools.

Papa, who was always gentle and respectful to us while growing up, said to me, "Love, why don't you try public school for a couple of days? To go to Popayan to get the school paperwork is going to take me a couple of days anyway.

I had put my foot down, being a true spoiled brat. I retorted, "I will go to a private school or I won't go at all!"

Papa sighed and rubbed his temples in resignation. "I promise you that upon my return I will register you at La Presentacion."

"No! You must register me *now*."

Such an unreasonable comment forced Papa to give me my first spanking, administered with a belt. As he expressed the need to discipline me, I could feel his gentleness. I could not imagine just how difficult this was for him. "My love, your behavior is wrong and I have the obligation to discipline you," he told me as he undid his belt.

At that time, my hands were sweating and I was turning ghost white. What had I done? He could see just how uncomfortable and scared I was. For a moment, I thought he would tell me to leave and never speak like that again.

But once the belt was loose in his hand, he whispered, "Please put yourself in a position that you won't feel as hurt." I had almost wanted to laugh at his comment. He was such a gentleman, even at the moment that he was about to deliver me the punishment I deserved. And so, I took his advice. The strap marks fell on the lower part of my legs, which was less painful than in other areas. When my father finished, he returned the belt to his waist and said, "I am leaving immediately to Popayan to get your school papers. I will be back as soon as possible."

I had run into his arms, thanking him for getting the papers so that I could go to a private school. I had almost forgotten that the same arms that delivered my punishment were now embracing me.

The following day, I wore a short skirt on purpose. If anyone asked me what had happened to my legs, very proudly I would say, "My father hit me with a belt." People would look at me in surprise, especially at the fact that I was so proud to share this information. It did not phase me, because I knew that I would be going to private school anyway.

Mama was the one with the heaviest burden on her shoulders. Now her responsibilities were limited not only to us, but also to my Aunt Ligia, her husband Alberto, and their five children. They would come from Bogotá to Girardot during the weekends and vacations. Maria Belisas's children also came from time to time. Many times, we were easily twenty-five to thirty people in the house.

Mama never complained about the extra work. She not only welcomed everybody, but also showered them with the same love, care, and affection she had for her children. Mama got up every day at four in the morning so breakfast would be ready, and made sure the children bathed and dressed on time to go to school. After we left, she went to the public market, by a long bus ride, sometimes three times a day, to buy fresh food to prepare a special brunch for Ligia and Alberto, who had to leave for the betting parlor by eleven in the morning. Once the older children left for school, Mama cleaned the house, did the laundry by hand, and ironed our clothing. At the time, dry cleaning was unthinkable.

The weather in Girardot was hot and would easily reach forty degrees centigrade, which usually doubled the effort put into every action. By noon, when we came back from school, lunch was ready and Mama would move on to preparing the dinner. Ligia and Alberto would not return from work until one or two in the morning. After feeding the family, Mama had to return to the kitchen to prepare their late dinner. Their meal was expected to be more elaborate and time consuming to prepare than that which our family ate. It meant fewer hours of sleep for Mama, without a spare moment for rest or even to sit down. She was doing all the work, and by four in the morning, she had to be up again to repeat.

Mama never complained or demanded help from any of us. She believed the children's responsibility was to go to school and receive an education. I wondered where she got the strength that permitted her to take care of such a big family under such impossible conditions. When I think about dedication and love to a family, I understand the meaning of the word by just looking at my mother.

The economic support that my Aunt Ligia gave us was immeasurable. Thanks to her we lived in a beautiful house and food was always on the table. My mother felt she had to compensate for her sister's kindness, and working hard was Mama's best way to say thank you. Because of the concerns and responsibilities she had with taking care of eight children, she felt she would create an adverse reaction in the family if she told them she was pregnant with a ninth child. And so, none of us, including Papa, were aware of it, until Mama was six months pregnant. She was so skinny, because of her hard work, that her pregnancy was not noticeable.

Pregnancy is supposed to be a beautiful experience in a woman's life. But unfortunately, Mama did not get support or consideration from anyone, including my father. So rarely were Mama's pregnancies glorified.

Papa became used to Mama taking care of us and creating solutions to any problems we were confronted with. He then adopted a passive and comfortable position. Their marriage started deteriorating as a result of my father's lack of responsibility. He was incapable of providing economic or emotional support to my mother, and his drinking intensified his lack of interest in making a change.

Since he was very young, Papa got used to having a strong person supporting his every move. His father made all the important decisions for him, so Papa would go along with them. Now that his father was no longer around, Papa did not know how to make his own life decisions. And so, Mama became the new strong figure in his life.

Papa was a romantic who liked to write poems and love letters to Mama. Before we moved to Girardot, he used to serenade Mama every weekend. Sometimes, I would get up in the middle of the night to listen to the serenades. On most occasions, there were three men playing the guitar and singing my mother's requests for two hours.

Papa adored my mother. He was a gentleman not only to her but also to his children. To Mama, he was the Romeo any woman dreamed to have in her life. Unfortunately, this Romeo forgot that when a woman has eight children and no money to support them, someone must face reality. Mama had no time to be a wife and gave herself up to be a full-time mother. The ninth pregnancy, and birth of Monica Patricia, was perhaps the most difficult one for Mama. It is very clear in my mind to this day. And every single detail of the night before she left for the hospital is engrained in my memory.

The house was big, located on a second floor with high ceilings and grandiose balconies. On the first floor was an open patio with a laundry sink. To access it, Mama had to use the stairs next to the kitchen. She made this trip countless times a day. The laundry had to be done by hand and she wanted to take advantage of any spare moment to not fall behind in her daily chores.

So, the night before Monica Patricia was born, Mama made sure all the house chores were complete to avoid any chaos in her absence. She was up until three in the morning washing and ironing clothing. After serving breakfast and sending us to school, she took a taxi with my father to the clinic where the baby was going to be born.

At the clinic, they told Mama she was not yet ready. Knowing that she could use a few more hours doing something at the house, Mama went back, did some more chores, and returned to the clinic at ten in the morning. As soon as she got there, Monica Patricia was born. It was May 4, 1971. The doctor was astounded at my mother's ability to birth the child after doing so much work. He said, "I wish I could have a thousand patients like you." All of Mama's babies were born at home with the help of a midwife. Monica Patricia was the first, and the last, to be born in a hospital.

Ligia and Alberto came immediately from Bogotá when they found out about Monica's birth. They became Monica Patricia's godparents. By that time, I was fourteen years old and had been so spoiled that I could not see what was happening around me. We were not hungry and had a stable roof over our heads. But it was something I could not appreciate at the time.

As a consequence of Mama's hard work, she developed five hernias, an affliction usually reserved for men. Mama did not want to go to the hospital because she did not have anyone to whom she could delegate the responsibility of the kids and the house. Because of the seriousness of the hernias, she was forced to give up, and remained at a hospital for a few days.

On the first day of Mama's absence, I received a phone call from my father and brothers who were working at the betting parlor. "Maria Isabel, what is for dinner?" Papa had asked.

I was absolutely silent and at a loss for words. All I heard were my brothers laughing on the other end of the phone. They knew I could not cook. It also did not cross my mind that I was supposed to take Mama's place in the household. The truth of the matter was that, at fourteen, I was not my own person yet. My character and abilities were just beginning to take shape, and learning how to cook was not part of my lessons. As funny as my father and brothers thought it was for me to take my mother's household responsibilities, it was even funnier to think they wouldn't eat as well as if my mother was home.

Two days later, Condorito, a friend of Aunt Ligia who owned one of the best restaurants in a nearby city, had to close it and stay at our house while he found somewhere to live. He was my savior because he taught me not only how to cook but also how to do the shopping at the public market. I learned so well that in the beginning, no one could believe the food they were eating had been prepared by me. They thought it was prepared by a chef.

While Papa and my brother Julio Cesar were working at the betting parlor, Papa decided he wanted to speak to his father, from whom he had been estranged for the last three years. During that period of time, neither of them knew what was occurring in each other's lives. Pipa was completely unaware of the financial difficulties we were experiencing and Papa was unaware of my grandfather's illness.

Papa called Pipa's house and the maid who answered the phone said to him, "Your father is in the hospital and he is very sick."

In desperation, my father called the hospital and Matilde answered the phone. The conversation was short because at that precise moment, Pipa was dying and the phone was beside his bed. My father asked Matilde, "How is my father? Tell me, is he very sick?"

There was so much commotion in the hospital that Papa could barely make out what was happening or what Matilde was saying. But he heard six desperate words before he lost connection. "Come as fast as you can," Matilde said. She hung up the phone and Papa was left with silence on the other end.

CHAPTER 10: Pipa's Last Words

By the end of March 1973, Pipa's health rapidly deteriorated. He became very pale, was tired most of the time, and had a constant fever. His appetite diminished, and he had no enthusiasm to visit the ranches. Instead, he was always looking for an opportunity to lie down.

Thinking that a change of weather was going to improve his health, Matilde and Pipa spent a weekend in Buga, a city near Cali where Matilde's mother lived. Manuel and his wife Esther also went to Buga to visit my grandfather with the hope of finding him in better shape. Unfortunately, it was quite the contrary.

Pipa's skin color had turned a sickly grayish yellow. He refused to get up from the bed. Manuel was scared to see the way his father looked, so he suggested for Pipa to return to Cali to see a blood specialist. Matilde and Manuel soon found out that Pipa had chronic leukemia. They were beyond devastated. They made an agreement with the doctor not to disclose the true extent of his illness to anyone, including Pipa himself. Instead, the doctor told Pipa that he was acutely anemic and they would try to treat this ailment. Aware of my grandfather's love for life and his fear of dying, they decided to also keep this a secret from his daughters, my father, and Manolo's wife, Esther.

Matilde dedicated all her time to taking care of Pipa. She even moved their bedroom to the terrace of the house, where an apartment had been built many years before for my uncle Manuel when he was single. The apartment was redecorated with new curtains and furniture, hoping that if he was surrounded by beauty, it would at least lift Pipa's spirit. Matilde's dream was that it would improve his condition. Unfortunately, that would not be the case.

To this day, Manuel says, "I resist to believe in another life, and if God exists, he has to be very different than the one that religion tries to represent. This is something that I accept because I have seen it and felt it many times. It is the energy every human possesses that, at the last minute of our existence, starts traveling to the more precious places of our lives."

Manuel remembers once there was a knock on the door at three in the morning. He had been fast asleep, but quickly woke up to the sound. He also woke up his wife, who was unaware of the extent of Pipa's illness. As soon as he woke her up, the first words out of her mouth were, "Someone is going to die and they are coming to say goodbye now."

Manuel felt paralyzed. He immediately thought about his father. Two minutes later, they heard a knock on the neighbor's door. That was the home of a family that was very close with Pipa. Manuel had rushed to the door to see who was knocking. But there was no one outside their house or the neighbor's house. Manuel returned to bed, bewildered and disgruntled. He could not fall asleep that morning.

The following day, the neighbor confirmed they also heard the knocking, but when they went outside, they did not see anyone. Manuel's wife was right. Pipa had come to say goodbye. He was never coming back. Manuel went the following day to visit his father, begging him to come visit his house one more time. Pipa, in his poor state, answered, "Do not insist. I do not want to go back there anymore." His soul had been there already the night before to say goodbye.

After this experience, Pipa's health got even worse and the persistent fever robbed him of any strength left in his body. The chronic leukemia was already taking over a body that everyone thought was made of steel at one point. The many pills, blood transfusions, and healthy soups Matilde was preparing worked to no avail. Pipa stopped looking in the mirror. Instead, he would watch his hands nervously as they shook. They were a constant reminder of his fatal disease.

One Sunday morning, Pipa woke up with intense pain coursing throughout his body. The medication he was taking finally occluded his intestines. The doctor had prescribed morphine for the pain and because of the difficulty in getting it, Pipa had to be hospitalized.

Reynaldo Henao and his son Gerardo were at his bedside the entire time. Fortunately, Pipa had become very wealthy before he became bedridden with disease, so money was not an issue in the attempt to save his life. The future trustees of his estate were interested in taking over his two largest ranches, Rio Bamba and El Paraiso, as well as all of the livestock. In these last painful moments, they were supportive and consoling towards my grandfather's condition and Matilde's needs.

Doctor Chatin, the oncologist taking care of Pipa, told Matilde and Manuel the seriousness of his condition. Pipa was at the point of no return. His last two days were a nightmare for Matilde and Manuel, the only ones to know the magnitude of his illness. Doctors and nurses were constantly in and out of his room. On Monday afternoon, May 29th, while my Uncle Manuel was holding his hand, Pipa murmured, "I am tired of traveling."

"Shh, Papa, save your breath," Manuel had whispered in response. In fact, Pipa's words scared Manuel. Yes, he had been traveling to the places he loved the most. This was proven a couple days later because many people said they felt him and even saw a ghost of him in El Patia—one of his favorite places of all time.

After these few words, Pipa was sweating profusely, his face swollen and flushed with the fever. Suddenly, in a moment of clarity, he looked into Manuel's eyes. His hands tightened around those of his son. "How hard it is to die, my son," he said.

That phrase expressed by his beloved father dug deep into Manuel's soul. This was the first time that my uncle sat beside someone who was dying. Unfortunately for Manuel, the first time had to be his father.

Pipa always avoided talking about death. Just the word horrified him as much as it did anyone else. When Manuel asked my grandfather if he wanted to have a priest at his bedside, Pipa looked at him with surprise and responded, "Why? Am I going to die?"

"It is good to be prepared to go to the other side," Matilde consoled her husband as she sat on the other side of the bed across from Manuel. Pipa could do no more than oblige in his weakened state. And so, Manuel brought in a priest, who required everyone to leave the room. In the emptiness, Pipa made his confession and the priest spoke to him more about moving to the other side. Once the priest was done, he invited everyone back into the room to be part of the communion.

This was a touching moment for all those present. There was Merceditas the youngest, Matilde and her mother Doña Francisca, Fabiola, and the trustees of the estate. Pipa was quite aware of what was happening. He smiled for the first time since he was bedridden in the hospital and everyone cried.

By ten at night on May 29th, his agony really began. He was under the influence of morphine. At midnight on May 30th, Matilde and Pipa were celebrating their 18th wedding anniversary in the hospital bedroom. My grandfather had a beautiful black onyx ring that he believed had magic protective powers. In the hospital, as if the ring was the obstacle deterring him from leaving this world, he showed it to Manuel.

"Please, take it off, my son," he begged between breaths. The ring just slipped off his finger, falling into Manuel's open palm. Once free from the ring, he got the strength to sit up. He hugged every person who was surrounding him. When he laid back against the pillows, his eyes closed and he died. It was May 30, 1972. When my father arrived in Cali the following day, after a trip of eight hours by bus, it was too late.

It is impossible to write about Pipa's death and not take into consideration his loyal friend Terry, a German Shepherd with a gentle heart and enough toughness to protect his family.

Many would say, "You go to the cemetery to give company to a friend, but you do not bury yourself with him." This saying, however, had nothing to do with Terry. Since my grandfather became sick, Terry would lay under his bed and would not move. When Pipa died, Terry went to his bedroom and sat next to a pair of boots that he used to wear whenever he went to the ranches. Terry licked the boots and howled, crying for his lost owner and best friend. It was very touching to see him so sad, as if the best part of his life was gone and life was not worth living anymore.

In the beginning, Terry could climb the stairs to the terrace where Pipa spent his last days while sick. However, now that Pipa died, Terry stopped eating. He lost a lot of weight and reached a point in which you could see every bone in his body peeking out beneath the fur. He climbed the stairs with great difficulty, and would lay beside the boots and cry. Ten days after Pipa died, Terry was saying goodbye to this world as well.

There is another saying people use. They say, "It is possible that a friend not only gives us company to the cemetery, but it is also possible that he gets buried with us." This was true of Terry.

After my grandfather died, Dolores did not have a strong foundation anymore. Pipa promised that he would take care of Dolores for the rest of his life. Now that he was gone, he could not uphold his promise. And so, she went to live with her niece, Anita, who welcomed her with the love and tolerance of someone who understands. Dolores spent the rest of her years with Anita. When she died, we saw her in a different light. My Uncle Manuel was most adamant about describing this new side of Dolores. He had spent much time in front of her coffin on the day of her funeral.

"I saw her in that coffin lifeless, with a gesture of terror streaking her face," he said. "She seemed terrified of dying."

I had nodded in agreement. "I remember she used to tell us how horrible it is to have your soul ripped from your body," I reminisced.

Manuel chuckled and lifted his coffee cup to his lips. After taking a sip, he responded, "What's the most ironic thing is at our home, she was the one who always killed the roosters and hens." I shook my head, surprised that painful Dolores would have done that task.

"Since I was a little boy, it was always painful for me to witness the killing of anything that is alive. But when Dolores was ready to kill a hen, the episode would become a family drama. We, the children, ran to hiding, and covered our ears while Dolores dragged a lively, healthy, and fat hen to the slaughterhouse."

"Why did she have to kill the hen all the time?" I asked in wonderment.

Manuel shrugged. "I do not know if she actually liked doing it. She used to hide behind a door to sacrifice them. And when she came out of the slaughterhouse with the immobile hen, head down, it seemed like she had committed the worst crime in the world. At that moment, I usually felt like I hated her more than anyone else in the world. I would even promise to myself never to talk to her again, but whenever we had that tasty chicken soup, I would forget that promise to myself. And then, when I saw her in the casket, I wanted to cry when I saw those bony hands clasped on her chest. I thought, 'this is the same woman who used to kill hens forty years ago. Those same lifeless hands did the deed. Those hands took the life away from so many hens, but now, they did not even have the strength to swat a fly landing on her nose. Now she is dead. Just like the hens she used to kill," Manuel whispered. His voice was heavy;

much heavier than the bony hands clasped across Dolores' still chest.

CHAPTER 11: Forever on The Go

Soon after Pipa's death, Papa got into an argument with my Aunt Ligia's husband, Alberto. Alberto had become an uncle to us and we loved him for his unconditional support of the family. Unfortunately, Papa was in an argument with himself after his father died, and Alberto just happened to be the person to catch the brunt. This was Papa's way of venting his feelings of guilt for not having spoken to his father for three years and now it was too late for him to ask his father for forgiveness.

What we did not know was that, from that point forward, we would be confronted with one of the most difficult times of our lives. Chiqui said, "Mama, I'm going to stay here in Girardot with my aunt Ligia and Alberto. Fortunately, I can continue working with them at the betting parlor." He was a hardworking young man who was put in charge of the business when Ligia and Alberto went to Bogota. After his announcement, the rest of us left abruptly from Girardot to Pereira. Mama packed our few belongings that consisted mostly of clothing and the eight remaining children. Nothing was planned beforehand; so when we got to Pereira, we had no place to stay. Papa got a room in one of the cheapest hotels in the city. We squeezed into two beds, and the following morning, Papa brought coffee and bread from the local cafeteria. We did not complain.

We were slowly adjusting to this new reality, although we did not know how long it was going to last. Living in Pereira, even in the poorest area, was going to be unaffordable on my father's budget. So the following day, we went to a nearby town called Santa Rosa de Cabal, where we had more possibilities of renting a house. Luckily, my father found a one-bedroom house with a dirt floor, wooden kitchen, and a big backyard that looked almost like a farm. In the only room of the house, Mama put two beds that were shared by everyone. In the morning, my sister Maria Claudia used to get up early to buy fresh bread at the bakery. It was a large bread that Mama cut into eleven pieces and for us, it was like eating caviar. We ended up falling in love with this place. It was not in the nicest part of town, and it was small, but it was our home.

My father found a job in Pereira, and traveled every day fifteen minutes by bus to Santa Rosa de Cabal. His salary was not enough, and Mama had to buy food that had nutrients but at the same time was also inexpensive. One of those many inexpensive food days, Mama showed up at the house with the brains of a cow, and mixed them with scrambled eggs. Nobody wanted to eat them, but we tried hard and did it. Sometimes it would remind me of the time we refused to eat the chickens we had roaming around the house. It was during these times that I wished we had those chickens.

"I'm going to throw up," Carlos Augusto muttered as he played with the food on his plate.

"Hush now and eat your food," Mama said as she spooned a big chunk of brain into her mouth. She had the least egg of all of us so she wasn't able to cut the strong taste of the brains. She wanted to make sure that we didn't have to suffer as much.

"No!" Carlos threw down his spoon and tossed his arms in the air. Mama looked at him, a blank expression crossing her face. She knew we had to eat right to stay healthy, but because of our budget, we could not get any better food. In her frustration, she took the cup and the spoon and forced Carlos Augusto to have it. He shook his body from head to toe and clamped his mouth shut.

Mama got so angry that she broke the cup full of cow brains. It splattered all over him. Carlos was twelve years old already, standing up for his good taste in food. Mama stormed out of the house and we were left looking at each other.

"We all have to eat this, Carlos Augusto, otherwise we're going to starve and get sick," I whispered to him under my breath. He made a face at me before flicking some brains off his shirt. He did not eat anymore that day. Mama no longer tried forcing food down his throat.

We stayed in this house for two months, and after my father became stronger economically, we moved to Pereira. His income was not enough to support the family and Mama was forced to travel back and forth to Girardot to my Aunts Ligia's house. Mama kept doing the chores she used to do around the house when we lived there. Without Ligia's help, we would not have survived.

One day when we were expecting Mama to come from Girardot, Maria del Pilar and I decided to surprise her. We had been given a set of horrible dark purple curtains with ruffles. To Maria del Pilar and I, they were beautiful. When we hung them, they covered a whole wall in what was supposed to be our living room. When Mama came home from my aunt's beautiful house and saw that the house looked like a funeral parlor, she started yelling at us. Meanwhile, we could not understand her not liking what we had done because to us, it looked like a palace.

I understand now that it was difficult for my mother to be confronted with two different worlds. While she was working hard in Girardot, beautiful things surrounded her. Once she came back to us, reality was before her. It must have been very difficult for Mama to not be able to provide her children with the things that in a normal environment, a family would have.

Many times, when there was nothing to eat at the house, she asked the little ones to go to bed at six when they started begging for food. Softly she would say, *"Please, go to sleep."* Mama knew that if the kids were sleeping, they would not think about being hungry, and for her it was a way to relieve the pain of being unable to feed her children.

I was seventeen years old when I got my first job working for a friend of my father who owned a warehouse in the industrial zone of Pereira. I would say it was a favor John Monsalve was doing for my father. I was just a beautiful, young girl with an empty brain. I had not experienced life enough to have my own ideas and opinions about things and I was very insecure.

Shortly after I started the job, I noticed that when the warehouse opened in the morning, a man in his early thirties, with blond hair and blue eyes, would stand on the sidewalk near the entrance. I could not help but notice his unusual appearance. He had a dark tan and looked like he might have worked outdoors all his life.

He spent the entire morning just watching me. When it was time for me to go to lunch, he disappeared. This behavior lasted for approximately eight days, and the last day I saw him, he approached the pick-up counter near my desk carrying a book. He surprised me since I had not expected him to come into the warehouse, and when he did, I got up from my desk and walked toward him. We exchanged glances but no words. He placed the book on the countertop, turned, and walked out. I never saw him again. I picked up the book, "The Conquest of Happiness" by Bertrand Russell. This book became my first exposure to philosophical writings. I was rewarded with this wonderful gift of literature, for which I had no appreciation until that moment.

I resigned my position at John Monsalve's warehouse and went with my mother on one of her trips to Girardot. I had learned from one of my cousins in Pereira that my Aunt Ligia had a son out of wedlock. I used the opportunity of being along with Mama to inquire about his whereabouts. Mama was upset that I had found out, and asked me not to say anything because it was a family secret. I said to my mother, *"Whoever he is, he has a family and deserves to know about us. If you are not willing to look for him, I am going to."*

She sensed my determination and asked me for some time while she made inquiries in Armenia, the city where he supposedly lived. I was going to make sure that, late but better than never, he was going to make peace with his past. His name was Carlos Alberto Gutierrez.

CHAPTER 12: My Battle Against the Other Side

It had only been a week since I arrived at Girardot with Mama when I felt sick and came down with a fever along with a feeling of weakness in my body. The condition worsened over the next days, so my mother took me to a local doctor who failed to identify the cause of my illness. I had a constant fever and after the next few weeks of seeing two other physicians, Mama decided to take me to the public hospital. The symptoms had worsened to the point that I was bleeding internally from my intestines. After being admitted to the hospital, my mother spoke to the doctors who gave no hope for my life. Mama called my father in Pereira to tell him that I might die and he needed to come immediately.

For Papa and Julio Cesar, my older brother, to make the trip, they took our television set to the local pawnshop and borrowed enough money for a bus ride to Girardot. They arrived late that night and immediately came to the hospital to see me. By then, I had given up all hope—I could not even rise from the bed. I did not wish to go on any longer, feeling this sick, and did not care whether I lived or died.

The following morning, my mother returned to the hospital and when she came into the room and found me gone, she thought I died during the night. The hospital staff did not tell her that I was moved to another room. As my health kept declining, the doctor told my mother that I should be transferred to a private clinic. There was nothing more his facility could do for me.

Aunt Ligia referred me to her doctor, and that same morning I was taken to a private clinic where Doctor Moncada practiced.

Upon seeing my condition, he said to my parents, "The probability of Maria Isabel's survival is very low, however I am going to give her an injection. If that does not work in twenty-four hours, she will not survive."

Both Papa and Mama exchanged worried glances. Papa was on the brink of tears, but Mama did not say nor do anything. She was remaining the stronger of the two. Seeing her that strong in the face of possible death gave me the will to fight for my life as well.

Doctor Moncada realized that I was suffering from typhoid, which had already done a lot of damage to my body. Mama, Papa, and Julio Cesar returned to my aunt's house to rest while I fought for my life with all my will during that first night. The following morning, my father came to the clinic. The door to the room was open and I envisioned a screen on the door. On the other side, I saw faces of people and relatives I knew were dead. They were looking at me with unnerving expressions. I knew that if they passed through the screen door and reached out to me, I was going to die.

When I saw them pushing and trying to get through the screen, I yelled to my father, "Please, do not let them come closer to me. If they do I'm going to die!"

My father became frightened. He looked around but didn't see any of the bodies I was seeing.

"Love, there is no one else here except for me," he whispered in a shaky voice.

"I see them. They are right there!" I pointed to the screen, my eyes wide with shock. I was scared, and even more scared that Papa could not see them. Papa put a hand on me to try and console me but it was not going to help.

One of the dead got through the screen and walked towards me. I started crying and imploring, "Papa please do not let him come to me. If he touches me I know I'm going to die." Papa was confused and desperate in his inability to help me and began to pray.

The vision retreated behind the screen and all the images disappeared. What a frustration. I was seeing something that Papa was unable to see and, to me, it was the reality.

That night, Mama came to the clinic to stay with me. The door of the room was open to the hallway and Mama was lying in bed next to me when I saw the Virgin Mary kneeling in prayer facing the wall. I knew who she was even though her back was towards me and all I could see was her long blonde hair.

"Mama, I see the Virgin," I whispered, afraid the Virgin Mary would hear me and turn to face me. Mama had been quiet. She brushed the hair off my forehead. "Hush Maria Isabel. Be silent and pray," she murmured.

I started to cry because I was not sure if Mama believed what I was seeing. Then, the Virgin turned towards me and came through the doorway into my room. She was carrying a crystal rosary in her hand, stopped near my bed, and tossed it to me. I made my mother get up and search the room for the rosary. She could not find it.

"Maybe the Virgin is asking for our prayers. So, let's pray together," Mama said. She was trying in every way to remain strong, a stabilizing force, and make me feel better.

I had the feeling of being in another dimension, very similar to what people describe as an out-of-body experience. I was totally sensitized to the spiritual world. I could not see anything this time, but I could feel that everywhere in the clinic there were souls in limbo, not at peace, just floating in space, and at the same time, I could feel darkness lurking.

From this point on, I began to recover. My body, which was a little more than a skeleton, was beginning to accept liquids and small dosages of solid food. When it was time for me to leave the clinic, I found myself too weak to stand on my own, as I tried, unsuccessfully, to stand on numerous occasions.

When we arrived at the house, it was necessary for me to sit in a chair and be carried up to the second floor. Over the next few weeks, my mother took care of me, feeding me, bathing me, and helping me stand up. Within a few weeks of her loving care, my strength returned, my weight improved, and the crisis was finally over. However, I did not know that another crisis was just around the corner.

CHAPTER 13: Facing the Reality of Adulthood

It was three months since the cigarettes started to bother me and I could not tolerate the smell of them. I smoked a pack a day since I was fourteen yet now, not only did the smell bother me, but my body felt strange and I had this desire to eat anything sour. I slept the entire day and was supposedly responsible not only for the house, but for my brothers and sisters while my mother was away.

Every day I hoped to see blood in my underwear and I wished I did not have to think that I was pregnant. Economically, we were experiencing the worst times of our lives. We lived in Pereira, in a house that looked more like a toy than a real one. Everything was so tiny and it was hard to believe that ten people lived in it.

The front of the house was only a small door painted blue and a window that was so miniscule it never opened. In what was supposed to be the living room, there was a big wooden bed which was intricately carved and used to be a long time ago, Mama and Papa's bed. My sister, Maria del Pilar, and I slept in it now.

Across from the bed was a large cradle, almost the size of a twin bed, with four posts carved in great detail. At the top of the four posts hung a canopy with curtains tied back to each other. In this cradle slept my two sisters, Maria Luisa and Maria Claudia. These two beds were the only legacy left as proof of better times. They looked horribly out of place in this terribly poor neighborhood.

The men, Julio Cesar and Jose Carlos Augusto, slept in the only other room of the house. It did not have a door and other than two twin beds, the room did not have space for anything. In the middle of the back wall was an opening of nine-by-twelve inches that communicated with the kitchen, where Mama placed a beat-up radio that somehow still worked.

The house had a small hallway that was twelve feet long and three feet wide, with a bathroom located at the far-left corner. In the middle of the hallway, next to the bathroom, was an old-fashioned cement laundry sink, where everybody's clothing was washed by hand. To the right of the sink was the kitchen where Mama put another bed that took up practically the entire room, leaving just enough space to walk back and forth when we were cooking.

It was in the kitchen where Mama and Papa slept with the two youngest, Maria Alejandra and Monica Patricia; and of course, the rats and cockroaches that lived in the house on a forced diet, with the rest of the family.

Papa worked in a warehouse as a manager. It belonged to a friend of his and was two blocks from the marketplace and a fifteen-minute walk from the house. The money he made was just enough to cover some household expenses. Sometimes Papa even had the luxury of drinking some beers in a cheap cantina, smoking one cigarette after the other, listening to the old music he liked so much, and dreaming while awake.

To pay rent, put food on the table, and cover the house expenses, my mother traveled from Pereira to Girardot, a five-hour trip, to her sister Ligia's. Mama helped by taking care of her house and doing the same chores she did when we lived there five years ago. In return for my mother's effort, my aunt gave her money to barely cover our expenses.

Mama was gone for a month or two at a time and when she was not here, we felt unprotected and vulnerable. There was a bodega at the corner where we had a charge account, and when the list of purchases became too long, we had to wait for Mama to return before we could pay the credit. At times, we had nothing to eat.

To the left of our house was a family of color from the state of Choco. Their family was bigger than ours and the most important person in the household was "La Madre," The

Mother. She was a big woman in her fifties and married to a soft-spoken man half her size. At their house lived not only their seven children but some friends who had no place to go. In return for the favor, they collaborated in their sessions at night to invoke a drunken spirit who, according to them, liked to drink aguardiente. Jose Omar was seventeen years old and the oldest son.

During the evenings, we went outside and stood on the sidewalk to talk to him. He told us he had been with his mother at the apartments of very wealthy and important people in Pereira and had seen his mother invoking the devil. At night, we saw many people gathering at this house and we were well aware of how respected The Mother was by all of them. Two houses away lived Doña Gilma. On the block, she was the wealthiest of the poor, and her husband made enough money not only to feed his family, but also to have extra food to give to us when starvation arrived. Doña Lizbeth was married to a mechanic and had a fifteen-year-old daughter and twelve-year-old son. She had some basic nursing skills which allowed her to become the doctor of the neighborhood. She was the one everybody ran to when an injection needed to be administered or a medication to prescribed. These three neighbors played an important part in our lives when Mama was away. They experienced economic difficulties too, but were still willing to share whatever they had with our family.

The only valuable thing we had at the house was a black and white television set that was twelve by eighteen inches. Many times, to make ends meet, Papa would carry the television down to the local pawn shop and hock it for some pesos. This could cover a few days of expenses. For the children, the day the television was redeemed was a celebration, because it gave us a distraction from this little space where we had no privacy.

Many mornings, the kids went to school without having breakfast, and if there was something, it would be a cup of hot chocolate with three breads the size of a cucumber that had to be cut into ten pieces.

Sometimes at the end of the day, my younger sisters laughed about how they lied when asked by their friends what they had for breakfast. Their imaginary breakfast was composed of two eggs, cheese, bread, chocolate, ham, and anything else that came to their hungry minds. When the time came to talk about the furniture, they said very proudly that first of all, there was a television set, a radio (that hardly worked), and what else? A lot of beds. Those we had plenty of.

One day, I had been throwing up since I woke up and the only thing I wanted to do was sleep. The kids left for school early in the morning and I was lying in Mama's bed. It was very convenient because I felt lousy most of the time and to make lunch, I just had to get up, walk not even two steps, and place a pan on the stove with enough water to feed nine people. The ingredients were a piece of scallion, two bones that would give broth and protein to the soup, and two potatoes cut into small pieces.

Fortunately, with the way I felt, I did not complain of not having anything else to cook with, and at the same time my cooking did not require me to think or have some degree of imagination. That was the last thing I wanted to do at the time.

At noon, everybody returned for lunch and Papa was the most concerned with my health. He insisted on calling an ambulance to take me to the nearest hospital and I was almost begging him not to do it. I wanted to stay home as long as possible and I did not know what Papa's reaction was going to be when he found out that I was pregnant.

He called the ambulance anyway, and people from the neighborhood immediately came over to the house to find out who was sick. We left, and all the way to the hospital I was praying to God to give me more time. Not today, God. Tomorrow, I prayed repeatedly in my head.

At the hospital, we waited for a while before a doctor was ready to see me. "Please describe your symptoms, Miss," the doctor said to me in a soothing tone. I almost felt convinced that everything was going to be alright. However, when I told the doctor what I was experiencing, he looked quickly between my father and I.

"We need to do a urine test," he replied without looking at my father. At that moment, I could bet the last thing Papa imagined was that his favorite daughter was making him a grandfather. And so, I did the urine test. We were asked to wait. The silence was awkward, but I did not try to speak to my father. When the results arrived, I asked my father to leave me alone with the doctor.

"You are pregnant," the doctor said matter-of-factly. I bit my lip. I was seventeen years old and three months pregnant. This was my new reality.

I hastily told the doctor, "Please, do not say anything to my father, because at the house nobody knows I am pregnant and I do not feel this is the right moment for him to find out."

The doctor rubbed the crease marks over his bushy eyebrows before responding. His tone was loving, yet it did not make me feel any better. "Sooner rather than later you are going to have to face the reality of your pregnancy. For now, you do not have to worry because I will tell your father that you do not have anything serious, which is true. But you will have to tell him soon, before the belly becomes obvious."

As a result of my pregnancy, I started to experience a craving for different treats like unripe mango and pineapple. One day, I was walking down the street with Mama, when right there in front of me was a man with a pushcart, selling unripe mangoes cut in slices. I started to salivate. I asked my mother for some money and she said she did not have any. In desperation, I went to the pushcart vendor and explained to him my situation. Thankfully, he had a generous heart and gave me one at no cost.

Through the years, I still have the taste of that mango in my mouth. Time kept passing by and my stomach was starting to show a little. I was five months pregnant and my condition was not very noticeable because I was slightly underweight. I was not eating enough and most of my time was spent in Mama's kitchen. I was purposely isolating myself from the outside world and getting ready for the worst.

For the next few days, I harbored thoughts of leaving the house. I was getting tired of being nervous and apprehensive most of the time, and the waiting time to be punished once my parents found out was becoming too long. While I was trying to figure out what to do, with no money and no place to go, an old friend of the family, Milbia, came to visit us and stay for a couple days.

She was a nurse whom we met when we lived in Girardot five years prior. It felt good to have a new face around and it was good for Mama to talk to someone close in age. While Mama was washing clothing by hand in the laundry sink, Milbia stood next to her, reminiscing about the past.

I just recently began noticing some marks on my breasts that I did not have before. Now that Milbia was here, I thought it was a good opportunity to learn about the marks.

I approached Milbia and Mama at the laundry sink. "Milbia," I said, interrupting her discussion with Mama. Both women turned to look at me.

"Can you tell me what these marks on my breast are?" I inquired as I lifted my blouse so that she could see what I was talking about.

Milbia's eyes surveyed my breasts for several long seconds. "They are called stretch marks," she explained.

"But why do I have them?" I asked.

"They are usually associated with pregnancy or weight loss."

Mama now looked down at my breasts and then up into my eyes. Her eyes then fell to my exposed stomach. I felt ashamed. When Milbia said "pregnancy" I realized just how stupid I had been in exposing my stomach to them. All I could feel right now was Mama staring at my slight budge. It was too late: Mama knew.

I could not see Mama's facial expressions but I could feel in the atmosphere what was going on in her head. I was nervous but resolute about the end result. I just could not believe the day had come. I had a feeling that Mama did not want Milbia to know about my pregnancy.

Mama dropped a yellowed blouse into the sink, wiped her wet hands on her skirt, and jutted her chin at me. In a very subtle way, she said, "Maria Isabel, come with me into the kitchen."

I did, in very slow motion, as if a couple more minutes of not having to face the impending situation was going to make a difference. In the kitchen, Mama sat at the foot of the bed. I chose to sit against the wall at the far end, preferring to play it safe since I did not know what her reaction could be.

"Are you pregnant?" she asked very bluntly.

I did not, nor could I, play games with Mama. And so, I replied, "Yes." It came out in almost a whisper and it was my only attempt at wishing that Mama did not hear me.

She didn't say anything. She just looked at me, understandably confused. She could tell that my feelings of helplessness were just too overwhelming. I felt this adrenaline rush coming all over me and I was not done with the rush when I felt my body temperature change slightly, making me disoriented. Everything I thought important up to this point became irrelevant.

I tried to imagine a hundred different ways of how this moment would turn out. Many times, I gave myself hope; but sometimes you know deep inside your heart that no matter how hard you keep searching for different roads to bring the situation to a better outcome, it will not happen.

Mama did not touch me or try to console me. She just stared at me. The long, awkward moments of silence took over the room, making it feel even smaller than it was. I felt like I was suffocating.

"Well," she said, breaking the silence once and for all. I bit down on my lip, worried of what her final verdict was going to be. "We are going to have to send you someplace far away from here. Before the family and neighbors find out about this."

I did not respond. I looked down at my hands, not realizing that I had been squeezing them white while waiting for Mama to speak. And now she had spoken. Everything about the situation was extreme and the only thing I could think about was the reaction of my immediate family and those just outside the circle.

I had feelings of guilt because of how these people were going to perceive it, and how it would affect my family. There were the relatives, the close and distant ones, then the close relatives' friends, friends, and people from the neighborhood. It was an unavoidable chain reaction.

Mama left without waiting for my response. Her mind had been made, and I knew that I could not change it. Once she was out of the room, I crossed my hands, looked up to the crackling ceiling, and whispered, "God, from now on, my baby and I are in your hands."

Papa had been drinking at a nearby cantina when Mama showed up looking for him. It was early in the afternoon and when Papa saw my mother entering the place, he knew something was wrong. She grabbed a chair and sat across from him. Her face was serious, lines from weather and work etching her strong features. "Arnulfo," she began with no other pleasantries. "Maria Isabel is pregnant."

Papa did not respond. He waited for a few moments while his face conveyed his deepest thoughts. Once he found the strength to speak, he said, "Who was el hijo de puta, (son of a bitch) who did this to my baby? I am going to kill him."

Mama spoke to him slowly to calm him down. She had stayed with him at the cantina as he drank through three more beers and tried to process the pregnancy. Fortunately, he was calmer when he came home with Mama that night. He did not say a word to me. But, in a very loving way, he kissed my forehead and said, "I love you."

At that moment, I knew I had his unconditional support. His love was big enough to handle this burden. Being the oldest made me my father's favorite daughter. As for my mother, my pregnancy reignited in her the rivalry that existed between us when I was growing up. Mama always felt I was the one who drove my father and her apart. Now that I was pregnant, she had an excuse to be openly angry with me, even over the simplest of things.

She would begin using me as a scapegoat when she was disappointed by just about anything. Like a magnet, her frustrations were drawn towards me, allowing her to be more loving and protective to the younger ones. There was nothing worse that I could have done in her eyes, or in the eyes of everyone involved, than become pregnant.

CHAPTER 14: Hiding from the Truth

I was spending most of my time sitting in Mama's kitchen bedroom knitting sweaters for my baby. I could feel him moving and kicking in my stomach and very soon I would be able to see his beautiful face. Hard to believe that, less than a year ago, I was enrolled in one of the best private schools in Pereira, La Salle. How my parents were able to afford it, I did not know. I just remembered them being behind with the monthly payments most of the time.

It was an interesting time, since it was the first year the school was coed with only myself and another girl as the females in the class. This girl disliked me intensely because I spent my time during the breaks with the boys. Open fields surrounded the school and it afforded the guys the opportunity to smoke marijuana without being seen. I never tried it. I did not like to be poor, I did not want to be poor, and on top of it, I was embarrassed to be poor. I was trying to live a double life because I did not want the kids from school to find out where or how we lived.

To hide my superficial and empty identity, I got off from the school bus at my mother's uncle's house. It was in the best neighborhood of Pereira and gave me not only the opportunity to escape from the reality of my existence but also to be part of their social events. I slept many days of the week at their house. During weekends, I went to their farm near Pereira. Across from their house lived the Angulo family. They were descendants of the founder of Pereira so it gave them some importance among the people who knew them. They were not wealthy but were lucky enough to have a plain house in this beautiful neighborhood.

The couple was named Doña Alba and Don Fidel Angulo. Don Fidel was a handsome and proper man who did not talk too much. Doña Alba was a small lady, who was always busy taking care of the family. They had three daughters and three sons. The middle daughter, Patricia, in her twenties, was born blind and had some difficulty walking. Since she was born, Doña Alba's social life came to a stop. She dedicated the rest of her life to taking care of Patricia. Doña Alba could not rely on anyone else, since Patricia had a bad temper and only her mother could end a tantrum.

I knew them because their oldest daughter, Alba Sofia, became my friend. She was some years older and knew the cream of Pereira. When I wasn't at my mother's uncle's house, I was at Alba Sofia's house. With her brothers, I had a friendly, but formal, association. It never went further than a simple hello or small talk.

In my immaturity and lack of appreciation, I was joining a world I did not belong to and was escaping the world that was really mine. This is why I never took the time to get to know my own neighbors. These beautiful people, Doña Lizbeth, the doctor of the block, and Doña Gilma and her daughter Mary Luz, who came to visit me during my pregnancy and brought me juices, food and words of support. These were the people I used to underestimate before I got pregnant. The ironies of life only began to show. Those I ignored before came out to be kinder than my own family. Some relatives wanted to erase me from their lives when they heard about my pregnancy.

Besides being wealthy, my relatives were concerned about public and social opinion. The fact that I was to become a single mother embarrassed them the most. However, I refused to be intimidated by their behavior. When I walked down the street, I was proud to be carrying my child.

My head was held high, and if someone asked with a nosey tone, "Did you get married?"

I smiled and responded, "No, I haven't. I'm a single mother."

Becoming a single mother was a beautiful awakening for me. It brought me back to realize the importance of having my loving and supportive family next to me. It showed me who my real friends were.

We did not have money to buy clothing for the baby or for me. Fortunately, one of my mother's cousins, Elsy, who gave birth recently to a boy, gave me her maternity and baby clothing. It was exactly what we needed. With no place to put the baby's clothing, Mama went to a warehouse that was in the importing business and brought home a four-foot by two-foot wooden box. She made two shelves and decorated it with blue curtains as doors and beautiful ribbons. When they say that necessity is the mother of invention, Mama is proof of it.

Mama was as excited as I with the preparations. But what was sad was her inability to accept the fact that her oldest daughter, the one who should be setting an example for the rest of the family, failed miserably in her eyes. I don't blame her. She was raised in the old-fashioned way of thinking and for me to end up pregnant and not married was devastating to her. The economic situation we were going through was so precarious that, as any mother, Mama was counting on me to find a well-to-do-man to whisk me away from such hardships. One of the ironies with Mama is that she adored this unborn child already, as if it was her own.

December 31, 1975, New Year's Eve, was a special night of celebration. Doña Gilma, whose house was at the corner of the street, invited us to celebrate the New Year with her family. I was scheduled to be at the clinic at seven in the morning on January 1, 1976, to have my baby by cesarean section. I was tired and wanted to stay home. But the lesson I learned from the people surrounding me made me aware that this was a day to be cheerful.

So we left the party at four in the morning. By seven, Mama and I left the house for the clinic. We had to walk because we couldn't afford a taxi. The streets were empty and most of the people were home sleeping off their hangovers. In the afternoon, Papa arrived still drunk from the night before. He laid on the couch beside my bed.

I remember watching him snore so peacefully. I said to myself, "I wish the person on that sofa was the father of my son. He should be giving me the support I need during one of the most special moments in a woman's life."

I was having my baby by cesarean section because he was in a standing position. I could see and feel his head and butt sticking out of my stomach. The nurses came into my room and told me I was having contractions every five minutes even though I could not feel them. I lost so much weight that when I was laying down, my stomach was completely flat.

At seven in the evening, I was taken to the surgical room, and by seven-thirty, the doctor said with a huge smile, "It's a boy." That phrase made me smile with my heart.

The nurse took him outside for Mama and Papa to see. Then he was taken to an incubator because he was born with a breathing difficulty. I remained at the clinic for three days and when we returned home, everyone was excited about the baby. My sisters, brothers, and neighbors, who during my pregnancy helped me and gave me words of encouragement, were there waiting for us. I was beaming from happiness. I turned to Papa and said, "What a wonderful experience. I think every woman should have the opportunity to feel what I am experiencing right now, this fulfilling emotion of being a mother." He wrapped an arm around me and smiled. "Maria Isabel, you are one lucky girl. Never forget that," he replied.

The first night home, I slept with my little boy, even though we had a small, decorated crib for him. It was the only night I was able to sleep with my baby. During my pregnancy, I did not take good care of myself because of the stress, and as a result, my baby was small and weighed only four pounds. The whole night, he cried. He was hungry and because my body was unable to produce milk, I could not feed him.

The following day, Mama took the baby to sleep in her bed. When I protested and begged to keep him with me, she shook her head and simply replied, "I am going to teach him not to cry at night. He has to learn to adjust to this new schedule in our world." I did not object further because I knew Mama was the best at dealing with children. She dedicated all her life to raising kids, and she not only had the experience, but also missed not having a baby in her bed. The youngest one, Monica, was already four years old. Deep down, I had this feeling of being deprived of something that was mine. I was missing a wonderful opportunity of being a full-time mother, but at the same time, I was thankful for Mama, because without her help, maybe I would have been unable to do it at all.

We still did not have a name for the baby. Because he had little hair, Papa nicknamed him "Kunfuncito," or Little Kung Fu. Every day before Papa left for work, he used to say, "My love, be very careful with Kunfuncito because I will never forgive you if something happens to him." The reason for Papa's concern was that my son, like many new babies, had problems with excess phlegm. I used to stand next to his crib for hours just looking at him and making sure he was alright. Many times when my mother was not around, Papa and I would run into the street yelling to the neighbors for help while the baby was by himself struggling to breathe.

Because we could afford only a bottle of milk a week, I blended a plantain, called "guineo" rich in iron, with water to make the milk last. It really worked because my baby was able to normalize his weight and become a healthy boy.

We baptized him German Felipe. Mama was still angry with me and I felt that to compensate for her disappointment, I should stay home and avoid any social life. It was the only way to appease Mama because she was relentless day by day to accept what had occurred, no matter how much she loved Felipe.

CHAPTER 15: A Jungle of Opportunities

In 1974, my oldest brother Julio Cesar left Pereira with two friends, Roque and Chucho, without a fixed destination. While the three of them were on the bus, they talked about all the things they were going to experience. It was exciting and adventurous for these three young boys who felt invincible. They bought a tent, camping gear, pots, pans, and things they thought they would need to survive. After spending the night in Bogotá, they took a bus ride, which lasted four hours, and ended up in Villavicencio. From there, they went to the next town, Puerto Gaitan. It had approximately 6,000 in population. They arrived just when a festival was occurring. This festival features fashion and water sports that can easily attract 60,000 to 100,000 visitors. The three of them were having such a wonderful time that they remained in this town for eight days.

Unfortunately, one day Roque and Chucho got into an argument, so Roque decided to put an end to his adventure and return to Pereira. "I don't want to go back," Julio Cesar said to Chucho after Roque's departure.

Chucho had been silent. He was still angry at Roque but he was stubborn and also did not want to bring an end to this trip. "We will continue, wherever we end up." And so, Julio Cesar and Chucho continued their trip and took a canoe to another town, Oroque. The mosquitos fell in love with Chucho, and they made him so sick that three days later, he gave up too, and returned to Pereira.

"Please make it back safe and get treatment right away," Julio Cesar said to his friend as he waited with him for a bus.

Chucho put an arm around Julio Cesar in a brotherly gesture. "Thank you. Continue with your journey, wherever you end up," he repeated the words he said a couple days earlier. "But please come back to us sometime." Julio Cesar had laughed, patted his friend on the back, and left. He was excited for more adventure in his life, even though he was now all alone. Perhaps things happen for a reason.

Julio Cesar continued alone and decided to go to Venezuela or Brazil. He realized the easiest way to make the trip considering he had no papers was going through Puerto Carreno, a port in Colombia that bordered Venezuela. He asked for a ride from a truck driver who was going to Santa Rita, a famous town for producing the fiber used to make brooms. The truck driver obliged to have a traveling partner.

It took them six days to reach Santa Rita. From there, Julio Cesar took a boat to Puerto Carreno on the Orinoco River. In Puerto Carreno, he met up with five women in a bar who told him they were traveling to the diamond mining area in Venezuela, where they intended to work as prostitutes.

"I will go with you ladies," he said. "I will make sure you make it safely to Venezuela." The ladies were so thrilled that they bought another round of drinks. They continued chatting up a storm with Julio Cesar, telling him about the opportunities of making money working in the mines. Julio Cesar could not wait for this part of the journey.

He knew the tricky part of the trip was making it across the border to Puerto Paez, Venezuela, without papers or money. Having an outgoing personality, Julio Cesar talked to the local villagers and made contact with Arturo, whose business was smuggling gasoline from Venezuela to Colombia. Arturo agreed to take Julio Cesar and the five women across the border by boat.

They left during the night and from Puerto Paez, he and the women walked for seven hours through the jungle. They reached a dirt road and waited ten hours for a car to pass by. It was not a life-threatening situation since the women had enough food and water to last a couple of days. Carlos, an old man going to Ciudad Bolivar, gave them a ride to Caicara, the entrance to the mine in Guaniamo. Carlos was having so much fun with the prostitutes that he decided to take them into the mine and postpone the trip to Ciudad Bolivar. When they finally reached a village called La Culebra, the women got a job working as hookers in a cantina. For the miners, it was a day of celebration when new whores arrived.

"I think this is where we part ways," Julio Cesar said to the women one evening when they were heading into the cantina.

The women were upset to leave Julio Cesar, but they were starting new lives here and did not want to hold him back. "Thank you for taking care of us," the older woman said. She reached in to give Julio Cesar a big hug. The other women took turns hugging him and giving him kisses on the cheeks.

"Until we meet again," Julio Cesar said with a smile. The women waved goodbye as he turned his back on them to continue the next part of his journey. He started to walk, and two hours later, he came across a miner's shack where he met a Brazilian man in his early sixties. This generous man offered him a hammock to sleep in and a screen sieve to pan for diamonds. Julio Cesar did not even need to say anything or make an offer—the man just handed it to him. Again, he felt that luck was on his side and that everything was happening for a reason.

His first attempt at panning for diamonds was successful, so he brought his findings to a local diamond buyer. With this money, Julio Cesar bought clothes. At that moment, he knew he found his place. It was the opportunity to use his own abilities to reap the fruit of his efforts. Julio Cesar remained at the mine for four years and then decided to return to Pereira. Julio Cesar was frightened when he realized that we no longer lived there. Through relatives, he found out we had gone to live in Ibague. It made us happy to know he was fine. For four years, we did not know anything about him, since at that time, the communication in the mine was nonexistent. Six months later, Julio Cesar was missing the rush of adrenaline and excitement he got from taking risks, so he decided to return to the mines.

"Mary," he called me by my nickname. "Please come with me to the mines."

I did not have to think long about this proposition. Since a very young age, I would look forward to adventure. After all, we were moving so often. Now, I was looking forward to new adventures and better opportunities in my life, so I said, "Of course I will go with you."

Julio Cesar was thrilled. But I did not receive the same enthusiasm from my father. He was devastated when I told him that I was leaving. The night before we left, I could see the sadness in his eyes. He knew that I was going to be gone for what probably would be a long time. This was also the first, long time I would be separated from my son and family. Felipe was two years old.

"Don't forget to come home to us," my father said at my departure. "We love you very much. Please be safe."

"I love you too Papa. And I will be thinking of all of you every day while I am away." With tears in my eyes, I hugged my father, kissed him on the cheeks, and then said goodbye to my son. The goodbyes were much harder than I thought they would be. But deep down I knew that I was going to return to my family. I would never leave them behind.

Julio and I left Ibague, with only enough money for the bus to Villavicencio. Once we arrived, Julio Cesar had to find a way for us to travel further to the border with Venezuela. He easily located a cattle barge, which was going up the Meta River to pick up cattle at Puerto Carreno, the next step of our trip. The barge took six days, and the crew gave us a spot to sleep in. They even shared their food. On the barge, we met two sisters who were also headed for the mine to work as hookers. It was becoming a common thing for Julio Cesar to befriend hookers during his trips. The route we were taking was the easiest way for people without papers to reach Venezuela. That is why, just like Julio's first trip, we were in the company of whores.

When we reached Puerto Carreno, I was surprised to see how small it was. At the end of the street you could see the Orinoco River, and across the river was Venezuela. Julio was now more experienced and able to contact old friends. We went to a bar on the waterfront where he met a man who had an outboard motor canoe. We made a deal for him to take us and the sisters across the river. He dropped us at Puerto Paez on the Venezuela border. In this village, the Venezuelan government had a border-crossing to furnish entry approval for travelers into the country. Julio talked to the officials and made a deal with them. They would give us temporary permits that would allow us to travel to Venezuela, in return for the favors of the two whores.

This whole scene, the officers, hookers, and my brother's ability to negotiate such a deal, was a new experience for me. I was now beginning to become exposed to the realities of our adventure, and what had become so normal in my brother's life. After the permits were issued, the hookers decided to make their own way to the mine, so Julio and I took a different route. Since we did not have money, we had to rely on taking the trip towards the mine in short steps, accepting any opportunity that would take us closer to our destination.

In Puerto Paez, we met a man in his forties named Ramon, who had a machete scar across his face. He was good enough to give us a ride in his canoe to Orupe, a tiny fishing village on the Orinoco. The fishing village was primitive and consisted of only a few houses with dirt floors and families who made their living fishing the river. These people welcomed us and, while poor, gave us a place to sleep and food to eat.

"Although our house is very small, please stay with my family," Ramon offered when we got to the village.

"I wouldn't want us to impose on your family," I replied when I saw how poor the people living here were. But Ramon had waved a hand at my comment as if he were brushing away a fly on his shoulder.

"You are friends, and now our guests. We would be more than happy to have you and your brother stay with us for a while."

"Thank you," Julio Cesar responded cordially. He also offered to help Ramon with any of the daily chores he or his wife and children had to take care of. Ramon lived in a one-room house with his wife, a son in his twenties, and a nine-year-old daughter. We slept on the kitchen's dirt floor. The family spent all of their lives in this village and were very curious about big cities with buildings and shopping malls. During the evenings, we would sit on the beach near the river and make them dream by answering their simple questions. We would talk about how we grew up, which to them seemed like a luxurious life. It was during these moments that I realized how fortunate I was in comparison to the poor living in this village.

Every day, Julio and Ramon left at five in the morning to fish while I helped with household chores. After fishing, Julio tried to find someone going to the mines. On the fourth day, we got lucky. When Ramon and his wife Angela heard of our departure, they invited us to have a farewell dinner with some neighbors.

"You are our special guests. We want to share with you the traditions we have in this village. Consider it a farewell gift, and luck for the next leg of your journey." Ramon had us convinced. We stayed for the huge dinner and were humbly impressed by the meal we were served. The main course was turtle, which they call "morrocoy," a wonderful delicacy for them. The Orinoco River has an array of exotic creatures, and giant sea turtles are one of them. Unfortunately, I had to witness the turtle's execution, which was gruesome to watch. It was a giant one, and the fisherman and two other men chopped at the turtle with machetes until the shell was cracked and broken. It took them over an hour to kill the poor animal.

When it came time to eat the turtle, I could not bring myself to do it. All I could see was the poor turtle being chopped up alive, and the slow agony it had gone through. It was embarrassing having everyone looking at me, waiting for the moment I was going to have my first spoonful of the turtle. After all, I was their special guest. But I apologized to them and faked having a stomach ache. Julio Cesar was undisturbed, so he also ate my portion of the turtle.

The next day, Julio Cesar and I left at six in the morning in a canoe to Cabruta. The trip down the river was beautiful and peaceful. From Cabruta we went to Caicara, where transportation was available at any hour of the day. Since Julio Cesar was now in his environment, it was easier to get a ride.

Once we reached the point where the Jeeps could go no further, we walked into the mine at Guaniamo, which covers approximately fifty miles. Our first hike was three hours through the jungle. Julio was carrying my luggage, which was not only big, but also heavy on his shoulders. He was so strong and fast that I had to struggle to keep up with his pace.

On some occasions, he would stop, look at me and say, "Maria Isabel, you either keep up with me or stay behind. I am not waiting for you." The shoes I was wearing had little heels—they were not ideal for walking on these treacherous roads. It was hot, and there were no shacks or people to help satisfy our hunger or thirst.

I was almost running to keep up with Julio, when a snake crossed my path. It was two feet long. I started to scream. I was so loud that the snake decided to ignore me and keep on its path.

Julio turned to me and said, "Maria Isabel, this is a situation that you are going to be confronted with many times while you are in the jungle. It is better for you to get used to it, be smart, and be quiet the next time."

I had not responded. Instead, I closed my mouth and crossed my arms. I did not want to see any more snakes.

At the end of the first three hours, we came upon a miner's shack, which was empty because everyone was still working at the mine. Inside at the table, there was a bowl with corn grains and a bottle of ketchup. Julio put the corn and ketchup together and devoured it.

"Maria Isabel, come eat some of this," he said as he motioned to sit beside him.

My stomach was grumbling out of hunger, but I refused to eat it. I put my foot down and shook my head.

"No, I don't like it." I had my nose in the air as if I were a princess who could not, and would not, eat such food.

Julio gave me a cold eye. "Eat or be hungry," he said as if he didn't care. "There is nothing else for you." I chose not to eat. Although Julio was angry with me, he seemed somewhat content that at least he would be getting more to eat.

I said to myself as I watched him devour the rest, "I hope this is not what their diet is about, otherwise I will starve. We better find real food soon."

Julio became a good teacher to me—I just could not see it in that moment. Time had come for me to put aside my spoiled brat attitude, and I was going to have to learn to work hard if I wanted to survive in this environment. Most of the people who worked at the mine came from Brazil, Santo Domingo, and Colombia. They all arrived under the same conditions as Julio and I. That explained why they were so generous and willing to share what little they had.

We continued walking and reached another miner shack where an old man and his son lived. The son was away and

Julio asked Pedro, the old man, to take care of me for a couple days. Pedro was a sixty-five-year-old man who did not like to talk much about his private life.

According to what Julio told me, the wife had left five years before with a friend of his. She stole his hard-earned money. His goal was to leave the mine one day and live with his wife in Ciudad Bolivar. I think his heart was wrinkled forever after the painful experience of his wife leaving him. He was a man of few words with a permanent sad look on his face.

Julio had no choice but to trust Pedro. I could not go on with Julio, and it was necessary for him to be on his own in order to look for work for himself and a job as a cook for me. In this environment, the possibilities of work for a woman were severely limited. It was to be a cook or a hooker. I chose the easiest one.

I stayed with the old man for three days. In the morning when it came time for me to take a shower and go to the bathroom, I asked Pedro, "Where is the bathroom?"

He looked at me and laughed. "You're not going to find one of those around here." He then proceeded to show me the bushes. "That's our bathroom." Then he led me down to the bottom of a hill, where there was a sink with water and a bucket. Showers were taken in the open and supposedly there was no one around to see me. I just had a strange feeling that everybody was observing me while I was standing naked, pouring buckets of water on my body.

By the time Julio Cesar returned, I had become adjusted to the routine. Julio Cesar got a job for himself and found me a job cooking for five miners at a poor mining shack.

We left and moved to Barrial Largo, one of the mining locations. The miner's shack was built out of wood with a dirt floor and a roof made of palm branches and leaves. It had two small rooms. The first room where the workers ate had a table and a bench. In the other room was the kitchen. It had a small table, containing a one-burner kerosene stove, on which I was expected to prepare breakfast and dinner. One of the beautiful features of the kitchen was its open window, which looked out into the jungle. I placed the wash bucket for the dishes beneath the window. In the morning while I was washing dishes, I could look out and see people milling about.

There was no place for me to sleep in the cookhouse. Directly across the dirt path from the cookhouse, Cesar, the Brazilian man I was working for, erected a simple structure of walls of sheet metal. The space was no larger than 10 feet by 10 feet. A door was fabricated out of the same material and had a simple wire hook as a lock. People passed by all the time along the path and I was never concerned for my safety. People were respectful and supportive of each other's wellbeing. Today, however, the mine has become a dangerous place to live and work, even though living conditions are less primitive.

The only decoration I had in my room was my luggage. I did not have a bed or blanket, so I slept on the dirt floor. I insulated my body with layers of clothing, to serve as protection from the cold and dampness.

Because there was no shower and the bathroom was the bushes, I found a couple living nearby with a primitive shower, consisting of a curtain hung from a round rod. They invited me to make use of it, and at least it afforded me the minimum of privacy. I got up every day at five when it was still dark and cold, and walked across the dirt path to the cookhouse. I lit some candles to light the kitchen and made a simple breakfast that consisted of deep fried dumplings and hot chocolate.

Jose, one of the five guys at the camp, taught me how to make the dumplings, and told me that if I prepared the flour the night before, it would be more manageable. Before the men left for work, they would take turns bringing me big buckets of water from the nearby river to wash dishes and cook the dinner.

Shortly after my arrival, I got a high fever caused by mosquito bites. The swelling in my legs was so severe that I was unable to stand. In this part of the mine, we were completely away from civilization, so medical help was unthinkable. Fortunately, Julio Cesar asked a couple who lived a mile from us to allow me to stay with them while I recovered. They gave me a hammock and took care of me for eight days.

Usually, a miner's workday ends at five in the evening. All day long, the miners are standing barefoot in water up to their waist while using high-pressure hoses to loosen the dirt containing the diamonds. When work finished for the day, the miners return to their shacks. They take a shower usually at a nearby brook, put on dry clothes, and visit friends in nearby camps.

One day early in the evening, Julio was walking barefoot back to his camp, when he felt a needle-like bite on his foot. He looked down and saw a poisonous snake preparing to bite him again. Julio grabbed a branch from a nearby tree and clubbed the snake to death. When he saw the bite marks on his foot, he knew that at that moment the poison was entering his blood stream, and that if he did not get help quickly he would die. He started running.

The nearest medical help was in the little village of "El Milagro," two hours away walking distance. Nothing except jungle surrounded him. At that moment, Julio was not in pain, but he knew that he had to use all of his energy, and he started running toward the town. Within five minutes, the poison started to work into his system, affecting his ability to breathe. Nausea set in, creating the feeling of wanting to throw up but being unable to do so.

Time was running out when Julio spotted a miner camp at the bottom of the hill. The pain in his chest and the nausea forced him to crawl the remaining distance. Fortunately for Julio, there were some Brazilian miners who had a beverage that acts as an antidote against snakebites. The Brazilians gave Julio the drink, put him in a hammock, and carried him to "El Milagro."

One of Julio's friends came over to my shack that night and let me know of the seriousness of the situation. Unfortunately, there was nothing I could do but pray and wait. "He will recover. He will be okay, I promise you. There is a God looking out for him," his friend had reassured me. I was still not convinced, but at this point, there really was nothing that I could do to change the situation or help my brother.

The doctor left to Ciudad Bolivar and the nurse who was in charge when the doctor was absent was also gone. They placed Julio Cesar on the floor of the infirmary. It was the middle of the winter and it was raining hard. The only thing to do was fly Julio Cesar to Ciudad Bolivar, but that had to wait until the next morning because of the weather conditions. He developed a high fever and chills. The Brazilians gave Julio another dose of the antidote. At six in the morning, a small plane took Julio to a hospital in Ciudad Bolivar, and for the next twenty days, Julio was in the hospital receiving intravenous feedings and antibiotics. He lost a lot of weight but thank God, he survived. His friend was right; God was looking out for him.

Wherever Julio was working, regardless of how far away from me he was, he always managed to come to the shack to be with me during the evenings. Though he tried to show a tough attitude with me, I knew he was always concerned for my wellbeing, and always acted out of love. One day, he showed up with a hammock and I no longer had to sleep on the dirt floor. Eventually, the hammock got ripped and I ended up sleeping again on the dirt floor.

After almost one year of working as a cook in this poor miners' camp, I decided to leave. "I am ready to go," I told Julio Cesar. He did not argue, and instead, helped me gather my luggage and salary before beginning our journey through the jungle. Julio was tired because he had been working at the mine since five in the morning. After two hours of walking, he became so frustrated that he took the heavy luggage from his shoulders and threw it over the side of a cliff.

"What are you doing?!" I screamed at him, furious in the heat of the moment that I just lost all my belongings for no apparent reason.

Julio Cesar did not respond. So I stood on the edge of the cliff, looking down in disbelief at my clothing splaying out at the bottom of the cliff. Everything I had was in that big suitcase. I wanted to scream and yell some more at Julio for destroying all my belongings, but I knew it would not be worth it. He was going through something, and I did not want to get in the way. So, I closed my mouth, and we continued to walk for another hour until we reached "EL Milagro."

Since Julio had thrown away my suitcase, I had no clothes, no makeup, and no money. He kept the little money I had made to cover the expenses now that we had no work or place to live. I did not know how we were going to survive here without more money. "El Milagro" was primitive in its location but had all the amenities of a typical village. It had dirt roads, restaurants, clothing stores, hotels, and cantinas called "Botiquines." It was rich in cash because the diamonds that were sold by the miners were paid in dollars. As a result, everything sold to the miners had to be dollar prices. Supplies had to be either flown in by a plane or by land with a sixteen-hour drive from Cuidad Bolivar. The miners after work would come into town, sell their diamonds, buy new clothing, and spend all their money at the "Botiquines." New hookers were arriving daily and that was their incentive after a day of hard work.

The night Julio and I arrived, we walked across town and stopped in a restaurant with tables outside and live music. I was listening to the music while Julio was socializing with some people he knew. One of the men seated at a table came over and introduced himself to me.

"My name is Eloy Dasilva. I am from Brazil. I could not help but notice you when you arrived. What is your name?" the man said to me in a beautiful voice.

I looked over to my brother to see that he was fully immersed in conversation with a group of men. I smiled at Eloy and told him my name. We did not notice the time fly by as we talked until one of his friends whistled our way.

"Come sit with my friends and I, Maria Isabel," Eloy said to me. He took me by the hand and brought me over to the table. All the men went around introducing themselves. Ludo, a diamond buyer and exporter from Belgium, and the man whom Eloy worked for, wanted to meet me. I felt immediately attracted to him. He was handsome, had charisma and the self-assurance that money and power gives to a person. He was also one of the most important diamond exporters at the mine. I was twenty-one, young and unable to see ahead of my nose. I fell in love with him, and for the rest of the time I spent at the mine, I was just looking forward to the moment I was going to see him again.

Meanwhile, I got a job working for an Italian diamond buyer, Nino, doing the chores around his house. He was a short barrel-like man who drank a bottle of Chivas Regal a day. Cooking for him was the most important part of his day and as a good and true Italian, he made sure the people who sat at his table during the evenings had an unforgettable meal. The house had a tin roof as most of the houses in "El Milagro," and was just a long hallway with two bedrooms. The bathroom was a big room outside the back of the house with just a hole in the center and a cement floor.

One day, I got up and found the hallway full of blood. There were dismembered rats crawling slowly, finding a place to die. They were all over the place. Nino's German Shepherd had been doing his job during the night protecting the house from intruders. I started screaming with my eyes closed and got into a corner, afraid of having to see the horrible scene. I stayed quietly in that corner for what seemed to be an eternity until Nino, who had left early in the morning to the mining camp, came back and cleaned the mess.

Across the street was a restaurant owned by a married woman with a daughter. When her husband was not around, she used to come over to fool around with Nino. Nobody knew about their affair, and I was a good excuse for her to come over to see him without anyone finding out. She was my so-called "friend."

Communications at the mine were precarious at that time, and we were practically isolated from the outside world. Julio and I could not learn about our family's wellbeing and I was getting very homesick. I was ready to return. I was not making enough money to send home, and most of the time when I was eating, tears would run down my face. The thought of them struggling to make a living and my inability to help frustrated me.

"Why are you so upset?" Julio Cesar asked me one evening when I began crying over my dinner. I pushed the plate far away and covered my eyes. I did not want to respond because I did not want to sound weak. Julio Cesar wrapped his arms around me and pulled me into a hug.

"I miss the family. I miss my son," I finally confessed to him. Julio Cesar rubbed circles into my back for a long time as I cried into his shoulder. It never felt so good before to cry this much.

"Do you want to go back?" he finally asked me. Hearing those words was as good as winning the lottery. I pulled away and looked up into his face, a smile forming on my tear-stained face.

"Please," I whispered.

Julio Cesar nodded his head. "Consider it done." The next day, we packed our bags and left. Coming back from Venezuela, Julio and I were lucky to meet Arturo, the same guy who smuggled gasoline from Colombia to Venezuela. Once I got into Arturo's boat, it reminded me of the first time we rode with him. That first trip was when Arturo described the danger of piranha in the waters of the Orinoco. He told us about the horrible stories of people in small canoes being tipped over and never found again. I said a prayer for all of us.

There was a moment in which Julio was looking at the water, consumed in his own thoughts. I got close to Arturo to talk to him. He said to me, "I do not believe that he is your brother. But whoever he is in your life, he adores you."

I looked at Julio and back at Arturo, puzzled why he would think we were not related. I responded, "You are right. He has proven his love for me. All this time we were together, I never felt alone. And I learned so much from him."

Arturo just nodded his head and continued looking out across the water. I realized that Julio was here to protect me. As we kept going further into Colombia, darkness set in. The river was notorious for heavy currents and whirlpools, which could swallow a small boat under the water. It was for this reason that Arturo strongly suggested to wait until the following day. He was familiar with the shoreline and took the boat to a beach where he tied it up for the night.

We got out of the boat and climbed from the beach onto the sand hill. We slept on the sand under the open sky with no blankets or anything to make us comfortable. We were not alone, as the huge sea turtles also liked this spot.

"Why are all the turtles here?" I inquired, immediately remembering the turtle we were asked to eat when we began our adventure. I suddenly feared for the lives of these turtles.

"They come ashore to lay their eggs. Most females would return to the same nesting beach each year. Burying the eggs in the sand helps protect them from surface predators and helps the egg to maintain the right temperature," Arturo explained to me. I fell asleep that night watching the turtles, feeling oddly at peace with them resting beside me.

At five in the morning, daylight could be seen, at which point we returned to the boat. We continued our journey, and two hours later, we were in Puerto Carreno. Julio got a room in a cheap hotel. Once a week, a former World War II transport airplane left Puerto Carreno for Villavicencio. If you missed the plane, you were stuck in the town for another week. The plane was scheduled to leave at two in the afternoon with Julio and I on it. When time came for us to leave, Julio was nowhere to be found.

Since Puerto Carreno consists of one long street, I went looking for Julio at the hotel where we stayed the night before. I found him on top of a whore. I was furious because of his lack of awareness at that moment, but I also did not want to be in this town eight more days.

"Can you hurry up? We are going to miss the plane!" I yelled at him. He just looked at me with a shocked expression. I stormed out of the room and waited outside. When he finally came, we took a taxi, and did not say a word.

Once we got to the airport, we saw the plane was already moving. Julio told the taxi driver to go through the gates, onto the runway, and beep the horn while driving towards the plane. The taxi pulled into the path of the plane. Julio jumped out of the taxi, and proceeded to make a big scene for the pilot to stop and let us on.

Julio was screaming at the ground crew to stop the airplane because our luggage, money, and diamonds were supposedly on it. This was all an act to stop the plane so that we could get on. The plane did stop, but not because of us. It was having engine trouble.

All the passengers got off, and after two hours of work, the passengers began to board the plane again. We were boarding from a portable ladder, when the airplane began to roll. This caused the portable ladder to fall sideways and slowly hit the ground.

My brother was watching the whole scene unfold and ran towards me to prevent the swinging anchor tube from hurting me. This anchor tube was used in this type of World War II airplanes to secure the tail of the plane to the ground while it was parked. He got to me soon enough to help me away from the plane. This was difficult for me, as my right foot had been injured in the fall from the ladder.

Once in a safe place, we looked at my foot to see that it was badly bruised and painful to walk on. There was a tremendous lack of security and unfortunately for me, the whole incident went unacknowledged. I was surprised that no one from the airport came to see how the four of us involved in the accident were doing, not even the pilot. It seems to me that this kind of incident was not uncommon.

We made it back home with no other surprises. It was wonderful to see my son and the family, but my soul was uneasy. I was feeling like a fish out of water. I was not happy in Colombia, I was not happy in Venezuela but without knowing it, I had started my search for the place I could call home.

I was not ready for that place yet, and ahead of me were experiences that I had to go through to learn to appreciate it when that moment came. Fortunately, I continued my spiritual search.

I did not stay long in Colombia because I still felt the rush of adventure that Julio had injected in me. After a month, I decided to go back to Venezuela. I knew that if I waited any longer, I would not do it. This trip was going to be different because I planned on being in charge of my own adventure.

CHAPTER 16: Sometimes there are Angels, sometimes there are Devils

I took a four- hour bus trip from Bogota to Villavicencio, then a one-and-a-half hour plane ride to Puerto Carreno. I was familiar with this town, whose population was around 10,000, because of my previous trip with my brother. It borders north and east with Venezuela, on the Orinoco and Meta rivers. These two rivers are used by some people without legal documents, like myself to get into Venezuela.

I thought about calling the house from the airport, but in this part of the country, communications were not very good. I had mixed feelings of anticipation and anxiety. I had no idea what was going to happen next and I kept saying to myself, "What I'm I doing here?" I felt unprotected without my brother Julio Cesar.

At the airport, I took a taxi to the edge of town where outboard motorboats take people across. In a six-passenger outboard boat, I went across to Puerto Paez. It was a fifteen-minute ride in the Orinoco River, where I was able to get a permit to travel into Venezuela. From Puerto Paez, I took a twenty-minute ride in a similar boat to El Burro. I was tired, hungry, and all I wanted to do was reach Caicara before nightfall, which was seven hours away by bus. I had been riding the bus for approximately five hours when in Pijiguaos, a Bauxite mine, the police boarded the bus and asked for travel documents.

Young, illegal, and vulnerable women were their best prey, and unfortunately for me, I was the perfect one. I fulfilled all these requirements, and I knew they were not going to let this opportunity go. One officer stopped next to my seat and in rude tone said, "Give me your passport."

I got frightened and showed him the permit I acquired in Puerto Paez. Deep in my heart, I knew what was ahead of me. I was alone and worse of all, it was late at night when things usually got even worse. It was as if darkness had become an accomplice to the criminals. I stepped down from the bus and could perceive danger in the way the two policemen were looking at each other and smiling while looking at me. Everything was too quiet and nobody else was around. I knew that the next several minutes or hours of my destiny were in their hands. It was as if what was going to happen was part of the character I was supposed to play at that moment of my life, and I had no choice but to go with it.

They took me to the back of the building, in the bushes, and raped me. Once satisfied by their animal instincts, they did not even look at me and went back inside their office. I felt empty. It was as if my soul had been removed from my body and I was just a zombie. I sat outside on the sidewalk and waited for the next bus to take me further into Caicara.

I was young and inexperienced and did not know what to expect from life and of people's behaviors. Maybe that is why I was strong enough to make the choice to go on leaving that horrible episode in my life behind with no deep emotional scars.

This time I was on my own and being the victim was not going to help. Even in a painful situation like this one, God was on my side. I did not get pregnant.

When I finally arrived in Caicara, I did not know what to do next. I had no experience traveling alone and the painful situation I went through made me feel even more insecure and scared. It was early in the morning and I started walking towards the center of town with my small handbag carrying my few personal belongings. When I got to the main square, there were three taxi drivers waiting for people to go to Ciudad Bolivar. The taxi driver I talked to had one space left but told me that he was not leaving until the following morning. I had just enough money to pay for the trip but no place to spend the night.

I said to him, "Listen, the money that I have is enough to pay for the trip tomorrow. But I don't know anyone and I don't have enough money to pay for a hotel. I need your help, please." He was an angel sent to me by God. His name was Nicholas, a young man in his thirties willing to share what he had without expecting anything in return. I trusted him.

He responded, "I live with my mother and we are poor. The only comfortable thing I can offer you is a hammock, which hangs in our living room. You can sleep there and tomorrow we will leave at five in the morning." I could not thank him enough that evening.

His mother was in her seventies with a gentle soul. She welcomed me in her house and made me feel comfortable for the couple of hours I spent with her before I went to sleep.

Nicholas was a true gentleman and did not try to take advantage of me in that vulnerable situation. Just the opposite, he was helping me without looking for anything in return and it gave me confidence in the goodness of people. I was not afraid anymore of going to a city I had never been to before with no legal papers or money.

Before I left the mine on my previous trip, a friend of Julio's, Carlos, who was a detective at the mine and lived in Ciudad Bolivar, gave me his phone number and asked me to call him if I had a problem. After eight hours, Nicholas, the taxi driver, dropped me and the other three passengers at a street unknown to me.

Ciudad Bolivar is the capital of the state of Bolivar and is situated along the Orinoco River. I came to Ciudad Bolivar because this was the city where Ludo and the diamond buyers that worked for him, had their offices and was where they lived when they were not at the mine.

I called Carlos and a half an hour later he came to pick me up and told me he had a friend I could stay with while I found a job. Maria had seven children, most of them grown. The oldest daughter, Carmen, was in her forties and separated from her husband. The second daughter, Beatriz, was thirty years old and had a terrible temper. I never saw her smile and she was all the time creating conflict among the brothers and sisters. She had three small children and had her husband living with her at Maria's house. The rest of Maria's children were younger and some of them were still in school.

At the entrance of the house was a living room with a big refrigerator where Maria kept the beer she sold illegally to people who came to her house to drink and listen to music. The house had a big open patio with a cement floor and this was where people sat and drank. Maria had been separated from her husband for many years and this was how she supported the family. A job outside of the house would have been impossible for her since some of her children still required close attention.

Maria and her daughters were decent people and whomever came to drink at their house did so in a friendly and familiar environment. The men who came over were people she knew and trusted. I lived there for a while and Maria never asked or allowed me to serve a beer. She treated me like one of her daughters and even though the house had only three bedrooms, I was welcomed.

After two months, I found a job working for two Japanese sisters who had a beautiful store in El Paseo Bolivar, the commercial zone of the city. I worked in the perfume section. Meanwhile, I called Eloy Dasilva, Ludo's friend who lived in Ciudad Boliver, and updated him on my whereabouts. Ludo was away in Belgium and did not know that I was back in Venezuela. Now that I was working, I decided to move to a family house that rented beds for students. In the bedroom, there were two beds and a bunk. Because I was paying the least,

I got the upper bunk. I had no sheets, no blanket, no pillow, and no money. They rented only the bed and mattress, but at least I had a place to go to after work.

The salary I made was barely enough to pay rent and transportation. I did not have breakfast, and at lunch, a girl from Brazil who worked with me would take me to her house and cook something for the both of us. Her husband was working for the hydroelectric plant of Guri, which was being built at the time. One meal a day was enough for me to survive.

A few weeks later, Ludo returned from Belgium to Venezuela and showed up at the store. We renewed our friendship and he offered me his economic support. I needed his help desperately but my pride was stronger and stopped me from accepting the offer. At the same time, I wanted him to know that if I was with him, it was because of the love I had for him and not his money.

I felt lonely and unprotected most of the time since Ludo was traveling constantly and spending less time in Venezuela. He was established in Belgium at the time, so through all these difficulties, I decided to return to Colombia. One afternoon, Ludo and I were sitting in a restaurant with some friends of his. We were discussing my wish to return to Colombia and were looking at the possibility of getting immigration papers that would allow me to go to Colombia and come back to Venezuela with a legal status.

At that moment, a man passed by the restaurant and one of Ludo's friends saw him through the window and called him to join us. This man was the Assistant Director of Immigration in Ciudad Bolivar.

Ludo asked him about the possibility of getting me a piece of paper that would allow me to leave the country and come back without a problem. We waited at the restaurant for two hours until the man returned with a temporary permit that allowed me to leave the country with no problem within three days. It took me more than three days to get things together before I left Venezuela, so I went to the immigration building to get an extension. I went straight to the Director of Immigration and showed him the paper. His reaction was of anger and contempt. The permit had a seal, which expired over fifty years ago. The politics and personal animosity between the Director and the Assistant Director became exposed, thanks to me bringing things into the open.

Apparently, the Assistant Director was making money on the side, giving immigration extensions with an expired immigration seal as he was trying to get the position of Director of Immigration. Meanwhile, the Director of Immigration was looking for a good opportunity to get rid of him.

I begged him not to detain me. In my heart, I knew I had not done anything wrong because I did not even know the temporary permit was illegal, otherwise I would not have gone directly to the Director of Immigration for an extension. I was alone. Ludo had left for Belgium and I couldn't count on anyone else.

The Director said to me, "Do not worry. I am going to make sure you don't go to jail. I don't want you to leave yet, however, because I want to make sure everything is alright."

I trusted him. At the end of the day, when it was time for the offices to close, he said: "I am going to give you a ride, but first I would like you to come with me while I take care of some personal business."

I didn't have a choice, so I sat in the back of his car and did not say a word. Ten minutes later, he stopped the car and asked me to go with him to an office across the street. Once there, I realized it was a police station. He asked a policeman to keep me there until the following morning.

This station was set up to keep people overnight, which meant that I was going to be moved to a different place. It had no beds and I had to sit in a chair the entire night without sleeping. I did not know what was going on nor what was going to happen next. No one would answer my questions either. The next day, I was moved in a police car to another building where they detained people for thirteen days before they were released or sent to jail. I was not dressed for this kind of place. I still see myself in a beautiful, dark blue dress with small white dots and high heels.

It was an old, dirty building. At the entrance was a desk with a policeman who asked me for my watch and diamond ring that Ludo had given me. Those were the only belongings I had. Then, two policemen took me through a corridor surrounded by more police. At the end of it they opened a door. It was dark and I could only see a stairway going down to the basement. One policeman grabbed my arm and led me down the stairs. As I was walking, the light began to fade and the darkness of the dungeon took over.

It was one big space with a cement floor, about forty by eighty feet, and one light bulb trying to light the whole room. The room was divided in half by bars and a gate that was open all the time. Further to the right were three cells and at the end, in the far corner to the left, was a little room with no door and a water faucet sticking out of the middle of the wall. Every aspect was depressing and demoralizing. There must have been another basement cell on the other side of the wall for men because I could hear them talking. The heaviness of the air constantly reminded me of where I was. It had a stale, musty, mildew cement smell. I actually could not only smell it but taste it too.

The policeman, whose name was Ricardo, pointed to an old dirty mattress on the floor and said to me in a friendly voice, "I wish I could offer you something better but it is the only thing we have." No sheets, no pillow, no towel, no soap, and no blanket. God, this situation was becoming all too familiar to me. The policeman turned around and went up the stairs.

I lay down on the mattress and stared up at the ceiling. About two hours later, he came back, offering me his lunch, which was supplied by the police department. "It's better than the horrible food that the prisoners are served," he said when I inspected the aluminum paper it was wrapped in.

Ricardo was in his fifties and it made me feel good to know that he cared about my wellbeing. Since I had no appetite, I placed the food on the floor next to the mattress. In no time at all, a wave of rats emerged from everywhere. They were all around, jumping over me to get the food. They even ate the paper.

I removed myself psychologically from the situation to the best of my ability in order to preserve my sanity. I do not really know how I achieved this, but I did. I was able to ignore the rats and the roaches falling off the ceiling onto the mattress and me. At the end of the day, before he left for home, Ricardo came downstairs to say goodbye. He noticed that I had not moved from the mattress.

In a paternal voice, he said, "You are going to be here for a long time and laying on that mattress is not going to help. Get up, take a shower, and do some walking or other exercise." "Thank you," I murmured in response.

He left without another word. He did not even look back at me as he walked out of the room.

That first night, at about seven thirty, I heard a noise at the door. One woman and six men were brought down. The woman stayed with me in the first cell and the police closed the gate that was kept open before she arrived. They put the men in one of the three separate cells next to us, separated by iron bars.

These people belonged to a guerrilla group who kidnapped William F. Niehaus, Director of the multinational Owens-Illinois glass making group in 1976, while trying to promote a communist revolution. Niehaus was with his wife in their home in Caracas when Carlos Lanz and five men forced their way in. They took him to the jungle and for three years and four months, Niehaus was chained to a tree. He was rescued on June 30, 1979 in the state of Bolivar, during a routine operation in which two members of the police searched for cattle thieves. Niehaus was forty-four-years-old and lost sixty pounds during the ordeal. It was the longest kidnapping in the history of Venezuela. Carlos Lanz went to jail for eight years and after that was an advisor to the Ministry of Education for the government of the President Hugo Chavez.

Political conversations went on the entire night between the women and men. I could tell by the way they handled the situation that they were not only educated, but also well aware of what was happening in the country. They never said a word to me, which was fine. In a way, I was afraid of them. The following morning, with a lot of security and handcuffs, they were taken to a security prison.

That night, after a peaceful day of being alone, I heard a scream at the door. Four policemen dragged a woman from the top of the stairs. She was fighting them with all her strength. Finally, unable to control her, the policemen had to convince her that she was only going to be there for the night and that the following morning she would be freed.

She was a drug addict and her arms did not have a clean spot from all her injections. She had no teeth and her hair was curly and long, completely messy. She was skinny and tried to commit suicide many times. Her body had scars everywhere from her failed attempts. When she came downstairs, I was frightened.

It made her happy to find out she was not alone and she started to make advances on me. She said to me in an evil tone of voice, "I like you and am going to make you mine. Otherwise, I'm going to kill myself."

I ran up the stairs and started knocking as hard as I could on the door. Fortunately, Ricardo was on guard that night. Tears were helplessly running down my face, though I struggled against them. I said to Ricardo, "If you don't lock her in a cell, I am going to try to escape and ignore the consequences. Anything is better than having to deal with this bitch!"

Ricardo knew her very well because this was not the first time she was arrested. He understood my desperation and came downstairs to lock her up in one of the cells. "Don't worry, you will not have to worry about escaping tonight."

From that night on, I spent most of the time sitting on the top step, next to the door, and talked to whomever was on guard for the day or night. Occasionally, the policeman on duty would open the door a little and talk to me. I left this spot only to go to the bathroom or take a shower. At the same time, I would ask questions about my case. The policemen told me the man who gave me the fake papers was also in jail. They also said that there was a big possibility I would be in jail for many years.

Four days later, a Colombian newspaper reporter came to visit me. I never knew how he found me, but he told me that he had published a piece about my injustice in a local newspaper. He also gave me a book to read called, *Contra los Traficantes del Poder,* or *Against the Trafficants of Power*. I read the book throughout the night, and by the following day, I finished it. It was a wonderful gift. It took me away from my situation and allowed me to transport myself to different places, and even to situations that were worse than mine.

Almost every night, because I was next to the door, I could hear from the second floor the tortures that took place and the men screaming in pain. I would cover my ears with my hands.

What broke the routine every night were the hookers who were brought in from the streets. They would sing and curse at the police the entire night. They were friendly with me and I never forgot one of them being drunk and singing out loud for everybody to hear, "She was a plastic hooker one of those I see around. One of those girls that when they sweat they smell Channel number three..." After six days in jail, Maria, the lady I went to live with when I got to Ciudad Bolivar, found out through the local newspaper that I was in jail. She sent one of her daughters to bring me clothes, soap, a toothbrush, and toothpaste. It made me feel human again.

One morning, a young man in his twenties came to visit and brought me flowers and magazines. I had never seen him in my life and before I was released, he came to visit me two more times. His name was Samy and I did not ask him how he learned about me. I was just happy to know that there were people who cared about me and my wellbeing.

After thirteen days of being detained, I was released without an apology. All of the problems I encountered while living in Venezuela were showing me that I was in the wrong place and that it was time to move on. Unfortunately, because of my lack of experience, I had not learned to listen to my heart yet.

The day the jail door opened, it was a surprise to see the Colombian reporter and a group of men in their late twenties. I had never seen them before, and found out later that they were the sons of people with businesses in Ciudad Bolivar. Why they were there I did not know nor did I ask. I just knew they were waiting for me on the other side of the door that I had been unable to cross for thirteen days.

They took me to a beautiful hotel to shower and eat my first real meal since I was arrested. The next morning, I went to Immigration and was welcomed by all the employees who told me how unfairly the Director used me to get rid of his Assistant Director.

The damage was already done, and being illegal did not give me the right to voice my opinion about what they had put me through. Unfortunately through my journeys, I had not been able to find better opportunities for my son German Felipe and I. He was the main reason for my searching and I was disappointed with myself, as a fisherman would be to come home with nothing to offer his family. I felt as if I had not accomplished anything except the experience of time rushing by.

I was overwhelmed with mixed emotions. With nothing to offer my son or myself, I felt trapped without a new opportunity in the future. I was twenty- three years old, a single mother, with no formal education, and feeling desperate to provide hope for my son's future. My son was in my heart, and I knew the older my Felipe got, the more determined I would be to give him the opportunities in life that so many take for granted.

And so, I left the next day for Colombia.

CHAPTER 17: A Mother's Quest to Provide for Her Son

Now that I was home, I would help my mother, going to the supermarket and doing house chores. At the same time, I was trying to gain back the time I lost with Felipe. Mama made Felipe a small puppet with a dark blue dress and small flowers. The puppet's head was a clown and Felipe called him, "Pancho."

When Felipe and I went to the supermarket, we would take Pancho with us. While walking, we made Pancho part of our conversations. If Felipe was upset with me, he would not talk to me, but I would put my hand inside Pancho, and like magic, gave him life. I would talk to Felipe through Pancho and Felipe would confide in Pancho as to why he was upset with me. As soon as I stopped talking through Pancho and tried to talk on my own, Felipe would say, "I'm not talking to you. I will only talk to Pancho, because I am upset with you." Pancho became Felipe's best friend and a vehicle for me to communicate with him.

We were living in a building with three floors. Each floor had an apartment and ours was on the second floor. On the third floor lived the owner of the building, and on top of it there was a terrace with the hand laundry sink and many wires to hang the clothing. It was in this apartment that Felipe showed he was sensitized to what can only be described as out-of-body experiences. One day, he was fooling around and put a piece of chalk up his nose. We did not find out until a few days later, when he mentioned that it was bothering him. Across the street from the apartment was the firehouse. I called Cesar, a friend of the house who worked for the Fire Department, to help me extract the piece of chalk from his nose.

"Please help me Cesar. My son has a piece of chalk in his nose and I don't want to hurt him getting it out," I pleaded.

Cesar rushed over without hesitation. He had inspected little Felipe's face before turning to me.

"Can I have some oil?" I paled in the face and responded, "Why do you need oil?"

"I need to lubricate the nostril so that it is easier to get the chalk out. This way it will hurt Felipe less." I trusted him, so I sent Monica, my youngest sister, down to the store on the street corner to buy some oil. Felipe got scared, and as a result, removed himself from his body and went to the store with Monica while his body was lying on the bed. When Monica came back from the store with the oil, Felipe proceeded to watch Cesar perform the chalk removal from his nose, from outside of his body.

On another occasion, Felipe was in the apartment playing with his toys. He sensed that in the hallway, something was happening. Felipe removed himself from his body and saw in the hallway that the landlord was falling down the stairs screaming for help. When people started showing up from the apartments, Felipe returned inside the apartment where his body was surrounded by his toys.

Felipe would confide in me about the experiences he was having, and I said to him, "You have an unusual ability." He said, "I did not tell you before now because I honestly thought everyone else could see the same as I see."

"No, my Felipe. You are very different. You are unique," I would tell him as I put an arm around his shoulders and brought him into a hug.

Every day while Mama was in the kitchen cooking dinner, she gave Felipe a newspaper and made him familiar with the alphabet. He was only four years old when he learned how to read. One afternoon at the end of February, I received a phone call from Enrique Farinango, the son of an Ecuadorian family. We were neighbors when we lived in Popayan, and our friendship became so strong that whenever we moved, we made

134

sure he and his family knew how to get in touch with us. They were well educated Indians from Otavalo, Ecuador, and had a very successful business of wool sweaters, ponchos and other original crafts native to their town.

When I met his family, I was only ten years old and Enrique could have been twelve. What I admired the most about them even at that early age was how proud they were of their race. A major part of their identity was the way they dressed. His mother, father, brother, and sister-in-law, kept their traditions even though they were living in a city where aristocracy and having the right last name was important. The women wore a white blouse, blue skirt, and necklace of gold beads. The men wore white pants that were calf length and a long braid down to the waist.

"Do you want to go to Otavalo?" Enrique asked me very bluntly. I was taken aback by this offer, since it came out of nowhere.

"Why would I go to Otavalo?" I asked.

"I need help managing a fast food business that my cousin just bought. I think you would be a good fit for the job." This was another opportunity presented to me in my search for the right place for Felipe and I. Colombia and Venezuela were out of the question, and this time I was not only listening to my heart, but also open to miracles. I was paying close attention to the thoughts that came to mind during the day. I knew they could change the course of my life forever. I had started to live my life with courage, thanks to my brother Julio, and I was not afraid to look for the path of life that God prepared for me. This time, I was listening to His advice.

"Deal. I will go to Otavalo and manage the business."

When I left Colombia, I went by bus because it was the cheapest way to travel. It was a twelve-hour trip, and as I crossed the border of Pasto into Ecuador, I could not believe the intensity of green in the mountains and the lushness of the vegetation. At the same time, I had the frightening feeling of embarking again into the unknown.

I did not have any prior information about Otavalo, the town where I was going to live, and it surprised me to see how small it was. There were about fifty thousand people and most were Indians whose specialty was wool products.

When I arrived at the house of the people I was going to work for, they welcomed me and made me feel at home. Mercedes and Antonio were a young couple in their late thirties with an eighteen-year-old son, Arturo. Every day at eight in the morning, a taxi picked me up to take me to Ibarra, a twenty-minute drive from Otavalo. Ibarra was a bigger city and the help I received came from hard workers and reliable people. Unfortunately, the people in Ibarra were not ready for fast food, and this was one of the first of its kind. During the evenings and weekends, I was introduced to very interesting people. The Ecuadorian Indians are proud of their heritage and are people of honor. Most of the new generations go to the university and are well-educated.

After three months of working, Rene, a German man, came into the restaurant to buy a hamburger. He told me he had a resort on the San Pablo's lakeshore with log cabins surrounding it. He asked me, "Are you interested in working there for me?"

"I have decided to go back to Colombia. Business over here is not going well. I think the owners are going to sell it and stick with the traditional business," I responded.

He looked crestfallen, so I quickly added, "Give me your business card and if one day I decide to come back, I will give you a call."

Three months later, I got the urge to return to Ecuador and asked my sister, Maria del Pilar (Pilly), if she wanted to come with me. She agreed. She had vacation time coming and she decided to take it for the trip.

We had enough money to pay for our bus tickets, and without checking with Rene in Ecuador about the availability of the job, I took the chance. We got to Ecuador during the afternoon and made our way to Rene's resort. Fortunately, he was there and asked me to start the following day. He provided us with one log cabin to live in, which gave us free room and board.

The resort was a beautiful place. It was located in a valley, facing the famous San Pablo lake. In the middle of the resort there was a small zoo, surrounding by individual log cabins. Each one had a fireplace. The restaurant was located at the right side of the building, so the windows held views of the big lake. The help included local Indians who lived higher up in the hills. People came from all over Ecuador to spend their weekends and we were always booked.

Rene and his wife, Rosa, had a four-year-old baby called Anita. They also had an apartment in Quito where they spent their weekdays while Anita was in school.

The resort was closed during the week and Rene would return on Thursdays to get ready for the weekend. My job was to make sure everything was in order while they were away and to help during the weekends to run the resort. Pilly did not like the adventure and decided to go back to Colombia. I took her home and came back to the resort.

After working at the resort for eight months, Rene asked me if I wanted to stay with them. He could arrange with his lawyer to get me a permanent residency or working permit. Felipe was in my thoughts all the time and many nights were spent crying until I fell asleep. Unfortunately, this was not the place for either of us.

I was looking for the possibility of staying, only if I could have Felipe with me. The closest school was a ten-minute walk from the resort, and its academic level was not good enough for me.

"It is not worth to put Felipe through such a change if it's not for the better. I would travel to Colombia every other week to see him, though, until you find someone to replace me," I told him when I denied the job offer.

And so, I would return to Colombia, stay for four days and then go back to Ecuador to help on the weekends. The trip by bus took approximately twelve hours and after doing this traveling for a certain time, I got very sick. I was spending too many hours sitting on a bus and my kidneys could not handle it any longer.

On my last trip back to Colombia, the police stopped the bus in Ibarra and asked for travel documents. When it was my turn, I showed the policeman my passport and he started questioning me. I had them in proper order and I felt that he was being a little unreasonable. This situation reminded me of the previous behavior I had been confronted with during my trip to Venezuela. It made me both sad and angry.

Furious, I said to him, "Carajo! Don't you see that all my papers are in order?" While this is a common phrase to use in Colombia, it was an offensive one in Ecuador. So, the policeman accused me of being disrespectful to his authority and had me arrested. The irony of the situation is that, even at the present time, I do not know what the correct interpretation of the phrase even is.

The pain from my kidney infection was getting worse, and at that moment I was more concerned of taking care of it than going to jail. When I got to the detention center, they put me in a small cell with five other women. One had a baby only one-month old who cried constantly because he was hungry. The mother was unable to feed him and did not have money to buy milk. What surprised me the most was that the guards knew the baby was hungry and did not do anything to help the situation.

Directly across from the women's cell was the men's cell. Among the group of men was one in particular who, from the moment he saw me, started singing the same song the whores used to sing when I was in jail in Venezuela. When you talk about coincidences in life, this was one of them. I had some money with me and asked the guard to buy milk for the baby. At that moment, they realized that I was one of them under the same circumstances.

Two nights later, my back pain worsened and I got a high fever. My condition became so critical that it forced the police to take me to a doctor. The doctor prescribed me a strong antibiotic by injection every eight hours to stop the infection that developed in my kidneys. Because of my condition, they let me go and I returned to Colombia. When I got home, I found out that Rafael Frieri Maccedo, the owner of the racetrack in Bogotá, Hipodromo de Techo, had decided to close it. More than 200,000 people in Colombia suffered from this decision and found themselves without a job. We were among them for the betting parlor, and Pilly's salary was helping the family with daily expenses.

My brother Jesus Fernando (Chiqui) was also affected. He had been living in Girardot with Aunt Ligia and her husband since he was ten and, while going to school, he was working at the betting parlor. When he was thirteen, he had not only the authority of hiring and firing, but also became my aunt's right hand. With the closing of the racetrack, Chiqui came to live with us in Ibague. He was already twenty.

We moved to a new apartment in the center of the city that was noisy by day and night. It was a three-bedroom apartment, and if one of us couldn't sleep, we lay quietly in bed so as not to disturb the others. Mama stopped having children and there were only ten of us with Felipe, and twelve with Mama and Papa, who had not been sleeping together since

Monica was born. We learned by experience and practice how to create our own privacy in a small space.

At the corner of the apartment there was an empty space, and Chiqui decided to start his own business there. It was a very small cantina, but with a man like my brother in charge, it became a success. Because the cantina was not even a half-block from the house, Mama helped him during her free time. Our economic situation began to improve.

The apartment had a small patio and Mama put out birdcages and a hundred plants so the place looked like a jungle. Mama had two favorite pets, a monkey called *Muñeco, (male doll)* and a macaw called *Niño, or little boy.* In one of the patio walls was a water faucet that Mama used to wash clothing. Above the water faucet, the monkey was tied up to keep from running away. No matter how complicated we tied the knots, Muneco would slowly undo all our efforts.

Nino, the macaw, was a talker and was constantly teased by Muneco, the monkey. Poor Nino had no feathers because the monkey hung on them and pulled them out. These two pets disliked each other and were constantly fighting. When Mama gave Nino juice to drink, the foam would get all over his beak. Before he could enjoy the taste, Muneco would sneak up and lick the foam.

Getting a job with no skills was becoming difficult for me. I decided to go into politics and joined the Conservative party. I supported Dr. Guillermo Angulo Gomez, a senator running for reelection. I contributed to his campaign by working as a secretary in his office. When Dr. Angulo won, he assured me a position at the City Hall in Ibague, working as an Executive Secretary for the Department of Finance.

It was typical for Felipe not to ask for anything before I got the job. When his only pair of shoes began to rip on the side, he came home from school and without asking for a new pair, sat on the bed and sewed the tear. It was not long after that they would rip again and he would sew it back up. It made me happy to know that by the time the shoes were beyond repair, I had a job waiting for me. I could even pay for Felipe's private Catholic school, which was only five blocks from the house.

In an effort to find a way for Felipe and I to share more time together, I decided to enroll us in a karate program. The sessions were five days a week. Every night after work, I would meet Felipe at the academy. His progress was very rapid and many times he was asked to lead the adult class in the warmup. This was a real honor for someone who was only nine years old. During the weekends, we took classes of Nitjitsu. This training was more intense. In the morning, we ran up the mountains without water, and during the evenings, we were taught to fight in the dark. This kind of training instilled a competitiveness and self-assurance in my son, which contributed to his ability to place demands upon himself in excess of what might otherwise be considered normal.

One day, before break, a bully approached Felipe.

"I want to fight you. I will be waiting in the yard after class," the bully said in a threatening tone.

Felipe had nothing to prove, and this situation was of no interest to him. The kid did not know Felipe had been taking karate for over a year. But Felipe had no intention of hurting the kid either.

Unfortunately, the bully was persistent and followed Felipe home day after day, provoking him to fight. Finally, Felipe approached the situation from an angle that this kid did not expect. One day, he simply said to the bully, "Why don't we become friends instead of fighting?"

The kid was so taken aback that he would follow Felipe home just to talk with him as a friend. When Felipe first introduced this kid to me, I did not like him.

When I expressed my opinion, Felipe's answer was, "Mary, I understand you don't like him because you think he is a bad kid and that somehow I will be influenced by him. But don't worry, I think we can learn good things from each other."

Felipe was an old man in a little body. I was always learning from him and sometimes it made me feel a little embarrassed.

I would keep telling him, "Felipe, learn from me only the good side that you see in me, because even though I am your mother, I am not perfect."

Felipe was the child I never had to yell at. Responsibility is one of his strong points, and while he was going to school I never had to help or question him. He was always thirsty for knowledge and for him learning was a pleasure. His sense of responsibility went hand-in-hand with his independence. He liked the challenge of accomplishing varying tasks. One of his beautiful qualities that surprised me when he was growing up was the understanding and consideration he had towards people.

My brother, Carlos Augusto, and Felipe shared many of the same qualities. Carlos Augusto would always try to better himself without the help of others. The age difference between them was big enough that Felipe looked up to Carlos. It wasn't always this way, however. Carlos Augusto would tease Felipe who would retaliate by hiding Carlos Augusto's schoolbooks. This created fights, but as time passed, it became a game.

Unconsciously, Carlos Augusto was teaching Felipe a variety of lessons without trying to so. Carlos Augusto was eighteen years old and about to finish high school when he got the offer to own a betting parlor in Ibague. Two wealthy families in Colombia decided to open a racetrack. A man who knew my brother made the offer. Carlos Augusto went to a friend he trusted and offered him a partnership. His name was Dario. From that moment on, they included each other in future deals. The first deal of the betting parlor was a great success, and as time passed, Carlos Augusto could save some money.

One day, Dario offered a deal to Carlos Augusto. "Here are four newspaper stands. They are for sale and come with the guarantee of permits from the city hall so that you can place them in strategic locations. It's a win-win situation for you," he told his friend.

Carlos Augusto thought about it for a little. "I will take only two, and I will rent one to my friend, this way I can make more money," he explained. It was a smart decision, because with that money, he was able to pay all expenses to attend university. Once those expenses were paid, he returned to Dario and said, "I will take another stand because I want to give it to my mother. It will be my contribution to support the family."

At the newspaper stand, Mama sold newspapers, magazines, cigarettes, and candies. She left the house at four in the morning and walked ten blocks to pick up a bundle of newspapers that weighed at least thirty pounds. Then Mama carried them five blocks to the stand. The busiest time was from six to eleven in the morning, when my sister, Maria Luisa Fernanda, arrived to relieve my mother. Mama took the money she earned and went to the public market by foot to buy food. Without asking for help, Mama carried the groceries seven blocks back home to start the job of cooking lunch for the family.

Lunch was the only time the family got together during the day, because the offices were closed at twelve and reopened at two. Although we loved this time, it did not help Mama. After she fed the family, she had no time for her own rest. Until now, she had been working ten hours straight and didn't sit once. After lunch, she returned to the newspaper stand and worked until six. She would return home to cook dinner. After dinner, she spent the evenings washing clothing by hand. Her bedtime became two in the morning and she had twenty-two-hour workdays.

This was a physically punishing schedule for Mama. She was underweight, overworked, and exhausted. We tried to help as much as possible with the house chores, but Mama preferred to do everything her way. I don't think we were aware of what it took for Mama to run a house of twelve people and work full time. When relatives showed up unannounced for lunch or dinner, it usually created a big commotion at home. The lunch that was expected to feed the family now had to be stretched out to feed an additional unexpected amount, sometimes more than six people. Mama never complained, however, and always made them feel welcome.

There was so much tension between Mama and Papa that their relationship could no longer last. It came to the point where Mama had no time for Papa. Her feelings of attraction were nonexistent and her dedication to the family and towards accomplishing what she knew she must do left virtually no time for her to even consider a romantic involvement with Papa. He could not contribute financially to ease the struggles we faced as a family, which left Mama with even less interest in him.

And so, as they separated their romantic lives, Papa became interested in other women. In 1985, he started dating Daysi. She had two children: Alex was four and Elena was six. Her husband had been unfaithful so many times that she left him and carried the burden of supporting herself and her children on her own. She had no money, no job, and no place to live, so she turned to her sister Rosa who owned a beauty salon for help. She said to her sister, "Listen Rosa, if you give me a room where I can sleep with my children and feed us, I will help you with the chores of the house and whatever else I can do at the salon." Rosa agreed, and Daysi and her children moved into her sister's home.

At that time, Papa was working for IMI in Ibague and everyday he would walk the same streets to work. After work,

144

he would go to the cafeteria for a beer, which was nearby Rosa's salon and, since the salon was on his way, he would get his hair cut by Rosa every two weeks. Often, they would chat and would learn about each other's lives, so much to the point that Rosa told Daisy, "You should pay attention to a man like him because he is not only good looking but also well-spoken."

Daysi did not want to take her sister's advice because she was afraid of trusting a man again. What scared her the most about Papa was their age gap. Papa was fifty-three and Daysi was only twenty-one. However, as time passed and he continued to be so kind, she decided to give a second thought to Rosa's words. "Perhaps I can have a comfortable life and a father figure for my children," she thought to herself.

One day he blurted to her, "I separated with my wife and I have never felt so alone before." Once she heard that, she knew they could be together, especially since she felt the same way, and the age gap was no longer her concern. They continued to see each other, and became so comfortable that they decided to move in together. Daysi did not hesitate to pack up her children, leave her sister's house, and trust a new man who waltzed into her life unexpectedly.

On November 13, 1985, I was working at the city hall in Ibague, when the Nevado del Ruiz volcano erupted. It killed 23,000 of its 28,700 inhabitants. Armero is almost two hours from Ibague and thirty miles from the volcano. Before the disaster, Armero was one of the largest producers of rice, cotton, and coffee in Colombia. The day after, Armero was no more than a grey mass, like cement covering the entire town.

Because its hospital was destroyed in the eruption, Ibague provided shelter for the survivors. I was at my office when a man stopped by and introduced himself as Fernando. "I am a lawyer, and three days before the tragedy, I went to Bogota to take a job," he explained to me. "I have five children;

the oldest is fifteen and the youngest is five. I need your help," he pleaded with me.

"What is wrong?" I asked him as I urged him to join me in the conference room of the office. He sat down and his hands shook as he told me his story.

"The day I was ready to leave Armero for Bogota, my youngest begged me to take her with me. My plan was that in eight days, the entire family would move to Bogota. So, I did not take my youngest daughter with me and I told her that I would be sending for the whole family as soon as possible."

Fernando began to cry and I tried to console him. Through tear-stained eyes, he said to me, "Please, take me to the shelters. I need to find my family otherwise I will never be able to live with myself."

I obliged, and we went from shelter to shelter, hoping to find the family. We came across many people who knew his family. One couple said that during the eruption, they went to Fernando's home and banged on the door, begging for his wife and children to run with them. Fernando's wife refused to leave. She locked them inside the house and they were killed. The house was buried under a mudslide. Early in the afternoon of that fatal day, the local officials instructed the people to stay inside their homes and remain calm, which I assume, is exactly what Fernando's wife did.

It hit him as hard as the mudslide hit the town of Armero. He knew that he would never see his family again. There wasn't even a picture, a child's toy, or a piece of furniture that could remind him of this wonderful life he shared with the people he loved. After realizing that his family was dead, Fernando became angry at his wife. He was frustrated because she was stubborn and did not want to go with the neighbors to safe ground. There was nothing I could do to help him get out of this mental state of anger, regret, and frustration.

Afraid of another eruption, we decided to send my sisters and Felipe to Bogota. Cecilia, a friend of the family, offered her house as soon as she heard about the tragedy. My other two sisters, Maria Alejandra and Maria Claudia, went to Cali to our Aunt Merceditas. They remained at these new locations for over a month until we were certain that it was safe to return to Ibague.

My brother Chiqui lost his business in the little cantina when the landlord asked for the place back and, being broke, had to find a new way of making money. Carraca was a friend of his that made his living selling clothing and shoes in the nearby towns of Ibague during the weekends. Chiqui decided to learn the business from him. It was 1981 and he was only twenty-three years old.

Chiqui had been working for two months with Carraca, when he met Martha Machado Alcazar. Martha was raised most of her life by her oldest sister, Angela, who lived in a town near Ibague called, "Cajamarca." Angela was a teacher and her salary made it possible to afford private school for Martha and give her a comfortable life. When Martha was seventeen, Angela took her to Ibague on Mother's Day to visit their mother. This was when she met Chiqui.

They fell in love, and Martha refused to go back to her previous life. The two of them went to wholesales and purchased clothing and shoes in bulk for a flat amount of money and went to the small towns near Ibague to sell what they got. Martha and Chiqui would arrive early in the morning at the town they had chosen the night before and lay out the merchandise on a plastic tarp on the ground for people to walk around and see what they might like. Chiqui was a good salesman and with all the energy he had at the beginning of the day would shout, "Fifty cents for anything that you see!"

Everything they sold was so inexpensive that he quickly attracted large crowds. Most of the customers were local

147

peasants who returned from their farms on Sundays to do shopping and sell their products. When some people did not have money to buy his goods, Chiqui offered to trade. It could be a chicken, a pig, or vegetables. This worked well for them, because when Martha and Chiqui were hungry, they would go to a restaurant and exchange the traded goods for a cooked meal. Such goods would also get them a night in a cheap hotel.

Being only the two of them, it was hard to watch what was going on. At the end of the day, Martha and Chiqui found themselves with old pairs of shoes, which customers had left when they walked off without paying for Chiqui's new shoes.

The following day, Chiqui announced in the plaza, "If you purchase a new pair of shoes, I will give you a second old pair for free. Or you can take a used pair for half price!"

On one occasion, a peasant came to Chiqui wanting to buy five pairs of shoes for his kids. However, he was without money and offered Chiqui two six-month-old pigs in exchange. In the evening, Chiqui came to the apartment with the pigs and put one in the bathroom and the other in the laundry sink.

The squealing and smell of pigs was more than Mama could bear. Two days later, she threw Chiqui and the pigs out of the apartment. He took them to Martha's house and when the pigs were old enough, they became food for Martha and her family.

CHAPTER 18: Carlos Alberto Gutierrez Reality

I asked my mother again about my cousin, Carlos Alberto Gutierrez, who was given up for adoption. Her older sister Maria Belisa, and her husband Fabio Gutierrez, had registered the baby as theirs before giving him to Camilo Isaza and Gilma. Eight days later, Mama went to Armenia and found him. It was easy, since he lived one block from my mother's aunt Trinidad.

He came to Ibague to meet us, and we were very happy and excited. When I asked him what his life had been like all these years, he said, "I was born in Sircacia, a small town in the state of Quindio, on January 13, 1954. Camilo Isaza and Gilma adopted me eight days after I was born. Fabio Gutierrez was a friend of theirs and he knew that they could not have children on their own. He came to them one day and said, 'Would you like to have a child?' That's when he offered me to them. They were very happy to have me. I remember when I was three years old and they dressed me in a cowboy outfit. Camilo, my new father, owned a bicycle shop in town. He took me in my outfit to the shop and put me on display in the window.

I felt at that young age that he really loved me. Camilo used to come home drunk at night and cry. I did not understand anything and did not know why, just that he cried a lot. When I was five, Gilma gave birth to Liliana. The love they had for me became less, and two years later, when she had a boy, Ruben Dario, the love for me seemed to end. This is when my suffering began."

Carlos had become quiet. I thought he would not continue his story. I could tell that it pained him to recount his past with me, but eventually, he continued.

"I was eight when Gilma and Camilo separated. The man left and I stayed with Gilma and her two children. Camilo gave no economic or emotional support to us. I used to go to the bicycle shop and he made me clean the bicycles. One day, I found an oil can and began to write on the floor with the oil dripping. That man came from behind and slapped my face very hard. When I was leaving, he yelled at me, 'don't ever come back again!'

I went home crying, and at that moment I knew that he had completely stopped loving me. Gilma used to disappear for ten-to-fifteen days and Liliana, Ruben, Dario and I were taken care of by her parents. I slept on a bedframe with no mattress. Burlap bags covered the metal straps on the base of the bedframe. I had no sheets and no blanket; as a pillow, I used my pants that I rolled up in a ball. During the day, I went to school, and in the afternoon, I worked in a bowling alley setting up the pins. I was only ten and worked from six in the evening to one in the morning. They did not pay me a salary and all I got was grape soda. Sometimes I got tips from customers. At one in the morning, the house would be locked, so I slept on the street with my friends from work. We would go to a cantina called, "El Niagara" and entertain the drunks by wrestling and fighting with my street friends. These drunken people used to have a wonderful time watching how we beat each other up and would tip us for the entertainment."

I could not imagine growing up as Carlos did. Every string in my heart was pulling toward my cousin and I wished I could have helped him from the start. He continued without me saying a word, "When I was eleven, I started selling a local newspaper called *El Diario del Quindio*. I started at four in the afternoon. There were about fifteen kids my age and we ran while selling the newspapers because it was competitive. Food was hard to come by at home so while selling the newspapers, I stopped at the Chinese restaurants. I watched the people who were eating and what they left on their plates. I asked a waiter, 'Sir, can you please give me the leftovers you would otherwise throw away?' He looked at me and saw how skinny and malnourished I was. So, without a word, he obliged. I ripped out a page from the newspaper and he wrapped the leftovers in it and gave it to me. I would go to the street corner, sit on the sidewalk, and eat everything.

One day while delivering the newspaper, I walked by a bar, looked in, and saw my mother Gilma with some friends. I was so happy to see her that I ran inside and said, 'Hi Mom!' The reaction was devastating. She looked at me and quickly turned her head as if she was embarrassed that I was there. I had become a street kid selling newspapers and I was barefooted.

When I turned to leave, I stepped on a lit cigarette butt and burned my foot. My mother Gilma thought it was funny and started laughing at me with her friends. I left feeling sad and embarrassed. I was walking away from the woman I thought was my mother. That day I felt so down that I spent the money I collected from the newspaper, which I was supposed to turn in to the main office. I could not go back to work the following day since I spent the money, so I lost my job. I went to sleep at the house of a neighbor, Puresa, who had eight children. They were also poor.

When you are a child, you like to eat, and because there was not enough food at the house, we were hungry all the time. With some of her children, we used to go to the North neighborhood of the city where the rich lived, begging for food, holding out tin cans as we knocked on doors. I slept most of the time on the streets and for a long time, was unable to afford a pair of shoes. One time in the middle of the night, I was at the central plaza and that man, Camilo, who was my father, was drunk and happened to walk by.

We had just looked at each other. His first reaction was to raise his hand to slap me. That was not going to happen twice, so I ran away. While I was running, I couldn't help but think why he hated me so much if he was my father. He had so much money and I was so poor. Even though I was a street kid, I did not steal money and I never did drugs.

When I was fifteen, I became a waiter in a restaurant. The owner was not a friendly man, and besides not being paid much, I had to pay for my own food. I went back to sleep at my mother's house. Because I did not have a bed, I slept on top of a small desk and had to crouch to fit. It was so uncomfortable, but it was a luxury compared to the streets. One day when my mother returned from one of her disappearances, her parents told her that Ruben Dario, her son, had been accidentally burned on his hand by me. She took a belt and beat me. Then she said, 'That's what happens when you raise a son of a bitch.'

I started to cry and turned to her brother and said, 'Why did she say that and why does she treat me the way she does?'

He simply replied, 'Because you are not her son.'

I continued working at the restaurant and one day I was asked to deliver some food to a whorehouse, La Casa de Leo. When I got there with my delivery, the door opened just enough for me to look inside and I saw my mother Gilma, surrounded by men, drinking and working as a prostitute."

I gasped in shock. I did not want to believe this was the truth, but the pain in Carlos' face as he retold the story made me see otherwise. He continued, "I left in disbelief of what I had seen. It was painful beyond belief. I understood why my mother Gilma disappeared for so many days at a time and how she was making money to pay some bills at the house. She did not know that I saw her and I never said a word.

When I was eighteen, it was time for me to apply for a national identification card. I needed my birth certificate and when I asked Gilma's mother for it, she said, 'They are not your parents. Your birth certificate is in a little town called Sircacia.' That town was only a half hour away from Armenia, and Gilma's mother came with me. The birth certificate showed that my name was Carlos Alberto Gutierrez Munoz, son of Fabio

Gutierrez and Maria Belisa Munoz. When getting my card, I was asked what my parents do. I simply responded, 'They were killed a long time ago in a car accident.' The officials did not question me and I got the card.

When I was twenty-one, I got a job in a modernized bowling club with respectable clientele. I started dressing better and socializing with the cream of Armenia. It did not take long to realize that it took the same effort to have nothing as it did to have many possibilities. It almost seemed that if I wanted a door to open for me, it would. This gave me an outlook on my young adult life that I never had dreamed of before. The world was becoming mine.

I was still working at the bowling club when a woman came to my house. When I got up in the morning, I went to the patio and when I turned my head to the right, I saw that she was looking at me through the window. I did not know who she was but my mother Gilma called me over and said, 'Carlos Alberto, I would like to introduce this lady to you.'

She introduced herself as Marleny. She had a warm look in her eyes and showed a great interest in getting to know me. After getting comfortable, she asked for me to visit her family in Ibague. She left almost immediately and went to Puresa's house, a half block away. Puresa was related somehow to Marleny's family.

When she left, my mother looked at me and said, 'Go to Puresa's house. There is a surprise waiting for you.' When I got there, Marleny started to cry. I asked her if she was okay. And that was when she told me the truth. 'I am your aunt. My daughter Maria Isabel has been asking me to look for you for the longest time."

I nodded my head. Now the story was sounding more like I would expect it to be,

"I found out that my biological mother was a wealthy woman. It brought me back to the time when I was a little kid.

153

On Christmas Eve, I always wished to have a toy microbus, but when I got up, there was nothing for me. I remember when I was three and I got a bicycle for Christmas. That was the first and only real gift I got. Once my sister and brother were born, there was nothing for me.

I decided to go to Ibague and meet my aunt Marleny's family, which was actually my blood family. Little by little I was finding out more about who I was and where I was from. This left me with mixed emotions about what I thought was my real family, the one I knew until now. At my aunt Marleny's house, I felt like I had a place where I was always welcome. I went back to Armenia and Ligia called me to the club. She did not say she was my mother. It was as if it was too painful for her to say it. I will never be able to call her my mother. I never did and I never will.

On the phone one day she said to me, 'I would like to help you. Would you like to go to the United States to study?' To me, this was the biggest door opening. It seemed like out of nowhere, people were suddenly kind and wanting to help me. It made me think a lot about where I came from. Things like this didn't just happen to any street kid.

At the end of the phone call, she asked me to meet her at a restaurant in Girardot where she lived. I had no idea who I was going to be looking for, but neither did she. On a Sunday I left for Girardot. My friend came with me to sit in a restaurant and wait for her. She arrived with her niece nicknamed 'La Nena.' I looked at them and they looked at me without saying a word. She showed up in a fancy car; meanwhile, my only agenda was to impress them as if I had money. I did this by putting a checkbook on the table. What they did not know was that there was nothing inside.

Once she saw me and realized that I was her son, she appeared to be less than pleased. She was satisfying her twenty-six years of curiosity about who she had given birth to. The entire way back to Armenia, I was thinking about how I met the person who hurt me the most. It was a different pain than the one the rest had done to me. This woman who claimed to be my mother hurt me in a hard, scathing, and emotional way. Once she gave me away, she sealed my fate and all the opportunities she could have easily provided me.

When she met me twenty-six years later, it was as if she was shopping, looking at an object and deciding if she liked it or not. The biggest humiliation of my life was when my cousin Jesus Fernando, Chiqui, said to me: 'Cousin, I am going to tell you something and please, don't get upset. My Aunt Ligia asked me to tell you not to tell anyone that you are her son.'

Many times if I was hungry and cold, it was because no one who cared was there to guide me. It is like having a car with no one to steer it. It will crash. In my life, everybody is guilty. The ones that abandoned me and the ones who adopted me. God forgive them. I know there is no perfection in this world, but no matter what, life will grant you good things.

When I went to my Aunt Marleny's house, I felt loved like I never felt before. Sincerity like that you cannot mistake and those moments when she made me feel at home, I will never forget. For that, I love her more than anyone else.

On the other hand, if I had had everything handed to me on a silver platter from a wealthy family, I might not know how to appreciate anything. Through all my struggling and hard times growing up on the streets, I may say 'thank you' to know that I can survive many things, and to this I owe my success today.

I went to work in a supermarket in Buevavista. One day, I went to a disco and met a woman named Margarita. Since the moment I saw her, I knew she was the woman I was going to spend the rest of my life with. This little town was not giving us the opportunity to grow, so Margarita said, 'Let's move to my brother's town. He has a fish market and we can learn the business.'

After spending one year with him, we decided to come back to Pereira to buy our own fish market. Now, I'm a successful businessman, have one daughter Lina, from a previous relation, and two sons with my wife Margarita named Victor and Carlos. The lesson I learned is that in this life, it is not who you are but what you appear to be that controls other people's thinking. Many people, even after they get an education, will still judge a book by its cover."

I nodded my head in agreement and opened my mouth to say the first words since Carlos began his story.

"And sometimes, the picture on the cover is not a pretty one."

My grandfather, Antonio Arbelaez Giraldo, on his way to a
cockfight

Antonio Arbelaez Giraldo and his second wife Matilde Giraldo Londoño

Rafael Muñoz Ospina, my mother's father, holding Maria
Belisa

Camila Murillo Gomez (My mother's mother)

Mother Marleny M. Muñoz and father Jose A. Arbelaez

My mother and her sisters
From left: Maria Belisa, my mother Marleny M. Muñoz, Ligia,
and Maria Teresa

My father Jose A. Arbelaez

My brother Julio Cesar Arbelaez in the mine

Me in India

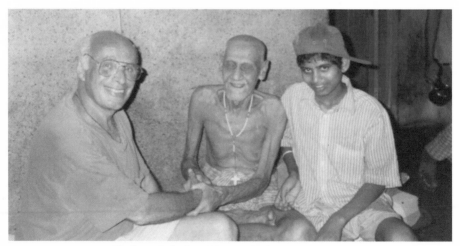

Bob at Mother Teresa's house

My sisters and my son. From left: Maria Claudia, Maria del Pilar, me, German Felipe, Monica, Maria Alejandra, Maria Luisa Fernanda

Joseph John Seviroli & son John Joseph Seviroli in Aspen, CO

My brother Julio Cesar Arbelaez and John Joseph

My brother Jesus Fernando (Chiqui) and his wife Martha
Machado Alcazar

From left: Eva Catherine LaMere, Victor Manuel, a US Marine Corps E4-Marine, and my sister Maria Claudia

From left: my brother Carlos Augusto, Juan Camilo, and Sandra Bonilla lopez.

My husband Jeffrey M. Norton and I

From left: Camila, Natalia, Isabella and German Felipe

From left: Isabella and Camila Arbelaez Parra

From left: Christian Arbelaez, my sister Maria Luisa Fernanda, Erika, Rosario Asta, Marco Arbelaez

Mama making arepas

My sister Monica and her boyfriend Carlos Mario Garces
Ramirez

My brother Jesus Fernando (Chiqui) with my sister Maria Alejandra

Dr. Joan Digby, Professor of English at LIU Post in Long Island, New York

CHAPTER 19: The Start of Many Dreams Coming True

When Felipe was eleven, I decided to create an opportunity for the both of us to be together. We lived all our lives with the family and I wanted to experience how it felt to be a full-time mother.

My sister Pilly was working as an Executive Secretary for the Finance Corporation of Transportation. It was a big company with offices in every major city. I went to their main office in Bogota and spoke directly to the company's president. During our meeting, he asked me where in the country I wanted to work. I told him my preference was Pereira, since I was familiar with the city. He then asked me to start the paperwork while I was in Bogota because coincidentally, they needed an Executive Secretary in Pereira. I went back to Ibague and resigned my position at City Hall and received my severance pay, which covered the five years I worked there.

Mama came with me to Pereira to help me get established. We had to find a place to sleep for a few nights while we searched for a permanent apartment. We looked for a room in strangers' homes that was close to my new job. After many disappointments, we found ourselves at a block of condominiums and started knocking on doors, asking to rent a room for a few days. We did not go to a hotel because I needed to save as much money as I could to pay for the month of security plus the month of rent.

As I look back on that time in my life, I realize the lessons I learned from Julio Cesar during our jungle journey instilled in me a sense of self-reliance. It was crazy and optimistic of me to go knocking on strangers' doors asking for a place to live.

Finally, that night I convinced an old lady to let us stay with her for three days. I paid in advance to win her trust, and we had to give her a long list of relatives who lived in Pereira. For the next three days after I finished work, Mama and I searched the streets for a small apartment to rent. Finally, I saw an empty one on the street level. We knocked on the door and the owner told me the apartment had been rented to someone else. I was so desperate that I said, without begging, "I am ready to take the apartment right now and will not take no for an answer."

After much convincing on my part, he relented, took my money, and a difficult situation was averted. What was ironic is that the apartment was located two blocks from where Felipe was born eleven years earlier. I felt it was meant to be. The next day, Mama and I purchased two beds, a small hot plate, pots, pans, dishes, and some utensils. The apartment was so tiny I did not need many things. It had a small window looking out onto the street and one bedroom. Next to it was another small room which I made into a kitchen. To the left was the bathroom. The place had no closets and in the corner of the bedroom, I hung our clothing.

This was the first time since Felipe was born that he and I were together as mother and son. It was the most fulfilling experience of my life. One of the first tasks I dealt with was sending Felipe to school. All his school life, Felipe attended private schools, even considering our economic situation, and it was my intention to have him continue on this path. I found a private military school, and with his good grades, Felipe was accepted to eighth grade, even though he was only eleven. He was, by far, the youngest student in the class.

This school in Pereira, *Rafael Reyes*, had a rigid military discipline. Improper behavior resulted in a strong punishment of physical work and many unpleasant reprimands. Each school day lasted from seven to five o'clock, and lunch was provided. I could go to work after the bus picked up Felipe and be home before he returned. Despite Felipe being the youngest, he was academically at the top of his class. I tried to give him a little money to spend during his breaks at school, but he never accepted it.

"Mary, you need the money more than I do," he would always say. We interacted with each other as partners more than mother and son. On the corner of our apartment, there was a small bodega, which fortunately extended us credit between paychecks. I got paid every two weeks. We also made use of my credit card to help month to month. This afforded Felipe and I the luxury of occasionally going to a restaurant or movie.

Alba Sofia was a friend I had met long before I got pregnant. She came almost every day to say hello. At that time, she oversaw the Mental Control Silva Program, a mind-enhancing course attended by professionals. It had both adult and child sessions. Felipe was eleven, and after being interviewed by the program directors, they realized he had a maturity level far beyond his years. They placed him in the adult program. I thought it was a nice learning experience for him.

One day, Felipe and I decided it was time for him to receive his first communion. "My love, next Sunday we are going to Mass and you will receive your first communion," I said. He was humbled and excited to have this experience. After Mass, I treated Felipe to an ice cream. I will never forget his expression. It made him happy that we were celebrating together during an important day in his life.

"Thank you," he said through the biggest grin. "Having this ice cream with you makes me happier than any party."

Felipe and I were living in Pereira when we found out that Mama received a visa to go to the United States. It was 1986. For many years, her oldest sister Maria Belisa, who was living in New York for the past twenty years, tried unsuccessfully to talk Mama into joining her. When Aunt Maria Belisa travelled to Colombia for vacation, she always looked for us no matter where we were. Aware of our economic difficulties and of Mama's suffering, she promised herself that one day she would talk Mama into changing her mind.

She never gave up; and so Mama obtained her visa on her first request and made plans to leave two days later. Mama was leaving with the hope that one day she would reunite the entire family in the United States. She wanted all of us to have a bright and successful future.

Felipe and I had a conversation about paying the rent or going to Ibague to say goodbye to Mama. Without giving it much thought, we decided to leave that night. "Let's worry about paying the rent when we return. We don't know how long it will be before we see Mama again," I told Felipe. This opportunity for Mama may have been what saved her life. When she got on the plane, she weighed ninety-four pounds. I think she couldn't endure more of the constant overworking and the lack of consideration for her health.

Soon after she left for the United States, I resigned from my job in Pereira, and Felipe and I moved back to Ibague to live with the family. Four months later, my brother Julio Cesar invited my father, Maria Luisa, and Maria Claudia to vacation at the mine in Venezuela.

The day after Maria Luisa's high school graduation, the three left to join Julio Cesar, who was waiting for them in Puerto Carreno. He had already arranged with the border guards to permit them safe entry into Venezuela illegally.

Julio took them to his house in Salvacion, a village built inside the mining location. His girlfriend, Yolanda, was pregnant and ready to have the baby, and Maria Claudia decided to go to Ciudad Bolivar and stay with her until the baby was born.

She was a beautiful, healthy girl, born on February 5, 1998, and was baptized, "Yahaira." A couple days after Yahaira was born, Claudia found out she was pregnant, and she and

Papa decided to return to Ibague. Her son's father, Victor Manuel, was waiting for them in Bogotá.

When Luisa arrived at the mine, she met a friend of my brother named Jesus Antonio Campos Chacon and three months later they got married. She did not know what to expect from life or what to ask of it, and the relationship that she jumped into so quickly became a new world at which she smiled.

CHAPTER 20: When All Hope was Lost, A Dream was Reborn

Back in Ibague, I realized that there was no future in Colombia for Felipe and I. I did not want to spend the rest of my life sitting at a desk making a salary just to survive. I decided to apply for a visa to the United States and follow in my mother's footsteps. It was not as easy as I thought it would be. It was not the right time for me to leave, and with my inexperience and impatience, I was forcing a move without it being in God's will.

Six times I tried and six times my visa request was denied. Each time, a little piece of me died. Not only was the denial emotionally painful, but economically difficult, since I had to pay for a bus and expenses to go to the American Embassy in Bogotá. Sometimes, the hardest part was leaving the Embassy with my Colombian passport without a visa, which contained all of my dreams. I felt like all my hopes were disappearing and all the doors of opportunity were closing.

A year passed since I last attempted to get a visa, and Mama was getting frustrated. She was living with Aunt Maria Belisa, her husband Ramiro, and their son Kevin. They had a beautiful home on Long Island and a successful dental laboratory in Queens. When my mother realized my difficulties of getting a visa, she told my aunt the possibility existed that she would return to Colombia rather than be separated from her children. Every time we talked on the phone, I tried to encourage Mama to hold on to the dream.

We saw, through pictures, the change in Mama. She looked younger and healthier than ever before. If she had remained in Colombia, we might have lost her at a young age.

When she left, she was tired and worn out from the hardness of her life and seeing how happy and lively she was made me push and try even harder to get a visa. The sixth and last attempt at obtaining a visa was when a dear friend, Don Eri, decided to help me. We went to a legal affairs office in Ibague and filed a statement indicating that we had been living together for ten years. The idea was that since he had the financial requirements to satisfy the American Embassy, we would go as a common-law marriage and obtain the visa for both of us. While Don Eri was not the least bit interested in a visa, as a friend, he volunteered to do whatever he could to help me get out of the country.

With just my luck, Don Eri got a visa and I was again denied. After these rejections, I said to my mother that I had used up all the resources I could find to go legally to the United States. I now was going to start searching for other possibilities. I refused to surrender.

Mama sent me eight hundred dollars that I used to try to buy a visa. My first attempt at buying a visa was through a contact in Bogotá, who supposedly had the ability to obtain a visa through an arrangement with personnel who worked inside the Embassy. He asked me to go to the Embassy, go through the procedures, and wait for my visa's approval. He said that he had already spoken to his contact. However, when I left the Embassy without the visa, he was outside waiting for his money. The truth was that he had no connections and was just hoping that a visa might be issued and he could have made some dollars by doing nothing.

My next attempt was through a contact in Cali, who had been successful in the past through a system where real visas were issued, however the picture would be changed to give the person a false identification, matching the name on the visa.

Fortunately for me, the day before I arrived, a bunch of people with forged visas were caught at the airport and my contact had been arrested. I returned to Ibague and gave the money to my sister for safekeeping.

One weekend, I decided to take a trip to Neiva, a city close from Ibague and while I was gone, the apartment was robbed. Carlos Augusto was home alone when there was a knock on the door. When he opened it, two men and a woman armed with a gun pushed their way inside. One robber hit Carlos Augusto on the head with the butt of a revolver and tied him up. They taped his mouth and threatened to kill him if he made any noise. They immediately went to the closet where Maria del Pilar hid my eight hundred dollars, took it, and left.

Carlos Augusto freed himself and began shouting out the window for help. When I returned home the following day, Jesus Fernando, Carlos Augusto, and Maria del Pilar asked me to sit down before telling me the bad news. I was absolutely devastated. My money was gone and I could not believe it. My last hope to go to the United States was gone.

Carlos Augusto had also been hurt badly. The blow to his head caused blood clotting under his skull and he was having terrible headaches. We decided not to call the police out of concern for our safety. We were scared that the robbers might return and take revenge. The morning of the robbery, a friend who knew about the money, asked Maria del Pilar to change a twenty-dollar bill for him. She thought that his request was unusual since in Ibague, the use of dollars was unnecessary and all business was done in pesos. However, she went where she kept the money, followed by him, and made the conversion. Later that day when the thieves forced their way into the apartment, they knew exactly where the money was. Obviously, someone told them about its location. All these setbacks to my plans to leave Colombia were messages from God telling me that the time was not right to leave.

One day, after I had given up all hope, I received a phone call from Aunt Maria Belisa. She asked me if I would take the risk of traveling to the United States illegally, and without giving it any thought, I said yes. She had contacts in Mexico and was going to make the arrangements for the trip.

By this time, Mama had been living with my aunt for two years, and in her frustration, she was planning to return to Colombia. Without Mama knowing, my aunt was planning for my arrival in New York to be a surprise Christmas present. My dream was reborn, and I had the feeling the right moment had finally arrived. I obtained my Mexican visa, which at that time was easy, and left a few days later and flew to Mexico City. I was going to stay in Mexico City with the mother of an old friend of my Aunt Maria Belisa who had recently died of AIDS.

Because I had a fear of flying, I asked the flight attendant if she could give me a pill to calm my nerves. She said they were not allowed to give out medication. I started drinking gin and tonic instead, not realizing that my behavior was creating much suspicion amongst the crew. As soon as we arrived in Mexico City, I was the only person detained on the flight. Immigration kept me in a room under observation for more than an hour. The lady with whom I was supposed to stay sent two friends to pick me up. As time passed, I became concerned that these people might leave the airport and I had no address, phone number, or a way to tell them that I was detained.

From that room, I was taken to another location where a rude woman ordered me to remove all my clothing. She searched my body and bags. She threatened that if no one was waiting for me outside, she would send me back to Colombia. I told her that I had been held for two hours and I was afraid that by this time, the people picking me up would have left. My biggest concern was that I had no money, not even for a taxi. Unable to find anything, she let me go, and at the Customs exit, I met the couple, just as they were getting ready to leave.

For the next fifteen days, I stayed at Carmen's apartment. I enjoyed the opportunity to visit the Virgin of Guadalupe, who brought many miracles to my family, and saw

179

the most beautiful places in Mexico City while waiting for my aunt's money to arrive for me to continue the journey.

After the fifteen days, plans were made to continue the trip, so I left Mexico City by plane to Tijuana. Two girls who took me to their parent's home on the outskirts of Tijuana met me at the airport. The father was responsible for getting me across the border and was supervising all the arrangements. I slept at their home for one day, and at two in the morning, left the house with the son-in-law who took me to a location in Tijuana.

Two men responsible for taking me across the border met us. My aunt, in an attempt to assure the success of the trip, made arrangements for me to be the only person they guided that day. Usually, there would be a group of ten or more people. My aunt and I kept in contact by phone during the whole trip, and Mama still had no idea I was coming.

The two men and I walked for three hours in the darkness. It was raining and I had no idea where we were, so I just followed them. They never spoke, and when I tried to make conversation, they answered me in as few words as possible. After three hours of walking, we hid in a small drainage tunnel. One man stayed with me while the other went ahead to check on the changing of border guards. He returned to where we hid and again, we started to walk at a fast pace.

Once we crossed into the United States, we started running through the back streets of San Diego. It was already six in the morning, dawn was quickly approaching, and the streets were empty. I knew that it was time for us to get off the streets, so we found ourselves at a hotel in downtown San Diego.

I waited there with the two men until the two daughters of the man who made the deal with my aunt showed up. They came by car from Tijuana with my luggage and airplane ticket. The clothing I had worn to cross the border was dirty and wet and the girls immediately threw them in the garbage. We sat in the hotel room and the two men who guided me were silently waiting to be paid by the girls. I took a shower, changed my clothes, and then they took me out for breakfast. We then went to the airport in San Diego, where the girls put me on a plane to John F. Kennedy International Airport.

When I got off the plane, I knew I was home. This was the place I had been looking for all my life, and all the efforts and tribulations I had been through were worth it. I spent many years of my life in the wrong places and everything I tried to accomplish became more challenging. But now that I was here, I knew that opportunities would present themselves at the right time and place.

At the same time, this was the beginning of a new life for my Felipe, the family, and myself. Cecilia, a close friend from Colombia, and my aunt met me at the airport. Meanwhile, my aunt's husband Ramiro stayed with Mama in Westbury, New York. He kept trying to feed Mama drinks of aguardiente, hoping the alcohol would calm her, so that when she saw me after all this time, the impression could not be as strong.

I was nervous the entire car ride to the house. When we arrived, they led me through the garage, and when Mama came to say hello to my aunt and Cecilia, she put her hands on her face and hugged me in disbelief. Her dream had started to come true. I was the first of her children to reach the United States.

Dreams do come true.

CHAPTER 21: Adjusting in a New World

I arrived in New York on December 16, 1987. We enjoyed the holidays with my aunt, and when January came, it was time for me to find a job. Since I spoke no English and had no papers, my choices were limited. The only options I had were babysitting and any other work that did not require a social security number. I did not have a driver's license and did not know how to use public transportation. So, my job would have to require me to live-in, except for the day off.

Since I would live-in for six days, I was isolated from the family. I felt trapped. It was winter, cold, and no time to be outdoors. At the end of the week, my aunt would pick me up and I spent the day off with the family in Westbury. I was not happy and my spirits were down. Every time I saw someone with his or her own place to live, I could not picture it happening to me. I realized that by working hard for the first four months, studying a small book of basic English and committing each page to memory, I was moving slowly toward my independence and opportunities for a better job.

My last job babysitting was in Long Beach, Long Island, working for a family with a three-year-old son. They immigrated to the United States from Turkey.

The mother was beautiful and was a famous belly dancer in Turkey. She used to host parties at her home. One day, she invited me to one, and I had the opportunity to meet Abdula.

He was an American citizen from Turkey, and it was with him that I started to practice my English, getting my ear used to the sounds and developing a vocabulary. He also exposed me to his wonderful taste in music. His knowledge covered everything from classical to Spanish music.

After four months of working for this family, I resigned my position. Abdula came to the house in Long Beach to pick me up and take me back to my aunt's. When we got there,

Mama came outside, telling me that she and I had to leave. My aunt had a problem with her husband Ramiro, and our presence at the house was no longer acceptable. I couldn't help but think what a time it was to give up my job.

That night, Mama went to stay at Cecilia's and Abdula offered to let me stay at his house. At that moment, we felt in limbo, not knowing where to go or what to do. But thank God it happened, because it was the only way for us to be forced to do something on our own. Three days later, my cousin Jorge called and told me that he found a house in Westbury. We decided to share it between the three of us. Fortunately, I saved money during the four months I was working, so we pooled our money to cover the rent and a month of security.

Overnight, like a miracle, we had our own place. All of our friends, including my aunt, gave us furniture, bedding, and kitchen appliances. We ended up with a completely furnished house, all through the gifts of wonderful people. It is amazing to think that just a couple days before, I could not fathom that we would ever have our own place.

Meanwhile, Felipe was in Colombia with the rest of the family and attending school. I was moving ahead with my plans to have Felipe with me in the United States. My abilities in the language were improving; I was finding my way around Long Island easier; and most importanly, I developed enough confidence so that when Felipe came, I would be secure in my capabilities to help him adjust to this new life.

We were in constant communication by phone and letter. There is one letter Felipe wrote when he was thirteen which impacted me the most:

Mary:

I did not want to worry you. You should know that above all, I love you and I always will, like someone who means more

*to me than just a mother: **A good friend I can always count on.
Remember that in life, friends are very scarce.***

*When I was a child, I never thought about you as a
mother. Mama raised me and I understood because you were
young and with your own dreams. Also, Mama, who has a very
strong temperament, thought (I think) that you were unable to
raise me. You have no idea how much I regret not having had
the chance to grow up with you.*

*You should know that the best moments of my life, and I
can swear it, were when we lived together in Pereira. I felt what
a home was like being just you and I (it's becoming very
difficult for me to write. I am writing what I am thinking, and
thinking faster than I am writing and while I think in something,
I am writing something else).*

*Back to the writing, I assure you that when we were
living in Pereira, I held you in the highest esteem. I was very
proud sharing every single day with you. It made me feel secure
and besides everything, it was wonderful having you as a
roommate.*

*In this moment, I would like to revive those moments. I
know it will happen and when that happens, it's not going to be
too late. The truth is that I have always thought that for you not
to raise me was a mistake; because it created a big distance
between us and unfortunately, I became used to your absence.*

*For a father, I am not worried because I had never
count on one emotionally and maybe the education he would
have given me, would not had been as good as the one I got in
my family, and for that I am pleased. My aspirations in life are
to become a professional, even though right now I have not
chosen one. What you say about not needing you... let me tell
you that you are wrong because even though I aspire to be
successful, I want you at my side.*

*At this moment, you are for me the example and I am
proud of you because I see that everything you have wanted in*

life, you have got it no matter what and that is admirable. I hope I have inherited that quality from you. You have never deceived me.

About you getting married, I do not think it is a bad idea. You are young and beautiful. Only look for a person who is good for you and do not think about me because as you well know, I had never needed a father before and now even less. I just need you.

About my preferences, I like to read, play sports, and have fun. Maybe my biggest concern is not to become successful and not to be able to help with the support of our family. Sometimes, I feel like a parasite and think I should do something about it, and I know I will. I read a lot and I am getting bored with water polo. The training is excessive and monotonous. Since I do not write much, I am saying good-bye, asking you please do not worry for me. I love you and always will.

I hope to have you close to me physically, because you are always in my heart. I hope that soon we will be together and I pray to God for it.

P.S. Do you remember Pancho? I do.

Felipe's letter inspired me to do everything in my power to make life in America better for all of us. I got my first job working in an office for a TV station through a Hempstead agency. The job did not pay much, and sometimes they did not pay me on time, but it did not bother me. I was making enough money to contribute toward the rent and I now started to feel more comfortable in New York.

After a few months of having our own place, Mama decided to go to Florida to help her youngest sister, Maria Teresa, who was preparing for her oldest daughter Lynn's wedding. We were never close to my Aunt Maria Teresa. Since

185

she got married and came to live in Florida with her husband Octavio, they never attempted to keep in contact with our side of the family.

When Mama made the decision to go to Florida, it created an imbalance in our ability to cover the house expenses. We had just moved and were adjusting to new living conditions. That is why I did not understand why Mama, who had always been a practical person, now felt compelled to make the trip.

Shortly before the wedding, their sister Ligia arrived from Colombia. Around the same time, my Aunt Maria Belisa flew from New York, and for the first time in twenty years, all four sisters were together. It was three months since my mother left for Florida, and after the wedding, Mama, Maria Belisa, and Ligia returned to New York. That same night, I was sick with stomach aches and was throwing up all night. Mama tried some home remedies without success and at six in the morning, asked Cecilia to drive me to the hospital.

The diagnosis was appendicitis and I was admitted for surgery. After surgery, a doctor came to my room to see how I was doing and told me that he saw my last name on the admitting chart and realized I was from Colombia. He assumed from my last name that I came from a wealthy Colombian family, legally, and could pay the exorbitant hospital bill. He saw in me the opportunity to show the hospital staff a different view of the Colombian people. As I was lying in bed, listening to him, I was saying to myself, "if only he knew the truth."

While we were talking, a resident doctor came into my room to give me an intravenous. He was warned by the Colombian doctor to be careful and gentle as he inserted the IV needle. It seemed to me fifteen minutes before the needle was in place, and by the time he finished, I was full of little holes and my arm was black and blue. I was discharged from the hospital and sent home to recover from the surgery.

A week later, Maria Teresa called from Florida to see how everyone was and to say hello to her sisters. That night, my Aunt Maria Belisa with her husband Ramiro, Ligia, Mama, my cousin Jorge, and I got together for a card game. While we were sitting at the dining room table, the phone rang. I picked up and it was Octavio, calling from Florida and asking to speak to Mama.

I gave the telephone to Mama, and after a few moments I heard her scream. We kept asking her what was wrong but it took her the longest time to gather herself and speak. Finally, she said four of the heaviest words: "Maria Teresa is dead."

This was the first time in my life I saw Mama so devastated and out of control. I wrapped my arms around her and did not let go. She needed all the support in the world at that moment.

Octavio had been ready to leave for a business trip to Colombia, but due to bad weather he canceled it. That evening, Octavio was lying in bed as Maria Teresa massaged his hands. Suddenly, she stopped and asked him to take her to the hospital. He realized it was serious because my aunt, who was always concerned about her appearance, did not bother to change her clothing before leaving the house.

At the hospital, while they filled out paperwork, Maria Teresa rested all her bodyweight on Octavio's shoulder. Seconds later, she quietly died from a heart attack.

She was only forty-one and left behind Lynn, who just married, Jennifer, only nine, and the youngest, John.

Mama and her sisters returned to Florida for the funeral. After the funeral, Ligia returned to Colombia and Maria Belisa came back to New York. Mama stayed in Florida with Octavio and the children for the next month to help dispose of the painful remainders of my aunt's life. Mama did not return to New York until Octavio sold the house. She helped him move to a new apartment.

The television program I was working for failed, and I found myself without a job. I went to an employment agency in Hempstead and they sent me to a real estate office. They needed a secretary. I only worked there for fifteen days before they fired me because my English was not good enough.

The owner of the real estate agency had a friend who was the Director of the Community Action Council in a town called Port Washington. The purpose of this office was to serve the poor in that area. He gave me a job.

Since most clients were Spanish-speaking, my lack of English was not important. The office was located across the street from a restaurant called Louie's, and it faced the Manhasset Bay. From my desk, I had a beautiful view of the harbor.

I did a variety of tasks and it gave me a wonderful feeling of satisfaction to help these people. I loved this work, and in a way, it gave me a direction in what I wanted to do with my life. Helping people gave me a real sense of purpose and a rewarding feeling in my heart.

Every morning, the bus dropped me off four blocks from the office. It became routine to stop at Louie's to get a container of coffee to bring to work. One day while getting my coffee, a man approached me at the counter, told me his name was Bob, and asked for my name. When I told him that my name was Maria Isabel, he wanted to know where I was from and whether I had seen the movie *"West Side Story."* At that time, I could speak English but had difficulty understanding. I liked him and decided not to let him know of my shortcoming with the language. Two days later, he loaned me the video (which I thought was boring). This was the start of our relationship.

With my new job, we could afford a better place to live. Mama, my cousin Jorge, and I moved into a three-bedroom apartment which occupied the entire first floor of a house on Salisbury Park Drive, in Westbury. The owner of the house,

Adriana, was a young Colombian woman with a five-year-old daughter. Her husband was killed eight days earlier on a business trip to Colombia. She was forced to rent part of the house to help pay the mortgage.

It was not a relationship between landlord and tenant. It became a close friendship since she was from Colombia, had lost her husband, and was struggling to keep her house.

Jorge, who was working as a real estate agent, started to help Adriana save the house. They became romantically involved, and she was always involved in our family activities. During the evenings, Aunt Maria Belisa, her husband Ramiro, and Kevin, their son, would come over to visit and play cards. They lived only a few blocks from us and it was like having one big family all the time.

Adriana, realizing that Ramiro was apparently successful, having a beautiful house and nice cars, thought he would be the perfect solution to her problem and started flirting with him. On many occasions, she would ask me to take care of her daughter and sometimes she would even leave her daughter alone upstairs for hours. We would hear her little girl cry.

What we did not know then was that while we were taking care of her daughter, she was having an affair with Ramiro. When the situation became obvious, my aunt and her son Jorge decided to follow Ramiro. It was no surprise to see Ramiro and Adriana together.

It was painful for my aunt to see *her* marriage of twenty-five years destroyed. Once my aunt confronted Ramiro, he dropped all pretenses and brought the affair out into the open.

Jorge was in love with Adriana and had a difficult time accepting his stepfather's relationship with his girlfriend. Mama and I decided to leave Adriana's house and moved to an apartment on Ellison Avenue in Westbury.

Ramiro, realizing his marriage was breaking up, decided to sell his dental laboratory business in Queens and go back to

Colombia. My aunt, in her desperation to save her marriage, followed him, leaving behind the house and letting the bank take it over. Unfortunately, once back in Colombia, my aunt and Ramiro were unable to stay together. Finally, she left with her son Kevin to restart their lives in Miami.

CHAPTER 22: One by One, We Followed Each Other to New York

Back in Colombia, my sister Pilly, in charge of the rest of the family, was an Executive Secretary for the National Corporation of Transportation and was attending the university pursuing her degree in business at night. Even though Mama was not there, they kept the family values and traditions. It gave me peace of mind to know that Felipe was in good hands. Pilly became the mother figure of the house and Maria Alejandra, Monica, and Felipe became attached to her. Carlos Augusto was living and working in Cali. Julio Cesar, Jesus Fernando, Maria Claudia, and Maria Luisa lived in Venezuela.

Once Mama came to this country, those left in Colombia set their minds to join her. Maria Alejandra was studying finances and Monica, the youngest, did marketing. Felipe was fifteen and a senior in high school. In Colombia, when a boy finishes high school, he is required to serve one year in the army. Felipe was approved and his induction would occur upon graduation. I was aware of this and decided to accelerate my effort to get Felipe to the United States before the army took him.

Bob offered to help me with an affidavit of financial support and a letter of invitation written by his youngest son Eric asking Felipe to visit during summer vacation. This was the only way to get him to the United States. I was illegal and even my mother, who became a legal resident, couldn't do anything. We had no time to complete the necessary paperwork to get him out of Colombia before his military obligation.

Felipe went to the Embassy in Bogota and applied for a visa. Being a minor, he had to wait outside while Papa, who legally was listed as his father, completed the visa application.

That afternoon, Papa exited the Embassy with a thumb up—he had gotten the visa. The whole trip back to Ibague,

Felipe had his passport in his shirt pocket; he never took his hand away from it. All of his dreams were contained in that little book.

Twenty days later on July 7, 1991, Mama, Bob, and I picked Felipe up at JFK in New York. I had not seen my son for three years and only pictures showed the dramatic changes in appearance. He was no longer the little boy I left behind.

When we got to the airport I could not spot him myself. Bob was the first to locate him. At first, it was difficult to get used to his new look and the changes in his personality. He had become a young man. It was not easy for Felipe to adjust either, since he had been away from Mama and I for three years and was used to his independence. Mama and I worked during the day and Felipe spent this time alone at the apartment until school started two months later.

He had no friends, did not speak the language, and was struggling to reestablish a relationship with Mama and I. We had been without him for so many years that now that he was with us, we were overwhelming him with our attention and demands.

A month later, my sister Pilly, having successfully gotten her visa, made the decision to come to the United States. It invoked a conflict of emotions in her because she was not only following a family dream but also leaving behind the rest of the family for whom she was responsible. Maria Alejandra and Monica felt unprotected without Mama and filled the void by creating an attachment to Pilly. She was to them, not only a mother, figure but also their best friend.

In the mornings after Pilly showered, she would find a dress Monica picked out for her to wear. Monica would get up earlier to make sure the dress was clean and ironed. After Pilly was dressed, breakfast would be waiting for her, and after breakfast, when she would brush her teeth, Maria Alejandra and Monica would have the toothpaste on the toothbrush ready for her. This was their way of showing Pilly their love and appreciation for everything she was doing for the family while Mama was away. Pilly made arrangements to leave from Cali so that she could say goodbye to Carlos Augusto.

He was offered a job in Cali to complete his internship as an Agricultural Engineer with a well-respected sugar cane plantation. Carlos Augusto got along well with the executives of the company and when his internship was complete, he became an asset to the company and was pursuing his Master's degree in water and soils.

Pilly was not fully aware of the bond Monica formed toward her until the evening of her departure. Maria Alejandra, Monica, and Papa went to the bus terminal in Ibague to say goodbye. While they were waiting for the departure to be announced, they sat on benches in the waiting room.

Monica and Maria Alejandra sat on opposite sides of Pilly as Monica held Pilly's hand. Suddenly, Pilly noticed Monica's grip tighten as her hands shook. Pilly glanced over at Monica's face and at that moment, Monica slid from her seat onto the floor. Maria Alejandra immediately knelt beside her, noticing a trickle of blood forming at her mouth. She looked up at Pilly and cried, "She's dead!"

Pilly screamed for help. Papa was running around the terminal yelling in terror, and he and Pilly lost control of themselves in shock. What they did not know was that the stress of Pilly leaving caused Monica to have an epileptic seizure. Within a short time, Monica began to recover and Maria Alejandra breathed the words, "She's alive."

The four of them went to the hospital where the doctors confirmed it had been a seizure from stress. Pilly, out of guilt and concern for Monica's wellbeing, said, "I changed my mind. I am not going to leave you behind."

It was already morning when they went back to the house. Maria Alejandra went to the university and it was there where she, who the previous night held things together and kept control over the crisis, lost it and began crying uncontrollably. When Monica found out that Pilly canceled her plans to come to the United States, she said, "It is everyone in the family's dream to follow Mama. If you go, then the rest of us will be forced to follow."

Two weeks later on August 21, 1991, Pilly came to New York. Since Felipe was only fifteen, too young to go to college and still needing to learn the language, we decided he should repeat the last two years of high school. Mama and I were working full-time and Pilly spent each day alone, crying and saying, "What am I doing here? I want to go back!"

The girls were constantly on her mind and now she had to deal with this new life. Her first and only manual labor job was helping Gladys, a friend, clean a house where she was going to earn forty dollars a day. While Pilly was cleaning the house, all she could think of was, "God, please let this be the first and last house I will ever clean in my life."

She motivated herself by thinking of the bottle of perfume she would buy with the forty dollars. After that day, Pilly spent two months at home without going once. One day she said to herself, "Tomorrow will be the last day I will spend the whole day inside this house."

Coincidentally, the next day I called Pilly from the office where I was working. My boss, Rafael, president of Hempstead Hispanic Civic Association, told me about a job that he thought Pilly could handle. The following day, she went for an interview and was hired on the spot.

Fortunately, this job did not require her to speak English and her immigration status was not an issue. The company was an entertainment booking business that brought performers from Central and South America to the United States. She became the boss's right hand, and with her business administration background, was able to handle all the day-to-day business arrangements for the performances. Even though her salary was minimal, she felt that she was finally doing something worthwhile.

CHAPTER 23: Love and Hardship

Bob and I did not have a normal relationship. When we met, he was in a relationship that was moving in a destructive direction. He was with a group of people who reached a point in their lives where self-indulgence was the rule of the day and whatever pleased them was what they did.

While they were not hurting people outside the group, they certainly were not helping each other unless it was in support of their own desires. It was during this time that I met Bob. He did not want to give up the group, and chose to play both ends.

Bob was not coping well when we met and found being with me a soothing and predictable diversion from the day-to-day madness of his life. He had his youngest son, Eric, living with him in Port Washington. He was thirteen.

After dating Bob for three years, I decided to end our relationship. The last time I saw him, he said that he was unwilling to give up his friendships, which was not going to work for me. The first time Bob realized his life was going down the drain was after a heavy night of partying. He awoke the following morning with the right side of his face paralyzed and assumed the worst: That he had suffered a stroke.

After some tests, it was diagnosed as a facial muscle disorder called Bell's Palsy. The doctor informed him that it either went away by itself or just stayed the same. Fear set in, and he knew it was time to change his behavior.

The apartment where Mama and I lived became too small now that Pilly and Felipe lived with us. So we moved to a house on Carmen Avenue in Westbury, which gave us more living space. It was a move at the right moment, because my oldest brother Julio Cesar and his girlfriend Iris decided to leave Venezuela and join us in New York.

It was six months since I saw Bob when he came to my house looking for me. I was dating someone else and the only thing I could do for him was to offer him my friendship. Obviously, my decision was based on his past behavior, and I did not wish to put myself through that level of pain and exposure of my feelings again.

Some months passed until we agreed to meet in Westbury at a local bar. "Will you marry me?" he asked abruptly. I did say yes. It was January 6, 1994, and we agreed to get married three days later. We took Mama, Felipe, and Pilly out to dinner and told them about our plans. The next day, we went with Eric and his girlfriend to a restaurant in Manhasset. Eric was eighteen and Felipe turned seventeen a few days earlier.

Bob had two sons from his first marriage to Clarice. The oldest, Todd, finished medical school and started his residency in Washington D.C. Kurt, the middle, was attending the (Naval Academy) in South Carolina. Eric, the youngest, was from Bob's second marriage to Kathy.

We were concerned about Eric's reaction to our marriage. He had been living with Bob for four years and grew accustomed to his independence and Bob's undivided attention. To avoid complication in Eric's life, we decided that I would stay in Westbury with Mama and Felipe while he finished his senior year. This would give Eric time to adjust to having Felipe and I in his life.

The day before the wedding, I worked as usual, and that evening, Pilly and I put together ten dollars, the only money in the house, to buy a pair of shoes. We went to the most inexpensive shoe stores but had no luck. Ten dollars was not enough, but the following morning Mama was able to get another ten. With twenty dollars, I bought a pair of shoes to match my dress.

A judge in Garden City married us. That day was the playoffs of the NFL championship and I don't know who was playing, but the judge was pushing us to finish with the ceremony by the end of halftime. After the ceremony, my boss and coworkers gave us a reception at the office. By three in the afternoon, we drove to Sag Harbor and took a two-day honeymoon at the American Hotel. When we got back on Sunday night, I stayed at Mama's house and Bob went home to Port Washington.

Eric, who was supposed to spend the weekend at his mother's house, was nowhere to be found. So Bob called his ex-wife Kathy to find out where he was. She said that Eric was at his girlfriend's house in Manorhaven and had not come to her for the weekend. Eric packed all his clothing and the only thing left of his at the house was his television and stereo.

Bob went to Eric's girlfriend's house where he and Eric had an argument. Eric accused him of replacing him with me. Even though it was not true, this was how Eric felt, and I could understand. Bob tried to convince Eric that his fear was unwarranted and Eric agreed to return home.

One month after the wedding, in February 1994, Julio Cesar crossed from New Laredo Mexico into Laredo, Texas, by way of El Rio Grande. He and Iris made the crossing at night through the most dangerous part of the border because of the constant video surveillance and the presence of the border patrol, both on the Mexican and American side.

The trip was risky considering all the countries they had to go through to get to United States, and a single mistake at the last minute could ruin their success. They called home from Washington D.C. to let us know that they got there successfully and would be in New York that night.

It was nine months earlier that Julio Cesar left Venezuela with his girlfriend Iris and went to Colombia with the idea of coming to the United States. It was an idea that kept getting stronger as days passed by.

CHAPTER 24: A Coyote in the Family

It wasn't until I saw Julio Cesar in New York that I learned of his story and of the many hardships he endured to reach us. After traveling through Colombia to visit the family, he went to a small town near Cali called, "Puerto Tejada." He saw Carlos Augusto, who was working for a large sugarcane plantation. He was the manager of three thousand acres and one hundred and fifty employees.

Julio Cesar said to him, "Iris and I are going to Buenaventura. My plan is to get to Panama and from there I have to figure out a way to get to the United States." Buenaventura is an important trade center and the most important Pacific port in Colombia.

Carlos Augusto gave my brother and his wife his blessing and wished them luck. Julio Cesar then went to Iris and told her, "We do not have much money left. Let's see how far we can get." Iris was as determined as Julio to make it to the United States, so she was willing to take the same risks. So, they registered in Buenaventura at an inexpensive hotel in the center of the city, and in the morning, Iris got a job at a bakery. She was not making much money but it was enough for them to eat and pay the hotel. Meanwhile, Julio Cesar was trying to find a way to get illegally to Panama by boat.

Somebody told him about a guy named Pedro whose business was to trade wood and food to Jurado in a two-hundred-fifty-foot boat with twenty crewmembers. Jurado is a little town bordering Panama.

Julio Cesar knew this was a good opportunity for he and Iris to continue their trip, so he decided to look for Pedro at his office. When he told Pedro that they needed to get to the Colombian border of Panama, he said, "At the present time we are having a lot of problems with the guerrillas and it is going to be almost impossible for me to help you."

At the same moment, Pedro turned to someone else in the office and said, "Where is the guy who was supposed to wash my car?" Julio Cesar saw this as an opportunity to establish a friendship with Pedro. He thought to himself, *This old car, I will wash it.*

"I will wash your car," Julio Cesar said eagerly. He had a feeling this would be the only opportunity to win Pedro's confidence; so he made sure that the old car looked like new. When Julio Cesar was done, he said, "Pedro, please don't leave us here. We need to get out of this city and I will help you with anything you need." He was so determined and persuasive. He was not going to give up. Finally, Pedro gave in.

"Come back tomorrow at two in the afternoon, and I will see what I can do to help you," he said under his breath.

The following day, Julio Cesar and Iris were at Pedro's office waiting with their few belongings. "I will take you for free as far as I can, but I cannot guarantee to take you all the way to Jurado," he explained hastily. The couple thanked him repeatedly. They could not believe that they were finally going on to the next leg of their journey.

The boat trip afforded them an opportunity to see the beautiful scenery of Colombia's Pacific Coast. Pedro provided them with nice accommodations and plenty of food that the crew shared with them. The boat stopped in all of the ports to buy wood and plantain, and by the time they arrived to Bahia Solano, the boat was full of provisions ready to go back to Buenaventura.

Julio Cesar asked Pedro if he had any idea how they could continue the trip to Jurado, which was still a forty-hour boat ride away. Pedro pointed out a chalet, which was owned by Pablo Escobar, and looked after by a fisherman.

He said, "Go to the chalet and tell the fisherman you know me. He will allow you to spend the night. Tomorrow morning, a friend of mine is going to arrive from Buenaventura and he is going further toward your destination. You can get a ride with him, just mention my name."

Julio Cesar and Iris thanked him again and set off for the chalet. The fisherman, just as Pedro said, allowed the two to spend the night. The people in this village make their living by selling and trading wood, plantain, and fish. The following day, they boarded the boat that was recommended by Pedro. Juan was in charge and had five men working for him trading wood and food. During the evening, Juan decided to anchor and they went ashore in a dingy to a small village in order to negotiate some wood.

They were fortunate to meet a fisherman who offered them to stay with his wife and nine children for the night. His house was a simple hut with a dirt floor near the beach and they hang hammocks for everyone to sleep. On the table were candles, since they had no electricity, and the wife cooked a wonderful fish dinner on a wood fire.

As Julio Cesar started to tell them about his adventures, the fisherman brought a bottle of aguardiente, a Colombian cane sugar drink, and as the evening continued, they drank. One story he told was about his experience in a helicopter crash in the jungle in Venezuela, when he and the pilot luckily survived.

"I left the mine in Guaniamo, Venezuela, in March, 1989, and went to another mine called Karum, on the Brazilian border. A one-hour trip had to be made by a light plane from Ciudad Bolivar to Uriman, which is a small port town on the Caroni River. From Uriman to Karum, the trip took another fifty minutes and had to be done by helicopter, since this location had no runway.

The only alternative would be to travel in a canoe. The river has many rapids, which requires the canoe to be carried from one side of the rapids to the other, a trip that can easily take fifteen days.

Ninety percent of the production from this mine was high quality diamonds. Karum was discovered in January 1989 and active until 1992. Seventeen people died of what was believed to be the last traces of the Black Plague from the 1900's. The infection occurred so rapidly that people were dying in two or three days. Now the mine is re-opened. When I got to the mine, the workers were doing all the mining with shovels and hatchets. The location made it impossible to bring in heavy equipment by land, so the only way to do it was by helicopter, which was expensive." Everybody was excited listening to Julio Cesar tell his anecdotes in the mine.

He continued, "My first trip to the mine was as a diamond buyer, representing one of the largest companies in Belgium. The first person I met upon my arrival was an old Brazilian man, Mavesa. When I told him I was there to buy diamonds, he gave me the keys to his office and told me to use it. He was leaving that day in the helicopter I arrived in to Ciudad Bolivar.

I started buying diamonds without making any profit in an attempt to get to know the miners, have them trust me, and for them to spread the word to other miners that there was a new buyer in town. There was one street with the buyers' offices on both sides of the street. Since I needed to have an office of my own, I noticed that at the end of the street there was a large tree one hundred twenty feet high with roots of eighteen or twenty-four feet in diameter. I hired some workers to cut the tree down and this was where I built my office. I hired some workers to build it out of the wood from the fallen tree. It had two windows in the front and I paid some local Indians to weave a roof of large palm leaves. It was a strategic location so I could look out the window and see which offices the miners were going to before they came to me. Once I had a general idea of what the other buyers were paying, I knew that the miners were going to come to me first.

Once I spent the money the company gave me to buy diamonds, I went back to Ciudad Bolivar, delivered the diamonds I purchased, and when they gave me more money, I returned to Karum," Julio Cesar explained.

The government's Ministry of Mines regulates business at the mine. The way it works is that each person is permitted to have two acres of land providing that they clear it. That is the maximum amount of land one is allowed to use. Only four cylinder engines were allowed with hoses no larger than four inches in diameter. This way, the government was able to assure the distribution of land for mining was equitable.

The owner of the machinery receives sixty-five percent of the production value, with the remaining being divided among the workers including the cook. The owner of the machinery is called 'The Company' and he is responsible for the fuel, for the equipment, and food for the workers. This way, everyone can make money.

I met a Venezuelan guy whose nickname was, 'El Primo.' He had two companies and was willing to sell one to me. I went to look at the machinery. I liked what I saw and offered to pay half upfront and the rest in a month. I sent someone to look for Don Ovidio Herrera, an old miner, and offered him a job as my foreman. Every day, a group of Indians came to my office and offered me diamonds of good quality. I asked them where they were working and they told me Hueco Redondo.

I went with Don Ovidio to look at the location and met the Indians who told me that a Colombian guy named Jairo owned the area. I contacted him and we settled on a price. I asked Don Ovidio to set up the machinery, build a house for the workers, and clear an area for a helicopter to land.

The following day I arranged for a helicopter to move the machinery to this new location and then fly me to Urima. From Uriman I took a small plane to Ciudad Bolivar and purchased food and supplies for the workers. When I came back, I asked the pilot to fly to the new area to drop off the supplies and then to fly me back to my office. Before I left, I saw the soil they had accumulated already, and I knew that we were in a good location."

Julio Cesar stopped to take a sip of the drink before continuing. The fisherman and his entire family were silent, waiting to hear the rest of the story. And so he continued, "I became quite successful and asked my brother, Jesus Fernando, nicknamed Chiqui, to come with his wife Martha from the mine in Guaniamo. I started him off as an ordinary worker. A month later, I went to have lunch at a restaurant in town and met Wilmer, a miner from Santo Domingo, who told me he was planning on stopping by my office to sell some diamonds. I waited the entire afternoon and into the evening. At eleven that night, there was a knock on the door. I was told someone had been killed.

I took my gun and went to see who the person was. It turned out to be Wilmer, who was seated against a tree and had been murdered. Wilmer had been with one of the town prostitutes when her boyfriend, whose nickname was The Devil, found them together. The Devil took a piece of lumber and hit Wilmer over the head, fracturing his skull."

The children gasped as the wife covered her mouth with her hands. He took another sip of his drink before continuing.

"The next morning, a helicopter arrived to take Wilmer's body to Ciudad Bolivar. I asked Raul, the pilot, to let them wait for another helicopter and to take me to an area where they found a big diamond a week ago. When we arrived to the heliport, there was no one available to fuel it, so Raul got two five-gallon cans of kerosina and filled our tanks himself.

We took off, and after a half hour, Raul noticed what appeared to be a malfunction in the engine. He immediately got on the radio and called for anyone who could hear the transmission. A small plane flying to Uriman responded. Raul let them know that he thought we could reach the small village of Los Frijoles where we would have to do an emergency landing.

A few seconds later, the main rotor failed and we started a rapid descent. I noticed nothing but the tops of the trees in the heavy jungle. I was going to jump but then realized it was too high, and decided to ride the helicopter down. We crashed onto the tops of the trees. The helicopter came to rest on the ground and bent the right skid. It broke through the glass window and just missed Raul's chest. When I got out of the helicopter, I saw that Raul was bleeding badly. I got some green leaves and put them on his wounds. He started to shake and told me that he had been flying since he was a little kid. His father owned a flying service and he had already been in five helicopter accidents, but nothing compared to this one.

The crash happened at ten-thirty in the morning and though we had matches, we were unable to start a fire. I was unable to get kerosene out of the gas tank. We could hear small planes but they could not see us. By three in the afternoon, we succeeded in making some smoke. Soon, a police helicopter came overhead. It was on its way to the mine to pick up Wilmer's body and to arrest The Devil. They stayed overhead while waiting for a second helicopter to arrive. When it did, the police helicopter left for the mine. They sent out a chainsaw with some gasoline to run it, water, and an axe.

The plan was for us to make a clearing so the helicopter could land and take us out. On the first attempt with the chainsaw, the chain broke. By five-thirty, they dropped a rope which Raul wrapped around me, and told the pilot to lift me out to a safe location and come back for him, which they did. They took us to the little village of Los Frijoles and from there, we took a small plane to Ciudad Bolivar. Upon our landing, the first person I saw was Wilmer's father, waiting for the arrival of his son's body. The helicopter's owner then sent the engine to Caracas to be inspected. They found out that the kerosene Raul put in the helicopter was impure and clogged the fuel injectors, which prevented them from spraying the fuel to be burned in the engine."

After explaining the entire situation, the fisherman's family was speechless. They could not believe Julio Cesar had survived. And with that, they wished Iris and him a good night's sleep. The following day early in the morning, Juan, Iris, and Julio Cesar said goodbye to the fisherman and his family and returned to the boat to continue the trip. After approximately thirty hours, they made an entrance in Jurado, which was dangerous.

They barely made it to the shore after several attempts to fight the waves crashing on the rocks and rebounding against their boat. Many people drowned when their boats were overturned in such rapids. Luckily they made it, and said goodbye to Juan and his crew.

In Jurado, Julio Cesar met two men from Cali. They invited him to play pool and drink, even though they knew Julio Cesar had no money. Through them, he met Eduardo, a sergeant who was stationed nearby. The following day, the police, asking for documentation papers on the street, stopped him. When he told them that he didn't have them, they walked him to jail.

This was a small town and almost everything was within walking distance. On the way to jail, they met Eduardo, the sergeant that Julio Cesar met the night before. When he saw the police detaining Julio Cesar, he said, "Let him go. I know who he is."

The guys from Cali that Julio Cesar met the night before paid for Iris and Julio Cesar to take a boat to Jaque, which was forty minutes from Jurado. If they thought the entrance to Jurado was dangerous, it was nothing compared to the experience of getting into the harbor of Jaque. There were multiple waves coming from different directions, some from behind the boat and others in front that crashed off the rocks and pushed the boat back.

The captain was nervous and Julio Cesar could tell he was scared. He already lost a boat in the same conditions and it brought fear to Julio Cesar's heart, together with the thought that this would be a terrible way to die, having finally reached the border with Panama. In Jaque, the majority of the population is black and make their living cultivating plantain and illegally smuggling artifacts from Panama into Colombia without paying duty taxes.

Once they arrived, Iris met people who let them stay at their house for the night. The next day, Julio Cesar started to investigate the best way to get into Panama. He asked around town where they could find the Chief of Immigration, and this being a small town where everybody knew each other, made it easy for him to find the house. When Julio Cesar told him that he needed to get to Panama, and had no immigration papers, he said to him, "I don't have any problem helping you. The problem is my secretary who can't be counted on. There is a boat leaving soon for Panama and I'm supposed to inspect it before it leaves. If I see the two of you onboard, I will ignore you. Just try to be out of my sight," he told Julio Cesar.

The only issue was that the people who owned the ship wanted twenty-four dollars in return. All Julio Cesar had was a small leather briefcase which he used at the mine to carry money and diamonds. Desperate, he sold it for seven dollars.

They missed that boat, but finally with Iris working in a little bodega, they put together fourteen dollars, of which they used one dollar to buy some food. Julio Cesar was successful at convincing the captain of the next boat to take them for the twenty dollars they had left. They were on their way to Panama, a twenty-four-hour ride.

The boat arrived in Panama at five in the morning, and since Immigration did not open until eight, they could not get off the boat for three hours. Because the water was shallow, it was necessary to off-load the cargo and people into smaller boats to get to shore and to the immigration dock.

The difficulty was that the immigration officers had a direct view of everyone leaving the ship. It turned out that right next to the Immigration Office was an open-air food market. Julio Cesar quickly realized that the only way for them to make it was if they blended into the crowd at the market plaza. Julio Cesar told Iris about his plan.

"We are going to wait for the people to unload ahead of us and for them to create a crowd at the Immigration Office. Hopefully a chance will come up for us to get lost and slip into the market plaza. Iris, stay right by my side," he explained hastily.

Nervous, they got off the boat with some Americans, and after Customs checked their small bags, were told to check their documentation at Immigration. They followed the Americans and the moment it appeared to Julio Cesar that they were unnoticed, he pushed Iris toward the marketplace and started walking quickly to the other side of the market.

This was the first country for them to reach. Panama is a poor country. However, dice shooting is legal gambling and as a result, there is a great deal of robbery. Julio thinks that Panama was one of the most unsafe countries he had to go through.

Iris found a job making ten dollars a day distributing advertising leaflets on the street. Meanwhile, Julio Cesar met a guy who was in the used car parts business. He had his office directly across the market square from Immigration and he allowed them to use it to sleep during the night. From the office window, Iris and Julio Cesar could see everything going on at Immigration during the twenty days they were in Panama. They were careful not to be seen by the police.

Iris gave Julio Cesar seventeen dollars she earned and he realized that the fastest way to make money was to gamble with the dice. He went to the craps hall and met David, who was gambling with other guys. Julio Cesar gave David the seventeen dollars and asked him to shoot the dice for him. He made five straight passes and won five hundred dollars, of which he gave to Julio Cesar half. Julio Cesar left the craps hall and went to a bar owned by a Colombian, and through him, he made contact with someone who knew the best way to leave Panama.

He said, "There are two choices. One is to obtain Panamanian passports for twenty-five hundred dollars each, or to get smuggled from Colon to New Orleans in shipping containers at seven-hundred-fifty dollars each."

Mama and I sent them some money from New York and together with what Iris made and Julio Cesar won, they were able to put together fifteen-hundred dollars.

Julio Cesar finally told Iris, "No more work. Let's leave for Colon."

The bus ride to Colon took them from the Pacific side of Panama to the Atlantic side of the canal. Colon is a large shipping center and because of this, there is a lot of money changing hands. Once there, they found a hotel and Julio Cesar decided to check out the best way to get to New Orleans.

When Julio Cesar came back to the hotel, he told Iris, "There is a container ship and for seven-hundred-fifty dollars each, the containers' loaders will put us in a container and not load additional containers on top of us. This way, once the ship is at sea, we can get out. However, it is important that none of the ship's crew or the captain find out we are on board because if we are discovered, they will throw us overboard," he explained.

Iris was nervous with this plan but she was as determined as Julio Cesar to get to the United States. After everything was arranged, before they turned over the money, the ship was seized. The Panamanian government discovered five thousand kilos of cocaine on the ship. Because of this incident, their plans of going to the United States by ship evaporated. So they took an eighteen-hour bus ride to the Costa Rican border, the next country to pass through to get to the United States.

Since they had no documentation, it was necessary to walk through the hills at night, bypassing Immigration at the border. The first town they reached in Costa Rica was where they saw newspaper reports about the cocaine seizure on what would have been their boat to New Orleans.

Costa Rica is a country where most of the towns are named after saints. Their biggest businesses are coffee plantations and cattle ranches. On their way to San Jose, the capital of Costa Rica, the police stopped the bus and while they did not ask anyone for identification, they did search the luggage. The first night Julio Cesar and Iris stayed in San Jose, they called the family in New York and told us that they made it to Costa Rica. Iris and Julio Cesar also asked us for money, which we sent immediately. They were able to rent a room for two weeks in a cheap hotel.

One afternoon Julio Cesar was walking around the plaza in San Jose, where local artisans displayed their products to tourists, when he heard someone call his name. It was none other than our cousin, Luis Fernando. He had been on his way to the United States but fell in love with Country, and decided to stay and work with the local artisans. A few days later, Julio Cesar was having a cup of coffee at the public square when he saw a sign flashing the headlines of the day. Pablo Escobar, the big mafia king of Colombia, had been killed.

It took Julio Cesar and Iris three attempts to cross the frontier between Costa Rica and Nicaragua. This was one of the most difficult parts of their trip to the United States. Julio Cesar met a local coyote, a term used to describe a person whose business is guiding illegal people from one country to the next. He charged them two-hundred-fifty dollars for the trip to Nicaragua.

By the third attempt, they made the move with the coyote and fourteen other people. They entered an underground tunnel that used to carry rainwater beneath a highway. When they reached the end of the tunnel, they were near a river edge and had to walk through it. Soon, the water was up to their necks. When they finally got to the other side of the river, they worked their way through deep thickets and a jungle area which crossed them behind the headquarters of Border Patrol.

They left at four in the morning, and it took them two hours to reach the location where they had to wait until one in the afternoon. Meanwhile, one of the coyotes went ahead to pick up a car in a small town which was going to take the sixteen of them to Managua, the capital of Nicaragua. Halfway through the trip, the driver pulled over because he knew there was a checkpoint a little way ahead. They walked back into the jungle parallel to the highway, and a half hour later, after the car went through the checkpoint with only the driver, they met up again, and completed their journey to Managua.

The city of Managua is poor and lacks a central plaza, which was destroyed, along with the cathedral, in the 1972 earthquake. The only place for the people of the city to get together is the market square. Once there, Julio Cesar and Iris stayed in one of the coyote's homes, where they were given beans with ground cheese to eat. The way the coyotes work the trip is that once you are at their house, they ask you to call your family to ask for money for the next part of the trip. You are allowed to stay at their house until the money arrives. The coyote told Julio Cesar and Iris that it would cost fourteen hundred dollars for the two of them to cross into Honduras and then into Mexico.

Iris and Julio Cesar stayed at the coyote's house waiting to see if he was going to take them any further toward the border of Honduras. He told Julio Cesar that no one was allowed to leave the house, but they could make phone calls to families to arrange for the money. When Julio Cesar heard the guy telling him that he was not allowed to leave the house, he responded, "The only way I'm going to be held inside four walls would be if I go to jail, otherwise I will come and go as I please."

Julio Cesar knew that Mama and I were only able to send small amounts of money every week, which meant it would take them forever to put together the money the coyote wanted. They remained in Managua for fifteen days, waiting for the money. Once it arrived, Julio Cesar told Iris, "We are leaving now, but this time we are going to do it on our own."

During their fifteen days in Managua, Julio Cesar asked a lot of questions and looked at maps. He figured out how to make the next step for he and Iris to cross the border into Honduras alone. They made their way to a small town and went to a Western Union office to pick up some money from home. While Julio Cesar was waiting, he met two guys from the Dominican Republic, also receiving money from their families.

"Where are you going?" Julio Cesar asked them, out of curiosity.

They glanced at each other before one responded, "We are trying to get to New York." At that moment, Julio Cesar realized he had gotten a lot of experience getting from Colombia to here and watching how the coyotes operated. So, Julio Cesar decided to become one of them. Julio Cesar said to the two men, "The local coyotes are charging seven-hundred dollars each to take you to Mexico." They looked at each other again and asked Julio Cesar, "How much would you charge to take us?"

They said that they only had six hundred dollars, so Julio Cesar agreed to guide them from Nicaragua to Honduras, Salvador, and Guatemala. They agreed to give him the money when they got to Mexico.

The following day, Julio Cesar met a man at the hotel and asked him which was the best way to cross the border into Honduras. He pointed to a mountain in the distance and said, "One way is to walk around the back of that mountain and cross into the country, but it is dangerous because the area is covered with land mines."

The following morning, Julio Cesar woke everybody up, climbed into a taxi, and for twenty dollars, made it to a small town at the frontier. It was the twenty-third of December. At a restaurant Julio Cesar was told that on Christmas Eve, everyone gives away food to people who aske for it.

"I'm going on a diet until tomorrow, besides I'm sick of eating beans with shredded cheese, and tomorrow I will be able to have a real chicken dinner," Julio Cesar told Iris.

On the twenty-fourth, at one in the morning, Julio Cesar got a small plate with one chicken wing on it. On the morning of the twenty-sixth, a motorcycle cop stopped them and demanded to see their identification. Julio Cesar gave him a letter he got in Managua when he reported that his papers were stolen, which was not true. Everyone else showed their identification, but the cop was not satisfied with Julio Cesar's letter and asked him to wait while he checked on the temporary papers.

As soon as the policeman was out of sight, Julio Cesar said to the Dominicans and Iris, "Let's go." They ran through the bushes. During their escape, Iris and Julio Cesar got separated from the two men. After running for a while, Julio Cesar saw a man on horseback trotting along a dirt path. "How can we safely get to Honduras? We have to go right now," Julio Cesar pleaded with him.

He was a friendly man who said, "Follow this path, it will lead you to the top of the mountain. When you reach the top, you will see a flat field, look down into the valley, and you will see a farmhouse and another path. That farm is in Honduras."

They were careful trekking up the mountain for fear that land mines would go off with the wrong step. When they reached the top, they heard a rifle. Julio Cesar pushed Iris to the ground, whispering to her, "Get down low!" They ran and hid behind a guava tree for protection. At that moment, Julio Cesar heard a voice saying, "Don't move."

When Julio Cesar turned his head, there was a soldier pointing a rifle directly at them. Another one appeared in front of them, and soon Julio Cesar realized they had run right into a patrol of eight soldiers. A life-threatening situation was the last thing Julio Cesar had on his mind. Julio Cesar tried to relax and said to them, "Listen, we are coming from Venezuela and we are just traveling north. All we have with us are a few pieces of clothing and four hundred dollars. If you want, take the money and just tell us how to travel over into Honduras."

After they talked for a few minutes, one soldier asked Julio Cesar to follow them. They walked about a mile to a beautiful farm with horses and cattle. They were already in Honduras, and this patrol was part of the Honduran Army. The woman of the farm was kind, and after a while, Julio Cesar asked the soldiers what they intended to do with them.

"Don't worry. We are going to help you. Keep your money and we will show you the way to town," one young soldier responded.

The patrol leader asked the woman to take them by car to town, where they would catch a bus to Churutela. He then said to Julio Cesar, "Go to the restaurant I am giving you the name of, and from there, take a taxi to my family house. Tell my parents I'm fine and that I'm sending you to them and to allow you to stay for a few days. My father will help you get through Honduras to El Salvador's border."

They were beyond grateful for this stroke of luck and wonderful human nature. They followed his instructions exactly as they were told. When they got to the patrol leader's house, his family was happy to hear news about their son. There were fourteen children and the family made their living selling sodas and tortillas.

After two days, the father took them to the outskirts of Churuteca and flagged down a truck which was going to the border of El Salvador. Julio Cesar asked the truck driver for the best way to cross, and he said that everybody did it by river, which was not deep.

Since people from Honduras and El Salvador frequently go back and forth across the border, no one bothered them. Therefore, it was easy to cross the river into El Salvador. Julio and Iris took a bus from the border to San Miguel, and from San Miguel it was a four-hour ride to San Salvador.

The countries of Central America are small and you can cross each one in a few hours. Iris and Julio Cesar spent some time walking around San Salvador before boarding a bus heading for the border with Guatemala. They walked through the mountain range into Guatemala. From there, it was a two-and-a-half-hour bus ride to Tecunuman, a town close to the Mexican border.

They stayed in Tecunuman for five days and celebrated New Year's Eve. In this town, many coyotes are active and as a result, there are plenty of houses where illegal people wait for money to be sent from their families for the coyotes to take them across into Mexico. Iris and Julio Cesar had been lucky during the trip, since many people are usually caught entering Mexico, Nicaragua, and Guatemala illegally. They had come through six countries already, and the next, and final, move would be into Mexico. Once reaching that border, they could look forward to crossing into the United States.

There is a river named Hidalgo, which divides Tecunuman in Guatemala from Mexico. On January 1, 1994, with some other people, Iris and Julio Cesar decided to go swimming and celebrate New Year's Day. While they were swimming, Julio Cesar said to Iris, "I'm going to swim across the river and touch Mexico." When Julio Cesar got across, he met a Mexican Indian and asked him which was the best way to cross the border into Mexico.

"If you can get to Tapachula, which is the town where I live, I will help you to go a little further into Mexico. Take my address and phone number with you and when you get there, give me a call," the Indian explained.

Julio Cesar swam back across the river to Iris. They spent three more days in Tecunuman. Meanwhile, they saw many people being deported or arrested for trying to get into Mexico. Three days later, Iris and Julio Cesar swam across the river to the Mexican side and landed on the edge of a cemetery. From there, they got a bus to Tapachula, a two-and-a-half-hour ride, and fortunately, the road the bus took was only lightly patrolled by immigration officers. They did not get stopped.

They arrived at Tapachula's bus station early in the evening and took a taxi to the address the Indian gave them. He took them to a hotel near his home, and the following morning, he showed up at the hotel. He made arrangements for Julio Cesar and Iris to stay at the home of a young couple who were just married and close friends of his. They were invited to stay at their home for a few days while they planned their next move.

Julio Cesar did not know why they were fortunate enough to experience such wonderful generosity. It may have been because it was the beginning of a new year. Regardless, they took every opportunity they were given. They spent the next fifteen days in the house, for fear of running into the police.

One day, Julio Cesar was looking through the window of the house. Across the street there was a truck stop where the truck drivers refueled and rested before continuing their trip. Julio Cesar noticed a large thirty-two-wheeler truck and went across the street looking for the driver. Julio Cesar had the gut feeling this could be the truck to take Iris and him further on their jouney.

When Julio Cesar found the driver, he asked him, "Sir, would you take us to Guajata?" Julio Cesar knew this was a difficult part of Mexico to cross but that did not seem to bother the driver.

"Let me unload the truck and we will talk tonight," he responded.

Julio Cesar pointed to the house they were staying in, and that night, the driver showed up drunk. He wanted to know how much money they had and when Julio Cesar explained how short they were on money, he agreed to take them for two-hundred-fifty dollars. When Julio Cesar told him that they had only ninety dollars, he said, "Let me think about it."

The following day at nine in the morning, Julio Cesar heard a horn honking in front of the house. The driver called from behind the wheel, "Let's go!" Behind the driver's seat, there was a compartment which had a box, built like a coffin, with a mattress on top. It was for the driver to sleep on whenever he needed a rest. The driver, who obviously had taken illegal people before, told them that before they reached a checkpoint, he would let them know. This would give them time to open the box, climb inside, and close it. Inside, there was a cable attached to the cover and when you pulled on it, the top could not be raised.

When the truck was a few minutes from reaching a checkpoint, Iris and Julio Cesar climbed into the box, and when the truck stopped, they could hear the voices of Immigration Patrol questioning the driver and the two Indian passengers riding in front. Julio Cesar would pull down hard on the cable and waited to see if Immigration tried to open the box, sweating in terror. Fortunately, they never did.

The truck was a petroleum tanker, so the trip ended at a refinery in Guajaca. The driver was generous and invited them to eat and drink some beers. Later, he took them around town and introduced them to a fellow truck driver who gave them a ride to Veracruz. From Veracruz, Julio Cesar called me asking for money to pay the guy.

The following day, Iris stopped a truck and asked for a ride. The truck was carrying coffee and going to the United States. He said that he could take them only as far as New Laredo. They were traveling for two days and stopped only to eat. They traveled across the Gulf Coast of Mexico and into New Laredo, a few miles from the border to the United States.

It was cold in New Laredo, since it was winter, so they bought warm used clothing. Before they got out of the truck, Julio Cesar asked a guy passing by on the street if he knew someone to take them across the border to the United States.

He said, "I will take you for one hundred dollars."

They were invited to his house so they could call New York asking for more money. By keeping them in his house, the man was sure the two would go with him and not some competing coyotes. The next evening, he showed up with a small fifteen-year-old boy and said, "He is the one who will take you across."

Julio Cesar looked at him in disbelief. "Are you kidding me? He is only a kid," Julio Cesar replied. It turned out this kid had been arrested more than five hundred times in his young life for taking people across the border. He had a lot of experience making the trip. So Julio Cesar listened to this fifteen-year-old giving them instructions. "I will be waiting for you in a rubber raft on the edge of El Rio Bravo River," he explained. When the three of them got into the raft, they paddled to a spot beneath the international bridge which goes from New Laredo in Mexico to Laredo, Texas. It was seven at night and they were crossing underneath the bridge with Immigration inspectors of both Mexico and the United States patrolling above their heads.

When they reached the other side of the bridge, they crept along the river's edge until they reached the American Customs depot in Laredo. The kid ran to hide behind a truck. Julio Cesar grabbed Iris's hand and ran after him. They paused and in the next run, the kid got them to the bottom of a brick wall with barbed wire along the top.

"Are you crazy? We can't get over this wall," Julio Cesar said to the kid under his breath.

He did not respond, but silently put his back against the wall, made a cup of his hands, and said, "Come on."

Julio Cesar looked at him confused and replied, "No way. You cannot lift me over."

"I have done it with bigger and heavier people than you. Let's go," he said as if he was not going to waste any more time. The boy was right. He got them to the top of the wall and that was when Julio Cesar realized that they were on top of the concrete roof of a building. They ran to the end where there was a round column. They climbed around the edge to get to the other side. If they slipped, they would wind up on the ground with a broken limb or even dead. The kid went first, holding on to the column. Iris followed and Julio Cesar brought up the rear, almost falling. They jumped across to another roof and at the end was a window the kid climbed through. "Follow me," he told them in a whisper.

Inside, the building was filled with computers and they found an exit that led to the street. The boy warned them to look out for the police. They started to walk until they reached a motel. The kid told the desk clerk this was an emergency, which is a word used by coyotes that means, "I have illegal people with me."

Then he turned to Iris and Julio Cesar and said, "I will see you tomorrow." He left them at the motel. In all Julio Cesar's years working in the mines, he never met someone more courageous. And he was just fifteen years old.

From the hotel, Julio Cesar called the house and spoke to me. He told me that they were in Laredo, Texas. At the hotel, Julio Cesar met a Mexican coming from Chicago. He told Julio Cesar the most dangerous part left was getting past Mileposts 13 and 14 on Route 66, which is the only highway between Laredo and San Antonio, Texas.

The desk clerk told them that his girlfriend knew a guy who took people from Laredo to San Antonio. That evening, they went to meet her and she introduced them to a man who said he would take them for twelve-hundred dollars. While the distance was not long, the problem was if he got caught, the government would confiscate his car. He said that the price was not very high if you considered the risk. Julio Cesar called New York and Bob and I sent the money without hesitation.

At seven in the evening, Julio Cesar gave the guy half the money and agreed to give him the rest when they reached San Antonio. He picked them up and together with a friend of his started driving toward San Antonio.

They stopped the car at Milepost 12 and the guy's friend, along with Iris and Julio Cesar, got out, walked off the side of the highway, and ran parallel to the road. It was winter and cold; they had to run through sagebrush and burr bushes.

They knew that Border Patrol was using electronic surveillance to monitor the area. They had night vision binoculars, laser tracking, and seismic sensors buried in the ground which could sense the vibrations from bodies as they ran. It was imperative that they keep running so when the

Border Patrol reached the spot they had been, the immigrants were no longer there.

They could hear the Border Patrol driving around looking for them. While they ran, they heard the screams of a woman being raped by a coyote. Even then, they could not stop to help her. They had to save themselves.

They ran for two-and-a-half hours until they reached the Santa Fe railroad crossing where the car was supposed to pick them up. The man who ran with them took a glass and placed it in the middle of the road as a signal to the car. The three ran to the car and he took them to San Antonio.

In San Antonio they looked for a hotel. Unfortunately, unless you have a social security card, rooms would not be rented. They were exhausted. Julio Cesar said to iris, "Let's just go to the bus station and go to Dallas."

It was a six-hour bus ride. In Dallas, they bought tickets on a Greyhound bus to New York. Mama, Pilly, Felipe, Bob and I took some winter jackets, since it was November and snowing. We went to the Port Authority terminal in Manhattan to meet Julio Cesar and Iris. I realized that it had been six years since I saw Julio Cesar and I thought of how much my life had changed since then. I knew none of us standing there waiting for the bus understood the dimension of adventure and stress that Julio Cesar and Iris had been through. They had been traveling for nine months, crossing South America, Central America, and North America illegally, finally arriving in New York to be reunited with us.

As Julio Cesar got off the bus, so many thoughts came rushing through my mind. I was certain that he would find it difficult to adjust to life in this country. The environment he had come from at the mine in Venezuela was one of an individualist, getting by on his wits and strengths with little interference from government, police, authority, and even bosses.

Now, Julio Cesar was in a country with more laws than necessary to live. He would need to give up many of the important parts of his being. Independence, self-reliance, and freedom, in exchange for being with us. Sacrificing his personal values to be with the family was one step closer to fulfilling Mama's lifelong dream that the entire family be reunited in America. Half of the family was in New York and we looked forward to the day when Maria Claudia, Maria Alejandra, Monica, Maria Luisa, Carlos Augusto, and Jesus Fernando would join us too.

CHAPTER 25: America's Magic Touch in the Face of Suffering

For the next few months, we all lived in the house on Carmen Avenue in Westbury. After Felipe's graduation from Clarke High School in Westbury, we moved to Port Washington to be with Bob and Eric.

Bob had a C&C 36 sailboat moored in front of the house. During the summer nights we went sailing and tried different restaurants along the water. I learned how to sail, which made our sailing time more pleasurable.

Felipe did not spend much time with us. He was working full-time as a waiter and going full-time to school for a degree in electrical engineering. He used to spend many nights at Mama's house in Westbury, which helped him go through these adjustments with less stress.

Unfortunately, whenever there was conflict between Bob and Eric, Eric would take his anger and frustration out on the furniture, breaking and kicking things. I never experienced this behavior before—with Mama, that behavior would be unthinkable.

Eric kept threatening to hurt Bob and one day when we were preparing to sail with friends, Eric called Bob and told him not to dare show up at the house. When Bob told me, I said we could not leave until we dealt with the situation. I was fed up at seeing Bob unable to sleep, frustrated, and unable to deal with his son.

When we got to the house, Eric was with two friends. When I saw him pushing Bob and threatening to beat him up, I got scared. Bob just put his arms down and told Eric, "You can beat me if you want because I'm not going to hit you back."

Without thinking, I went straight to the phone and called the police. Eric and his friends got scared and left. A couple minutes after, the police called back and I told them not to come.

When we left the house to go back to the boat, Eric and his friends were waiting for us on the side of the road. When we passed by, Eric made a gesture to me as if daring us to stop the car. I jumped out of the car, without thinking, and went up to Eric. I said to him, "Do you know how unfairly you treat your father? Do me a favor, from now on whenever you want to break things out of anger, do it to your own things in your apartment and not ours."

It was painful because in some way I was trying to be his friend instead of mother. During this time, I put concern for Felipe aside because I knew he was alright. He had my mother and family to be with, which Eric grew up without. Eric was full of anger and resentment, and unfortunately, didn't know how to handle it except through violence. But like everything in life, sometimes we must learn the hard way. It gave me the chance to confront him and let him know that I was standing by Bob's side. At the same time, I tried to make him understand the pain that he was imposing on his father.

At the beginning of the summer, Todd, Bob's oldest son, and Alison, his wife, decided to take a vacation in Bermuda. They were living in Boston and Todd worked in the Emergency Medicine Department at Boston University Hospital. They left for Bermuda from New York, having driven from Boston and leaving their car in Port Washington. For four weeks, Felipe had severe headaches. Three doctors saw him during that month but none took the time to find out what the problem was.

They said it was stress and all three prescribed to him medications for headaches. By the end of the month, I was concerned and insisted an MRI be performed. After the MRI, the doctor told me that the person responsible for reading it was on vacation and if I had been waiting that long already, I could wait a little longer.

Felipe's condition worsened and I knew he had been throwing up and having difficulty focusing his eyes. When I asked him if he wanted to go to the hospital and he said yes, I realized how sick he was. I took him to a hospital in Port Washington where they did another MRI. After a neurologist read it, they told me everything was okay and that he had allergies. That night, I went to bed feeling better and less concerned about the diagnosis.

The following day, I went to pick up Todd and Alison at the airport. On our way home, I explained to Todd what had been happening to Felipe. When we got home and Todd saw Felipe's condition, he told me that a headache for that long was not normal. He decided to call the hospital and ask for more tests. We took him back to the Hospital and when they did a second MRI, it showed that his skull was full of blood from an old injury. The pressure on his brain was causing headaches and making him sick.

They immediately took Felipe by ambulance to a hospital in Manhasset. Felipe was in a lot of pain but since the surgery was scheduled for the next morning, the nurses couldn't give him medication to relieve the pain. At that moment, I wished it was me instead of him in that bed. It was going to be a long night for him.

The following morning, Todd met Bob and I at the hospital. The staff could not believe this young guy dressed with a Mickey Mouse tee shirt, cutoffs, and sneakers was a doctor. He stayed with us throughout the surgery. If it hadn't been for Todd, Felipe might not be with us today.

In March 1995, I received notification from the U.S. Department of State to return to Colombia and pick up my visa for permanent immigration and residency.

I had been in Colombia for eight days when my sister Maria Claudia showed up by surprise. Jesus Fernando, who had been living in Venezuela, found out that Mama and I were in

Colombia and decided to take the trip with his wife Martha and their daughter Johanna, who was only six months old. It also gave Jesus Fernando the opportunity to bring my sister Maria Luisa and her three kids to Colombia. We had not seen her since she left six years earlier, on the day after her high school graduation.

My brother saw this opportunity as his only chance to take my sister from the kind of life she was living in Venezuela, which we were unaware of. I cannot erase from my mind what I saw when I went to pick them up at the bus terminal. It was a mixed feeling of pain, anger, and frustration toward the man who allowed this to happen to my sister and her kids. At the same time, I experienced a feeling of guilt, for not knowing until that moment what was happening in my sister's life while she lived in the jungle of Venezuela.

I started to cry for my sister and her kids. Erika, the oldest, was four and was the only one in a decent physical and emotional condition. Marco was two and Christian was just an eight-month-old baby. Their bodies were covered with sores. Marco was the skinniest and did not speak. He emitted sounds and would not allow anyone to get close to him. If you tried, he would go against the wall, cover his face, and deny you physical or emotional contact. Maria Luisa had been a beautiful girl when she left and now I was looking at a completely different person, deteriorated from too much suffering.

Jesus Antonio Campos, was an engineer, who came from an aristocratic family with high positions in the government of Venezuela. Unfortunately, he was an alcoholic who used to disappear for three or four days at a time and my sister was forced to wash other people's clothing in order to feed her children. When her children were sick, she would run, carrying them to the infirmary. Many times she was turned away for not having money. The lack of food and continuously being undernourished caused the children to become dangerously ill many times.

My brother Chiqui offered to take my sister and her children away from that environment, but she did not want, nor was she ready, to leave the father of her children. Fortunately, an opportunity for a new life opened for the children and Maria Luisa. Now in Colombia, my mother began repairing the sores and illnesses of their bodies with a combination of medicine, practical knowledge (having raised so many children), and devoted love. She had the magic touch and always knew how to turn around a bad situation.

I called Bob immediately from the telephone company in Ibague and while trying to explain the conditions of my sister and her children, tears streaming down my face, "I just don't understand how we did not know what my sister was going through all this time," I kept saying to him.

Bob's answer was, "Do whatever you feel you have to do. You know I will give you my unconditional support."

It gave me a huge relief to know that I was not alone and I had not only a husband but a partner.

At the end of April 1994, my sisters Maria Alejandra, Maria Claudia, and Monica made the decision to come to the United States. Without Maria Claudia, they never would have made the trip.

She gave them the strength required for an adventure like this one. Her plan was to give them company during the trip and then go back to Colombia to be with her son, Victor Manuel, who was seven years old. She left to Venezuela five years before and had not seen him since he was two.

Maria Luisa stayed with her children in the apartment that Maria Alejandra and Monica shared. Bob and I made the commitment to help her with a monthly amount that would allow her to live comfortably without working. Everything seemed to be turning out for the best in our family.

CHAPTER 26: Three Sisters, One Camera, and the Journey of a Lifetime

Maria Alejandra is the eighth of nine children. She has a short temper, which I think she inherited from our mother. She also inherited Mama's talent for manual arts and a good imagination. From our father, she inherited a silence and depth of thinking. Too deep, I would say, sometimes. Maria Alejandra always loved adventure and being confronted with the unknown, even though she confesses to being a bit of a coward. She inherited from our mother the spirit for adventure. When she looks back and thinks of everything she went through to get to New York, she always asks herself, "If I had to do it again, would I do it?" her answer is always no.

This was the biggest experience of her life and once was enough for Maria Alejandra. She had to live for two years in Colombia with our youngest sister Monica. At that time, Maria Alejandra was only twenty-four and Monica was twenty-two. It was a unique experience to share life and not worry about confronting it *"alone."* Maria Alejandra says "alone" because the truth is that Mama, Pilly, and I were supporting Maria Alejandra and Monica economically from New York.

Because they were the babies, Maria Alejandra and Monica kept a close relationship with Pilly. They were like her daughters-they did not see her as a sister, but as someone more special. The day Pilly left to go to the United States was one of the most difficult times, especially for Monica. She suffered emotionally to the point that it became physical.

From that day on, Monica suffered from epilepsy. When they knew Pilly was leaving, Monica and Maria Alejandra felt completely abandoned. This gave Pilly a feeling of guilt. They did not have the words to express their pain, but deep down, they knew she had to make this difficult decision because it would afford her a better life.

Monica and Maria Alejandra were forced to take on new responsibilities, which was difficult to get used to. The truth was now they had to grow up. Like everything in life, time makes possible for all things to take their natural course, and they had to get used to this new, grown-up life. They shared house chores. One day, one cooked while the other cleaned the house, and the following day they would switch. Their daily routine was to go to the university during the day and come home to take care of the house. They felt overwhelmingly alone.

Every day when they came home from the university, the apartment was empty, with no one waiting with a hot plate of soup or somebody to talk to. During the evenings, Monica and Maria Alejandra sat on the balcony, drank a cup of coffee, and talked about everything.

Monica was studying marketing and Maria Alejandra was studying finance. She finished her studies, but Maria Alejandra only made it halfway because her mind was set on one thing: going to the United States. Unfortunately, all of their efforts were in vain because every time they went for visas, they were denied. They made seven attempts and came to the point of hating going to the Embassy to ask for visas. Maria Alejandra felt afraid for Monica since she was more affected with these denials, making her susceptible to epileptic seizures.

Maria Alejandra remembers one day when they left very early in the morning for Bogotá. The following day, they had an appointment at the American Embassy. They stayed in Bogotá, at Mama's friend Cecilia's. Maria Alejandra didn't know why, but all that day they felt very lonely. It was as if they had only each other in the entire world.

Monica got up at six to take a shower, since the appointment was at eight. Maria Alejandra remained in bed and ten minutes later, she heard Cecilia's sister, Ines, scream, "Somebody fell in the bathroom!"

Ines had a thirteen-year-old daughter, Paula, and Maria Alejandra thought it was she who fell. It never crossed her mind that it would be Monica. Maria Alejandra got up, scared, and the first thing she did was look in Monica's bed. She was not there. Maria Alejandra ran to the bathroom and tried to open the door but it was locked from the inside. It took them several minutes to find the key and get the door open. Maria Alejandra felt frustrated for not being able to help our sister.

When they got inside, Monica was lying in the bathtub, unconscious. She suffered a seizure, and as she fell, she hit her head on the soap dish next to the shower. Maria Alejandra quickly finished bathing her and put her to bed. At that moment, what scared Maria Alejandra the most was how badly Monica hurt her head. Maria Alejandra did not want her to know she had a seizure because Maria Alejandra thought it was going to make her feel bad. Once the seizure was over, she experienced severe headaches, and even though Maria Alejandra tried to deny it to her, she knew.

Before they left for the Embassy, Maria Alejandra called Oscar, a friend who was doing his internship in pediatric medicine at a hospital in Bogotá. They agreed to meet him after the interview. Again, the visas were denied. When they went to see Oscar, their spirits were down and he made an appointment with a friend of his who was a neurologist. He prescribed Monica Lamictal, which she still takes to prevent seizures.

A few months later, Monica and Maria Alejandra started to have conflicts with each other which affected their relationship as sisters and hastened Maria Alejandra's desire to get to the United States. Now that Maria Alejandra looks back, she realizes how foolish and immature they were. They had allowed a man, who was not worth it, to come between them and threaten their love as sisters. This incident became the motivation for Maria Alejandra to make the decision to attempt the trip to the United States illegally. She felt this was the only way to get away from the person who was creating such a bad impact in their lives. She wanted to start over again.

At the same time, our sister Maria Claudia just arrived from Venezuela and decided to go with Maria Alejandra and Monica to the United States. My mother and I, in New York, knew the only way for them to make the trip was if Claudia came with them. She had the experience and courage that Monica and Maria Alejandra did not have. Her intentions were to return to Colombia immediately after to be with her son, Victor Manuel.

They left Colombia by plane for El Salvador on a cloudy morning. The trip took a whole day because the flight required them to change planes in Panama. They felt like tourists without knowing what was waiting for them in El Salvador. Once they reached El Salvador, it was horrible. The three were detained by Customs because they were suspected of transporting drugs.

They assumed this because the girls came from Colombia. They interrogated the three of them and when they were finished, the girls were sent to separate rooms. All of their belongings were checked, and for three hours they were questioned and accused of something that was not true. Finally, Customs gave up and allowed them to leave.

Once outside, Pedro, a friend of Pilly, met them. He promised to take care of them while they were in El Salvador and would arrange their trip to New York. Much to their surprise, he took them to a cheap motel in a bad neighborhood. The room was full of cockroaches and was filthy. He left them alone and said in a calm voice, "I'm an important business person in this country and cannot afford to be involved with the three of you after what happened with Customs at the airport."

They were in this motel, frightened, not knowing even a fly in the country, and unaware of what was going to be the next step. They decided to get a grip on themselves and realized they had each other to count on. They had a camera and decided to take pictures of the horrible room they were in. The bathroom was just a hole in the floor, the walls were punched with holes, and rats walked around as if they owned the place and the girls were the intruders.

Finally, after two days, they communicated with Pilly. She immediately reassured them. "Don't worry. I have a friend in New York whose name is Jesus and he has a brother, Antonio, who lives in El Salvador. Antonio is going to pick you up at the hotel," she said.

Don Antonio took Maria Alejandra, Maria Claudia, and Monica to his house outside the city in a small town called Nejapa. They stayed for almost a month with his wife and two daughters. It was an enriching experience to live with them and be exposed to a new culture. They were wonderful people who were kind with generous hearts.

Meanwhile in New York, Mama, Pilly, and I were not at peace. We were frustrated with the obstacles we were faced with to get the girls to the United States. Antonio started looking for different ways to send them to us, but all efforts were in vain. The only option left was to go illegally from country to country. Because of the many stories they heard about the dangers of the trip, Maria Alejandra, Monica, and Maria Claudia were scared. But as time passed, they got more used to the idea.

The week they had to leave, they felt butterflies in their stomachs. "No matter what happens during the trip, we are going to stay together. If one of us is caught by the authorities, the three of us will surrender together," Maria Alejandra told them.

With that in mind, they started the journey to Guatemala, where they met the rest of the group—twenty in total. Maria Alejandra, Maria Claudia, and Monica were the only Colombians, and for some unknown reason, the couple organizing the trip took pity on them and treated them well.

Maybe they felt sorry for the girls because they knew the hardships that lay ahead before they would reach the United States.

They were taken by car to Guatemala and then dropped off at a wonderful motel with a swimming pool, a comfortable room, and hot shower. The rest of the group had to stay in a shack, sleeping on the floor. The following day, they were supposed to meet with the group and they were already saying to each other, "If the rest of the trip is going to be as comfortable as this, we are going to have a wonderful time."

Unfortunately, the couple was only sweetening the beginning of a painful experience. The next day, Maria Alejandra, Maria Claudia, and Monica met with the rest of the group and left for Mexico. What divides Guatemala and Mexico is a river that, during the summer, runs very wide and rapidly, and during the winter becomes even more dangerous. By this time, there were two hundred people crossing into Mexico.

They loaded everyone into small boats. When they reached the Mexican side, they waited for darkness to fall before they were loaded into trucks. Although these trucks were designed to carry thirty people they put seventy in each truck. They were forced to stand and were crammed so tightly they could not bend their knees. Breathing the stale air was miserable and suffocating. The trip lasted six hours. By the time they stopped, every inch of their bodies ached.

It seemed that the driver believed he was carrying a cargo of potatoes and forgot that they were humans. They got to a ranch on a mountain in the middle of nowhere. The coyotes, afraid of the police checking for illegals, made them walk up the mountain to hide.

The ground was so arid that it was dusty. The trees were dry and the heat was intense. They spent the entire afternoon on that mountain without drinking any liquid, only the refreshing feeling of the urine from the cicadas, falling on their faces. At night, the group returned to the ranch. It was completely dark and they took quick showers before it was time to leave again. That same night, they loaded thirty into a truck for the trip to Mexicali, and from there to Mexico City. This would become the hardest part of the trip.

The truck had been modified to create a false floor space, eighteen inches high by the width of the truck. Where the front axle was located, they built a small sixteen-by-sixteen inch removable window. It was through this small opening that thirty people had to crawl to be hidden from view.

The space above the false floor was packed with sacks of grain to conceal the fact that there was a false floor. Once the truck was moving, the only air to breathe came from that small window. For the next seventeen hours, they couldn't eat, drink, or move.

My sisters established a friendship with the guide in charge of the group, and although there were seven other women traveling, the guide positioned the girls next to the window and the other women directly behind them. Maria Alejandra felt sorry for the men because they were all the way in the rear with little air to breathe. Because the space was small to accommodate thirty people and the ceiling so low, they sat or knelt on their knees the entire trip.

After a few hours, they lost track of time and place. At one point, the truck was stopped at a checkpoint where police searched for illegal people. They had been told to be completely silent and not to move until the guide told them they were clear. From the outside, the truck looked normal but the police knew coyotes use unbelievable tricks to conceal their purpose.

The police started their search by poking sticks in the sacs to see if anyone was hiding behind them. They kept interrogating the driver while the group was sealed beneath with no air to breathe, begging to God for the police to let them go.

The heat was so unbearable that they were perspiring and using up the little oxygen left to breathe.

They were becoming desperate and the men in the back were suffocating. With difficulty in their speech, they begged the rest of the group to surrender before they died. The police did not want to let the truck go because they had the suspicion there were illegal people hidden somewhere and they knew they could not last much longer without air. Finally, thanks to God who was on their side, the truck was let go and they reopened the small window.

They left at night and arrived at three in the afternoon in a small town on the outskirts of Mexico City. They stayed in a house where they slept on the floor because there were no beds or mattresses. They took hot showers, which was the best shower Maria Alejandra ever took in her life. They rested for the entire day, some people watching television and others washing the little clothing they brought with them.

That night, they left by bus to a subway station. From the subway, they went to a house where coyotes were waiting to leave for Leon de Guanajuato. The trip by bus was scary. There were police everywhere, boarding the buses, checking for illegal people, and standing guard in civilian clothes. They became paranoid. The trip from Mexico City to Leon de Guanajuato took five hours. They were taken to a ranch outside the city where they were mixed with another group. Now there were three hundred looking to cross the border.

The ranch had three large empty rooms and a big kitchen where the women took turns cooking. Maria Alejandra, Maria Claudia, and Monica had to work in the kitchen only once during the fifteen days they spent at the ranch. The three empty rooms were full of people and many slept in the hallway, on the patio, or in the fields.

There was only one small bathroom located outside the house in a corner of the patio. It had no roof but high walls.

There was no plumbing so they had to ladle water from a bucket onto their heads.

Maria Alejandra remembers one morning when she, Monica, and Maria Claudia, took a shower together to save time, since there were three hundred people taking turns. Suddenly, they heard a stampede of people trying to climb the bathroom walls. People were screaming and running, trying to reach the other side of the ranch to escape from immigration police. Maria Alejandra, Maria Claudia, and Monica were half naked, covered with soap, and trying to cover their bodies with terror in their hearts, knowing they had nowhere to hide.

Maria Alejandra said to Maria Claudia and Monica, "We can't do anything but get dressed and surrender." When they got out of the shower, they found out it was a false alarm. Regardless, the three hundred decided to go into the hills to sleep for the night just in case the police came to the ranch.

The reality was that this trip could have been more difficult, except for the fact of how they were raised by Mama. Maria Alejandra, Maria Claudia and Monica's childhood required them to live in precarious conditions. Also, at least they had each other to count on during the trip. They were not alone.

They tried to look at the bright side of the situation and not dwell in the darkness of the true conditions. They laughed, made fun of each other, and with Monica's camera, made a picture collection of their adventure, so as not to forget in the future what they had gone through.

Fifteen days later, the coyotes brought the group together and told them, "You have two options. You can leave by bus from Mexico City to Tijuana or pay more money and go by plane." This part of the trip was easier because they did it by plane. The biggest fear was being stopped at the airport and being asked for identification before boarding. But once more, God was on their side.

Safely reaching Tijuana, another coyote was waiting with a group of twenty people. The girls walked with the rest of the group to the top of the hill overlooking the border. From this point, they could look down at the border crossing and see the patrol. They saw them talking to the coyotes and what was ironic was that later that night, these were the same people they would try to catch.

People from other groups kept joining them, waiting for total darkness. Despite this, helicopters were constantly circling the area with powerful searchlights. At eleven at night, they started walking and for the next three hours, they did not stop. They were divided into small groups of twenty. Again, they were the only Colombians. The road appeared to be never-ending and further on it became more difficult to walk because the ground turned to sand and made each step harder. On this part of the trip, three young Mexican boys led them.

Their job was to take the group to a certain point where they would hand them to other guides who would take them across the border into San Diego. The three were completely exhausted and Maria Alejandra was fearful for Monica's health. At that moment, when they did not know if they could take another step, one of the coyotes took Monica's hand, helped her along, and forced her to keep walking. It was a caring and sincere gesture on his part and once more, God was giving them His hand.

At five in the morning, they reached San Diego. After six hours of walking, it was time to run across the highway. They prayed the Border Patrol cars would not see them. When they reached the apartment the coyotes had for them, all they wanted to do was sleep. They were dirty and did not have clothing to change into. They lay on the floor and for the next three hours they slept.

They were moved to another apartment where they were supposed to call their families and let them know they arrived safely. That way, they could send the plane tickets from Los Angeles to New York. Maria Alejandra, Maria Claudia, and Monica took showers and rested a little more.

The guys responsible for the apartment were nice enough to share their hamburgers and soda in exchange for the girls cleaning the office. They laughed and even found pleasure in doing the work. The following day, Pilly sent money and airline tickets. All of this was made possible through Pilly's boss, Nohemi, who loaned Pilly the money for the expenses of the trip.

They bought new dresses, and that was when they realized how much weight they lost. When Maria Alejandra left Colombia, she weighed one-hundred-twenty-five pounds and now she was at one-hundred pounds. On May 1, 1994, they boarded the plane in Los Angeles at ten at night. They were laughing and giggling about how ironic it would be to have come this far only to be stopped at the airport by Immigration and be sent back to Colombia. The flight attendant came through the cabin and woke everyone up half an hour prior to landing. They got ready and all they could think and talk about was the anticipation of seeing our mother who they had not seen for three years. Maria Alejandra also couldn't shake away thoughts about the life they left behind. They walked away from the comfort and familiarity of the day-to-day environment in Colombia.

Maria Alejandra, Maria Claudia, and Monica arrived at Newark Airport in New Jersey, and being such a big airport, they got lost. Since they did not know the language, they could not ask for directions. A half hour later, they saw Pilly waiting. It was a very emotional reunion. Now there was Mama, me, Maria del Pilly, Maria Claudia, Maria Alejandra, Monica, Felipe, and Julio Cesar in the United States. Having the family together had been our goal from the beginning and even without a penny in our pockets, God showed them the way. Mama only thought about stuffing the girls with food. She was so happy her daughters were together again.

"Finally, we made it," she kept whispering under her breath, as if she was in too much shock to say the words out loud.

Luisa Fernanda and her three children Erika, Marco, and Christian received their green cards in Colombia. Finally, on April 24, 1998, they arrived at John F. Kennedy Airport. Mama knew she could not bring all of us at the same time, but when she came, she knew her children were going to follow her just like chicks to a hen. And so, we did.

CHAPTER 27: Hardships that Ruined a Fairytale Love

In November 1994, Bob decided to take the boat south for the winter, hoping to find a spot where on weekends it would be warm enough to sail. The idea was a good one because the winters of 1994 and 1995 were the worst in many years. It was cold enough that the water froze in the bay and Felipe even walked across the ice to a local marina from the front of the house.

We took the boat as far south as Williamsburg, Virginia, to a marina on the York River and drove down there every weekend. We had to move from the house in Port Washington, (New York), and after looking at many houses, finally agreed on Huntington and in January 1995, we moved in.

We made the return trip with the boat from Virginia in April 1995 and the following spring, we moved the boat from Port Washington to a marina in Huntington. We had been sailing on a Saturday afternoon and once we finished, we decided to stop at the local supermarket. We went different ways and a few minutes later, I heard Bob screaming. I frantically searched for him; I knew something was wrong because of the way he called me.

When I saw him, he was bent over, holding his arm. "I think I am having a heart attack," he said through shortened breaths. I started to yell for help but no one came. I got Bob to the car and drove to the emergency room at Huntington Hospital. Thankfully it was only five minutes away. When we got to the emergency room, they called a cardiologist. I called Eric immediately to let him know about his father and then called my family. A half hour later, my family was there.

They loved Bob and were deeply concerned. At the same time, they were there for me, sharing my worry. The following day, the results of a blood test showed that Bob had a heart attack. Arrangements were made to move him to a Hospital in Manhasset.

I called Todd in Washington. To me, just his voice telling me not to worry and that he would be here in the morning was a blessing. He arrived and Bob was transferred to a Hospital in Manhasset. Todd's presence and assurance was the same I felt when he was with us for Felipe's surgery. It is sometimes difficult to put into words the feelings of support that Todd brought to us in difficult times. It was as if God chose him to be a giver.

Kurt was in Japan at the time and unable to come home, but Todd was in contact with him so he knew what was happening. The day of the surgery, Todd and I sat in the waiting room. When I saw Bob after the surgery with all the tubes coming out from his nose and body, I realized just how serious his situation was. Todd stayed after the surgery until he knew the danger was over.

Felipe has an enormous love for animals so he bought an iguana around that time. When we moved to the house, Eric asked for the garage to work on his car. Felipe could not have the Iguana in his room so we put him in the garage on a leash.

At the time, Eric was dating a beautiful girl with an empty brain. When the iguana disappeared and I asked Eric about it, he said, "I saw the Iguana this morning with my father and you can ask him, because I even made a comment to my father about it."

In the afternoon, I overheard a conversation between Eric and his girlfriend Kara. They were laughing about the iguana. When Bob came home that evening and I asked him about the iguana, he replied, "That is not true. I didn't see the iguana." It was unexplainable the way the iguana disappeared. She was well secured by the leash and the garage door was always closed. The night before I had gone to see her and the following morning she was gone. I called my mother and let her know about the loss of the iguana and she drove immediately from Westbury to help us to look for her. Mama was looking among the grass and bushes, concerned about the iguana dying of hunger. It was not used to living in the wild.

Eight days later, I was driving home when the iguana crossed the road in front of me. I stopped the car and ran to the house where Felipe was with his girlfriend Monica. I started screaming, "The iguana is outside, let's get her!"

Felipe was so excited that he ran out and even tried to climb a tree where the iguana was hiding. That same day, Bob and I had our luggage ready to leave for our overnight sailing trip to Block Island. Just a few minutes before leaving, Eric came through the door. I said to him, "We found the iguana. We are leaving but please make sure she does not get lost again."

What happened next is difficult for me to explain. It is like a film, so vivid in my mind and at the same time so painful.

"You fucking spic, get out of my house," Eric threatened me. He then turned to his father and said, "I don't know why you married this fucking bitch!" I was in tears and speechless. Meanwhile Bob was sitting in a chair watching what was going on without saying a word. He was too afraid to say anything. I could not believe it either; this was the first time I was verbally attacked by Eric. I had seen him lose control with Bob, but with me he had always been careful.

He started kicking the garbage can and came into my face. "I'm going to smash your fucking face!" he screamed at me. I was so afraid of his aggressiveness and loss of control that I knew if I said something, he would become physical.

After constantly telling me to leave his house, I went to our bedroom, took all my clothing, and put it in Bob's car to take to Mama's house. I was so concerned for Bob's health and his recent heart surgery that I said to him, "Don't worry Bob, we are going to Block Island anyway." He took the days off as vacation time and I did not want to spoil them. At the same time, he had not recovered completely, and it wasn't the right time for me to leave him.

I did not blame Bob for not giving me a place in his life. His son was a priority no matter what and I respected that. Bob drove me with my clothing to Mama's. Even though it was a one bedroom apartment in Westbury with not enough space for the many people we were now, there was a lot of love waiting for Felipe and I. We had been so used to living in small places that I didn't think for a moment the change I was going to experience after living so comfortably with Bob.

Felipe was my biggest concern. He was not aware of what happened and I decided to keep it to myself, afraid of his reaction if he knew the truth. Mama hung my clothing on the doors of the apartment and in any available space. She did not say a word about the incident. She just welcomed me and let me know in a silent way that I still had a home with her.

We left immediately after for the boat, and sailed through the night. What surprised me was the detachment from Bob. He was so used to being abused by Eric that for him this was just one more incident. Meanwhile, the entire trip I was crying just knowing that my marriage was over and once we went back I was not going to the house I thought was ours—I would be returning to Mama's house.

When I called the house from the boat, they told me Felipe was upset with me. He spoke to Eric who, of course, didn't tell the truth. Eric told Felipe that Bob and I were having problems in our marriage which made Felipe wonder why we left for Block Island together.

When we came back, Bob dropped me off at Mama's. My mother made magic with the space in my short absence. In the small bedroom was her bed and Mama worked out a way to stack on the sides of the walls the furniture that she had from the previous house that did not fit in this one.

It meant that to get into the bed, we had to climb over each other from one side. In that bed slept Mama, Maria Alejandra, Pilly, Monica, and I. Maria Claudia improvised a small bed next to it.

For everyone to fit in the one king size-bed, we had to sleep side by side crossways, instead of head to foot. In the living room was a small bed in which Julio Cesar slept. Iris, his girlfriend, had broken up with him and moved to Queens.

Bob used to come every day, so we kept seeing each other. The problem was still there, but we did not talk about it. Fifteen days later, we had dinner in a restaurant and I told him I wanted to go back and save our marriage. The following day, I talked to Felipe about my decision and, as always, he was supportive.

Once I moved back to Huntington, Eric and his girlfriend Kara made sure I felt unwelcome. Even though he had his own apartment downstairs, he and Kara would come upstairs to watch television and make their presence known.

I stayed in the bedroom most of the time when Bob was not home. But it was like God was showing me that I did not belong there anymore. It was only ten days later that I was thrown out of the house by Eric and Kara. This time, it was for good. I never went back.

On the ninth day, Felipe bought a ferret which he named, "Rasputin" because of the smell it produced. That afternoon, Felipe was leaving for Washington, D.C. with his girlfriend Monica and as soon as Eric and Kara saw Rasputin, they asked Felipe to loan him to them for a couple minutes while they went to get something to eat.

Before they left, Felipe made them aware that he had a long way to travel and to please not be gone for too long. An hour passed and they did not show up. When they finally came back, Felipe said, "You knew I had a long trip."

Felipe left late, and as it had become usual, I was in my bedroom. Once Felipe left, I overheard Kara say to Eric, "We should have had that fucking animal killed." I never heard her curse before. She had always been so nice and sweet, so I could not believe this new behavior. I came out of my bedroom and walked toward the living room where they were sitting.

"Is this the Kara that I know?" I asked her. I never understood her reaction. Eric apparently liked women that were aggressive and mean.

Perhaps in her effort to impress him, she answered, "You fucking bitch, I'm going to beat you up."

Eric got up and said, "Come on Kara, beat this piece of shit." He was smiling as he said those words. It became a nightmare for two hours. Eric kept yelling at me, "You fucking bitch, you do not belong here, leave my house."

Meanwhile, Kara was saying, "You fucking illegal people should go back to your own country."

I remained quiet. I sat on the sofa in the living room because every time I tried to get up and go somewhere, Eric would follow me and curse. I just sat there watching everything that was going on. I felt like I was not there and was watching it happen to someone else. I became insensitive in a way to their torture and finally said to Eric, "This is why I can't have a relationship with your father."

Eric came and sat on the sofa, almost on top of me, and while pushing me aside, kept asking me to leave his house. There was a moment when I got up and went to the kitchen to try and call Bob. Kara followed me and pulled all the wires out from the wall.

"I'm going to break every fucking bone of your fucking body," she said through gritted teeth. Unable to make a phone call, I went back to the sofa. While I sat there, Kara pushed by Eric, tried to hit me. I tried to protect myself with my leg and pushed her away. She fell back against the piano and did not try to hit me again.

When they knew Bob would be returning from work, I was still sitting on the sofa. They stood in front of me with big smiles, looking at me, and planning everything they would say to Bob when he showed up. They started organizing all the mess they made while making their big show. God was so beautiful to me that for the two hours this horrible situation went on, I was so in shock that it allowed me not to feel anger. It was like I was watching the situation through somebody else's eyes. Both were showing their true nature and mean spirits.

As if nothing happened, Eric and Kara went downstairs to his apartment. I sat in the living room waiting for Bob. When Bob showed up, I tried to explain to him in five minutes what had happened over the past two hours. He was tired of driving from Manhattan and tired of dealing with his own problems.

I felt sorry for him. Bob sat at the kitchen table without saying a word. A few minutes later, Eric came upstairs and I made a cup of tea for Bob when suddenly Eric turned the table over and screamed, "I want this fucking bitch to leave the house."

Bob was so afraid that he didn't say a word. I cleaned the mess and said to Bob, "I have to leave."

The following day, I started to put my clothing in Bob's car again, but while I was doing it, Eric was in the living room watching me. I said to Bob, "Can you please ask him to go downstairs to his apartment while I put my clothes in the car?"

"Eric, please go downstairs," Bob said quietly. Bob was a person who did not need to be hurt. He had been a good husband, but unfortunately, he was the most affected. Bob had become to Felipe the father he never had. Now, everything that had been given to him, without asking, was taken away.

I went back to Mama's house, and that night I told Felipe, "Love, we need to talk." We went to a restaurant, and as it happened to me for almost a year, every time I remembered the incident with Eric and Kara, I started shaking. It wasn't out of anger, but rather a physical reaction to how I was affected emotionally. The problem was that the entire time, I was avoiding telling Felipe the truth in order to protect him and tried to present the situation in a less severe way.

"I will go with you all the way. If you want, I will rent an apartment for the two of us if you don't want to go back to Mama's house. Just keep in mind that I'm going to school and working full time. So you will be by yourself most of the time," Felipe told me in his warm, soothing, and understanding voice.

This was a twenty-year-old giving me one hundred percent support and I felt so inadequate as a mother. I brought him into this situation and now instead of me being the one giving him support, he was offering it to me. Felipe had to take his belongings from Huntington, but there was no space left at Mama's for them. Monica, his girlfriend, offered to keep his things in her apartment while we looked for a bigger place to live. Eight days later, my cousin Jorge took me to see a house that turned out to be one of the oldest ones in Westbury that was being renovated.

It was built before the America Revolution in 1750. As soon as I walked through the door, I fell in love with it. It had enough space to accommodate a big family such as ours. The house was for sale and with my persistence, we arranged with the owner to rent the house for two years.

Meanwhile, Bob and Eric left the house in Huntington and Bob got Eric his own place. Bob asked me if it was alright for him to stay at Mama's house while he found his own place. While Bob certainly needed a place to live, I knew that deep down he was hoping we might get back together.

The full realization of our separation became obvious to him and unfortunately, it was too late. I had enough of exposing myself and my son to an unwelcome situation. Eric was too young and inexperienced, so I excused him of his actions. It is important to take into consideration what Eric's life was about. As an adolescent, his mother was not involved in his life, and his home life with his father was unstructured. Without going into details, it is easy to understand why a young kid growing up like this carried such explosive anger. At least we all grow, and we have God to thank, because time heals all wounds.

CHAPTER 28: A Mission with Mother Teresa

One afternoon during the summer of 1996, Felipe, his friend Sherry, and Bob went sailing to Connecticut. During the trip, Sherry talked about her work in Calcutta, India as a volunteer for Mother Teresa and her Sisters of Charity. Sherry was twenty-five years old and had been to India four times already.

Felipe knew my dream was to go to India as a volunteer and once he told me about Sherry's experience, I said I wanted to meet her. Many months passed until we finally got together in March 1997.

It was difficult to believe this young woman went to India as a volunteer when she was only eighteen. Bob and I had dinner with her. She was trying to put some money together to go back, since nothing is furnished by the Sisters of Charity. Bob and I decided to help her with the ticket. We were going to meet her in May in Calcutta.

We left on May 21, 1997 and a dream that had been with me for the longest time was going to be fulfilled. When Bob and I got off the plane, the heat and humidity were so intense that it felt like being in a sauna. We were expecting Sherry to be at the airport and when we did not see her, we decided to take a taxi. Fortunately, the taxi was prepaid inside the terminal. When we stood in front of the window to prepay the taxi, I looked behind the person taking our money and saw a small window facing the street. Ten people were struggling to look in, hoping to be the lucky one to get our fare.

When we got out of the terminal, people came to us in desperation, trying to get some money. It took us a couple minutes before we could get into the taxi. The saddest part was the taxi driver's expression as he watched the people around the car begging for money.

I asked the driver to pull out, but he waited a few more minutes, excusing the delay because he was in a silent way hoping we might give some money to the beggars. All the way to Mother Teresa's home, I was fascinated with everything I saw. The cows walked on the street undisturbed. People slept on the sidewalks and took baths in pumping water on the streets. They made little huts into homes, and washed their dishes on the sidewalk, which had become a home in the open for many. It seemed to me that they were unaffected by this way of living.

I quickly realized the Indian people are courageous and hardworking, blessed by God with a special gift. They do not complain, they just live day by day because they have no other choice. I was in India because it was my choice, not by necessity, which made the difference.

Once we got to Mother's house, all the kids from the neighborhood came asking for money—they knew we were new volunteers. It was overwhelming to have this many people around us. Once inside, we thought Sherry would be there but she had gone to the airport to pick us up and our paths did not cross.

One sister explained that it was only 1:00 and Sherry would not be back until 6:00. That was the time when the sisters and the volunteers pray at Adoration. She recommended that we go to a nearby hotel called, "The Circular" until we could get in touch with Sherry. The idea of going out again scared me. There was no necessity to take a taxi because the hotel was only two blocks away. I kept telling myself, "We are not going to make it." Once we left the house, all the children huddled around us again, hanging onto our clothing and their arms holding me down.

They just wanted to take us to the hotel, expecting to get a tip in exchange, but we were told many times not to give them anything because the situation could become unbearable.

The fear came to the point that while we were walking to the hotel, I wanted to hide or become invisible. Bob mumbled under his breath, "We are going to get our throats cut."

I was waiting for Sherry to show up, like an apparition. I was hoping for a miracle. Thankfully, we made it quickly to the hotel. When we got there safely, we were impressed by its appearance, considering the poorness of the area. While we were registering, Sherry arrived. As soon as we saw her, we were no longer afraid.

We had a nice dinner at the hotel, and even though we were tired after a twenty-five-hour trip, at 5:00 the next morning, we headed to Mother's house for the 6:00 Mass. Before getting into the chapel, we took off our shoes. The chapel is a big room with windows facing Circular Road, one of the noisiest and busiest streets in Calcutta. The altar is in the center and is simply adorned with Christ in the middle and the inscription, "I am thirsty."

The sisters in training wore a white gown with their heads covered. The sisters that took their vows after nine years of preparation wore white gowns with two lines of light blue ribbon on the edges. Approximately one hundred sisters, dressed in white gowns, were positioned in a straight line. The advanced ones were in the middle, and near the door were the volunteers.

Love, peacefulness, and faith were depicted on their faces and not even the noise from the street disturbed them. When receiving Communion, the sister behind the one receiving would bow her head with hands in prayer. At the end, I was given a page which contained beautiful prayers repeated every day after Mass.

Once the Mass was finished, everyone went downstairs for hot tea, bread, and small bananas. Since there was more than one house, the volunteers could choose where to work. At 7:30, we left with Sherry to Prem Dan, which means, "the gift of love," given by a multinational to the Missionaries of Charity.

Most people we passed on the street said hello, so we no longer felt threatened or uncomfortable in the streets.

Prem dan, is near the train station and most patients there suffered from terminal tuberculosis. We walked across a bridge over the station and once at the top, we could see thousands of people living on the sides of the railroad in shacks built of cardboard. On the sidewalk, people built shacks of about six by four feet. Because there was not enough room in a shack, the adults would sit inside and the kids remained outside during the day. There were no bathrooms and as a substitute, the people used a large open sewer tube next to the sidewalk that ran from one side of the bridge to the other.

When we passed on our daily walk to work, we saw people sitting on the sidewalk with buckets of water, washing their clothes and dishes. The kids begged for money and tried to grab us. At the top of the bridge was a staircase leading to the entrance of the Prem Dan house. Once inside, a large patio with trees and bushes was bustling with sickly patients, milling around. The compound had separated areas for male and female patients and the volunteers were split between male and female.

The population of Prem Dam was usually three hundred patients, divided equally between male and female. On my first day, May 24, 1997, Sherry introduced me to everybody. At the time, I was in my last semester at Nassau Community College on Long Island, New York, studying surgical technology. Aseptic techniques were a must in this program and when I looked for a box of sterile gloves at Prem Dan, they showed me a bucket full of gloves. These gloves had been used by the volunteers and were thrown into the bucket, unwashed and ready to be reused. I was disgusted and appalled.

Later that day, I realized that I was free to express my love in any way I wished, so I allowed my heart to flow. You cannot do this type of service unless your heart is in it, giving these beautiful people love, and making them feel that you

253

really care for their wellbeing. All the chores were done in a primitive way without mechanical aids. Mother Teresa's philosophy of service requires that you live like the poor to be able to understand their needs.

At Prem Dan, beds were piled outside and cleaned once a week. The floors are washed with buckets of soapy water and swapped with a straw whisk, which is like a broom without a handle. The sheets, pillowcases, and patient gowns were soaked and scrubbed by hand first, and then beaten on concrete to loosen the dirt. The outdoor cleaning patio had three concrete water storage tanks. The first was for dirty rinse, the next for cleaning, and the last for the final rinse. Meanwhile, another group finished the squeezing and the clothing was hanged on the roof of the third floor to dry.

Around the perimeter of the patio were canals that were nothing more than open sewage pipes, used by patients as a bathroom. The Indian women that worked for Mother Teresa from time to time would throw buckets of water there to flush out the canals. The toilet, used by the nuns and volunteers, was very primitive. There was nothing to sit on, with two cement blocks on the floor, one for each foot, and a porcelain drain in the middle.

Lunch consisted of rice and vegetables. Meat was served once a week. We, the volunteers, had to clean wounds full of maggots and on occasion, a limb was amputated with a pair of scissors. No matter the pain, the patients always had smiles of appreciation. Language was not a barrier because the communication became spiritual, where words were not necessary.

The beds were one next to the other, with small aisles between. In the limited space among the beds, patients created their own privacy. No one complained. They supported each other and if somebody disturbed the harmony, that person was told that their behavior was unacceptable. The water they drank was stored in large containers designated exclusively as "drinkable water" and each had their own cup next to their bed.

A doctor showed up only once a week for a couple of hours to see patients. Many times with Bob's unconditional economic support, I took it upon myself to take people in serious need to the nearby hospital.

Mother Teresa has always had greatness associated with her life effort in helping the poor, and attached to that, there had been numerous foundations and private individuals willing to donate large sums of money. When you read about Mother Teresa, you think of this endless supply of money from around the world to help the poor in Mother Teresa's care. It seemed that these resources had not been used adequately.

During my first day, I met Adhira and Ishanvi. They liked to be bathed, so I helped them with a lot of pleasure since it was a way to become closer with them through the blessing of their physical contact. There was one bar of soap for everybody. The importance of cleanliness and sterile procedures did not apply here. This was the way things were done, and I did them to the best of my ability.

I was so caught up in the opportunity of helping these people that it never occurred to me I might become exposed and catch their illnesses. It was a fulfilling experience, when you lifted or helped someone, and you felt a kiss anywhere in your body or your feet of gratitude. Every day working there felt like I was receiving God's reward, and there is not enough money in the world that can replace this feeling.

Bob came to India right when he was needed the most. His first day at Pren Dan was a shock—he was overwhelmed. The physical work was intense and with his recent open-heart surgery, Bob thought that he would have another heart attack. He knew that he could not keep up with the younger volunteers, most of them in their twenties and in great shape. Bob kept doing the physical work for two days and by the third morning,

Sister Paulita, the nun in charge of the men's side, took pity on him.

"I want you to work in the infirmary for Paul Parker," she told Bob.

Paul was a young Australian who took over the responsibility of administering all medicine, shots, intravenous, and wound care. He was there for over a year; took his responsibility very seriously; and had a wonderful sense of humor. He and Sister Paulita would play practical jokes on each other all the time.

One day Sister Paulita gave Paul a white cardboard box with a ribbon around it and said to him, "This is a gift for you." Paul, who had volunteered with Sister Paulita for a year knew that something was up. When he opened the box, inside was a dead mouse.

Bob helped Paul for three days and learned how to clean and dress the wounds of more than thirty patients a day. On the fourth day, Paul did not show up, so Bob was on his own. It turned out that Paul had contracted tuberculosis and needed time to get treatment.

Sister Paulita told Bob that same day, "You have to take over Paul's job for a while. Do your best, listen to your heart, and God will help you."

Bob recruited three volunteers, one from America, one from India, and one from Korea. The first day on their own was exhausting. That night at Adoration, Sherry told Bob that Paul was not going to be back for a while; so the following day, he received a crash course from Sister Paulita about intravenous shots and administering medication. Bob was practicing medicine without a license in Calcutta.

One day after work, Bob said, "I have the feeling for the first time in my life that I am part of God's work. I will never forget this blessing."

India was precisely what Bob's soul needed. It was magic for him, even though other moments were painful. One day, he had to face the reality of losing one of his patients. That was the moment that Santiago de la Torre came into his life.

The way Santiago communicated with the patients was fully appreciated. He took on the most difficult of chores with the sickest patients. He cleaned their wounds, comforted them, and most of all, made them laugh. The day Bob's patient died, the nuns removed the patient from his bed and carried him to the entrance lobby of the chapel.

Santiago sat on the edge of the bed and slowly passed his hands over the man's limp body, never touching him. At the last minute, the man's eyes opened, Santiago said something to him in Hindu, and the man smiled, took his last breath, and passed away.

I am sure that Santiago was a conduit of God, a chosen one. Other volunteers felt that he was an ex-priest and maybe a person who had lived a life of pain. Either way, Bob was drawn to his side, and from that day onward, they worked together in the infirmary.

Patrick from Ireland and John from Australia were volunteers who chose to work in the two train stations in Calcutta. They looked for sick people that required immediate help and brought them to Prem Dan. Once at Prem Dan, they were brought to the patio to have their hair cut in order to get rid of the thousands of lice that had accumulated over many years without a shower and to avoid lice from spreading in the compound.

They cried when they lost their hair because they did not understand the need for sanitary conditions. These were humans beings who had been living on the streets for many years and were taken away from a life they always knew. It must have been demoralizing and humiliating to sit there naked while being bathed by strangers who weren't of their culture.

Meanwhile, the volunteers thought we were doing the right thing. The interpretation of those tears could have been that many of those people did not want the outsiders' help or just wanted to be left alone.

After this was done, the patient was fed and their clothing replaced by a clean gown. All the volunteers were willing to do what was necessary with love and care. I wrote in my notes: *This morning, while washing the clothing, a girl next to me was telling me that her mother would not believe it if she saw her going to Mass every morning before coming to work and doing the things she was doing.* It was like, no matter what the conditions of life you had prior to coming to India, your whole self changed.

Some of the patients spent most of their lives in a squatting position, so the muscles on their legs were atrophied. For that reason, they learned to walk sitting; with their knees close to their faces and with their arms, helped the legs to move.

At 11:30, lunch was served, so I decided to take care of three sick people. I put small dosages of water in the mouth of one that was already dying and stayed with her for several minutes. The following day when I returned, the first thing I did was to look for her. She was not there. "Where is the woman?" I inquired. The nun told me that she had died that morning. During our break, I passed a room and Sherry called me in, "There she is." I was shocked to see the woman I helped the previous day laying on a bed. I stepped into the room and saw her covered in a clean white sheet with fresh flowers placed on top of her. I prayed for her soul.

Baby was a fourteen-year-old girl with tuberculosis. She was an angel, always happy and helpful. The volunteers wore aprons with blue and white checker squares. Once, Baby came and took the apron off me and gave me a beautiful black and white apron. Because she spoke little English, I was unable to understand what she was trying to say.

I was trying to explain to Baby that I did not want to wear something if I did not know who it belonged to. At that moment, a patient who spoke English came in and said to me, "You are lucky and I want you to know that it is a privilege to be wearing this apron. It had been worn all the time by Sister Allen, whom everybody loved very much and she left only three days ago to her hometown." So I wore it the entire time I was in India. I was very proud of it.

No matter how humbled I was for this experience, I experienced many sad moments.

One day, the patients had been put outside on the patio while the floors were washed. Once the floors were cleaned and the beds changed, I went outside with a wheelchair to pick up the patients who were unable to walk. I saw a young girl on the floor, almost unconscious, with foaming saliva all over her face. I realized that she had had a seizure and when I bent to pick her up, she opened her eyes and punched my face with all her strength.

For a few seconds, I was trying to comprehend what had just happened. She caught me by surprise and then tried to bite and rip my apron. Fortunately, there was someone next to me to calm her down.

In June, as we left Mother's house in the morning after Mass, Bob, Sherry, and I decided to stop by the hotel to have breakfast before leaving to work. We were ready to leave, when an ambulance from Mother's house passed by and gave us a ride.

When we got in the ambulance, lying on the floor wrapped in a white sheet was a dead body. When someone dies, they are taken to Kalighat, The Home for The Dying, to be cremated. We took a detour to drop off the body before going to Prem Dan to start the chores of the day.

There was a patient who had been sick for many days and her whole uterus was completely outside of her body. She was unable to move, could not eat, and was in a lot of pain. I said to Sister Welsa, "Let me take her to the hospital. I will take care of the expenses." She said, "No." Two days later, when I was leaving at noon, she was crying and tried to tell me something that I couldn't understand. I asked somebody to translate what she said. Apparently she had been saying, "I want to go home. I want to be with my family."

I wrote in my notes: *Today I could not believe it. Her eyes were glazed, and when I took one of her hands, there was no response at all. How I missed her smile today. I would have wished to spend the whole morning at her bedside, just giving her company in her last moments, but there are other patients who need attention too.*

The following day, when I got to Prem Dan, the first thing I did was to go and look for her. Her bed was empty and I knew it meant that she had died. I went to the little room where they put the bodies while they waited to be transferred to Kalighat, but she was not there either.

I asked Sister Welsa about her. The sister said that she died at four in the morning and was taken immediately to Kalighat.

I kept asking myself, "Did I do the right thing? Could I have done better?"

The last day I volunteered at Prem Dan, I was ready to leave when a beautiful Indian woman was brought in. She was crying and begging me to help her get out of there. She said she had four children and just wanted to be with them. Unfortunately, there was nothing I could do. And so I left her in the hands of the other sisters.

Bob and I went to Mother Teresa's house to say goodbye to everyone. Sister Nirmala gave us an envelope and asked us to give it to Mother Teresa who was in the Bronx, New York, visiting at the time.

Before we left, we spent time with Shaheen, an Indian girl who spoke English very well. She was going to get married, and before the wedding, Sherry, Bob, and I went to her parents' house to be part of the preparations. One day, a young Indian man saw her on the street, liked her, and asked his parents to go to her family and arrange for them to get married. Shaheen's parents paid the groom's parents eight hundred dollars. They had been saving that money all of their lives in anticipation of this day.

The sleeping quarters and the kitchen at her parents' house was one room, seven feet wide and eight feet long. The bed of the family, which used almost the whole room, was supported by bricks. Directly beneath the family's bed was the kitchen.

We had some tea and I noticed that Shaheen was not as happy as expected. I asked her why she was so sad and she said that she was scared and did not want to get married. If it had been her choice, she would have come to the United States to go to college. I told her that she still had time to change her mind.

"If I do not get married, as it is already established by my parents, I will disgrace the whole family," she said, crestfallen. Three days before the wedding, her entire body was covered with a mixture of turmeric powder, chick pea flour and mustard oil, which was supposed to make her skin shine. The second day, her hands and feet were painted with henna.

The marriage took place in a two-story building. On the first floor was the future husband and his friends while Shaheen was on the second floor with her friends. After several hours of people coming in saying hello and bringing gifts, they were married separately, surrounded by their groups of friends. Once husband and wife, his friends brought him to the second floor on their shoulders. This was the first time Shaheen saw her husband.

After the wedding, Bob and I returned to New York. A week later, I called Shaheen, and she sounded happy. Her husband turned out to be a good and responsible person.

When we returned to New York, Bob and I went to the Missionaries of Charity in the Bronx and met Mother Teresa. We gave her the envelope that Sister Nirmala had sent, and during our conversation she asked us to go back to India. I told her that we would consider it.

I resumed my last semester as surgical technologist at Nassau Community College. But the first day of practice at the hospital was a disaster. I was so out of practice and had become far too permissive of the foul at Mother Teresa's house that I made a mistake with keeping the techniques and equipment sterile. That same day, I was dismissed from the program.

CHAPTER 29 : Finding Happiness in a Diamond-less Mine

Our older brother, Julio Cesar, who had been working at the diamond mine in Venezuela since 1973, constantly asked Chiqui to come to the mine and work with him. Finally, on May 5 of 1990, Chiqui decided to go, providing that Marta would come with him. Their son, Andres Fernando, was two days away from becoming seven and Chiqui was so in love with Marta that he could not imagine being away from her for too long. She agreed to come, but because this trip was an adventure, they decided to leave Andres Fernando with Marta's parents in Ibague.

Julio Cesar sent them tickets to fly from Bogotá to Puerto Carreno. When they arrived at the airport in Bogotá, there was only one seat available on the flight. "Go back to Ibague. Tomorrow is Andres' seventh birthday and you will come on a later flight in a day or two," Chiqui said to Marta.

Not only was the seating limited on this Second World War plane, but also the flights were scheduled infrequently- two flights a week.

Once he arrived in Puerto Carreno, Julio Cesar was waiting at the airport with false documents for him to enter Venezuela. Chiqui was excited to see our brother whom he had not seen for many years. At the same time, Chiqui was distracted and concerned due to the absence of Marta, and he was looking forward to the moment that they would be together again.

From Puerto Carreno, they took a small outboard motor boat to Puerto Paez, across the Colombian-Venezuelan border. The next part of the trip was to Caicara. This town was at the edge of the mine and could only be reached by Jeep because there were no roads, only trails and rough terrain, which made the trip slow and long. From Caicara, they took a small plane to

Salvacion which was the most important village at the mine, where Julio Cesar worked.

After thirty-five minutes they arrived at Salvacion, which was an exciting place. It had many restaurants and cantinas with new hookers arriving every day. The miners looked forward to the end of the day, and spending money on hookers was the best way for them to conceal how lonely they actually felt. When they came to the mine, they were forced to leave behind their loved ones in the hope that one day they would strike it rich.

Our sister Luisa was a couple of weeks from giving birth and was waiting for Chiqui and Julio Cesar with her husband, Jesus Antonio Campos Chacon. The following day, Julio Cesar taught Chiqui how to work the mine. It was completely different from the picture he had envisioned for finding diamonds. Chiqui thought the diamonds were in the dirt on the edge of the road where he could pick up a handful of dirt, move it around with his fingers, and find a few diamonds sparkling in his hand. This was far from the reality as he soon found out.

A crater is dug approximately thirty meters, where a variety of tunnels go horizontally in many directions at four to five meters long. One man crawls in with a candle or a flashlight to collect the material which could have diamonds in it. Since there is no structural support in the tunnels, it is not uncommon for these to collapse on top of the men, killing them, with no one able to provide help. Most men working at the mine are hispanic from different countries and cultures, backgrounds, and understandings. Even though they speak the same language, sometimes the interpretation are easily lost.

Four days after being at the mine and seeing such a different way of life, it was time for Chiqui to go back and get Marta. He was observant of how Julio Cesar handled the situation with Immigration to get Chiqui into Venezuela, so he used these same techniques to bring Marta.

As soon as they got to Salvacion, Julio Cesar said to Marta and Chiqui that he was going to Caracas to get a license to become a diamond buyer. He and his girlfriend Yolanda had two daughters, Yahaira was two and Alejandra was one. They took Yahaira with them while Marta and Chiqui remained at the mine with Alejandra.

It took Julio Cesar two months to do the paperwork and put the business in place. When he returned, they moved to Ciudad Bolivar. Julio Cesar already rented a house and gave Chiqui fifteen thousand bolivars to buy clothing to take back to the mine and sell to miners.

There were people who did not have money to pay for the goods, so Chiqui took diamonds in exchange which, given the fact that he had no idea of the true value of a stone, was risky. After doing this for many months, he grew tired of the work, which was providing just enough money to survive.

A year later, Julio Cesar became a successful diamond buyer and was working for one of the biggest companies in Belgium. He left the mine in Guaniamo and went to another, called "Karum" where ninety percent of the production was high-quality diamonds. He asked Chiqui and Marta to work for him. He was not only buying diamonds, but had become the owner of ten companies. So, Chiqui worked at the mine and Marta became the cook for twenty of his workers.

Two years later, in 1992, some companies were making money and some were losing. Unfortunately, the losers outnumbered the winners, so Marta and Chiqui decided to return to Ciudad Bolivar and Julio remained in Karum.

Two months later, Julio Cesar was on his way to Colombia with his new girlfriend, Iris, to start their journey illegally into the United States to be reunited with us.

Chiqui was broke and his choices were very few. He sat at a bus station in Ciudad Bolivar with his wife and the fifty bolivars that Julio Cesar gave him before he left for Colombia.

It was eight at night and he said to Marta, "There are two mines. I'm going to take a bus without destination and I will call you as soon as I get to someplace."

Marta went back to the house hoping a door would open for him. The next bus was going to Santa Elena and Chiqui was on it. His future was before him and he did not know what to expect. Chiqui arrived in the morning and his first stop was a small bakery that had warm, fresh bread, reminding him of home. Chiqui bought two breads and a Coke. An adventure like this with no direction required patience, and with no money, all he had was time. He went to a gas station two blocks away and at one in the afternoon a truck stopped for fuel.

Chiqui walked up to the driver and asked him, "Where are you going?"

"Icabaru," he said in a low, cold voice.

"What is Icabaru?" Chiqui asked eagerly.

He looked at Chiqui with surprise, as if he was supposed to know what Icabaru was. "It's a mine," he said flatly.

Initially, someone told Chiqui of a mine called, "El Polaco," where miners found diamonds larger than any other mine. The biggest one was 160 karats. Chiqui wondered if Icabaru would be the same.

"If you want to go to El Polaco, you are going to have to walk for two hours after the three-hour ride by car," the driver said, after Chiqui inquired about El Polaco.

So Chiqui asked, "If you give me a ride to Icabaru, what will happen?" He offered to take Chiqui directly to the mine. Chiqui did not reject this offer. It was pouring rain and he had to sit in the back of the truck, but he wasn't complaining. To get to Icabaru was going to take fourteen hours because of the weather conditions. Being a perfect stranger, Chiqui was lucky to get a ride. There are one hundred fourteen kilometers from Santa Elena to Icabaru and with good weather it takes approximately seven hours in a big truck.

The road was unpaved and there were large rocks and deep holes which made the driver go even slower. A careless move could mean disaster. This required a speed of only three to five miles per hour. The road was so narrow in certain places that one car would stop to let the other pass.

The rain never let up and the driver stopped for lunch at four in the afternoon. Chiqui was wet, cold, and hungry. He spent the last of his money when he bought the two breads and Coke, so he waited for the driver to eat. When he finished his lunch, he felt sorry for Chiqui and asked him to come and ride in front while his stomach was full. Even though Chiqui was hungry, he was happy with this offer to ride in the front and out of the rain.

Once in the front, the driver introduced himself as Jose.

"How many cases of beer are you carrying?" Chiqui asked. When he told Chiqui three hundred, Chiqui offered, "How much would you pay me to unload them?"

He shrugged. "Fifty bolivars."

"Fifty bolivars for unloading the truck?" Chiqui reiterated.

"No, fifty bolivars for unloading the three hundred cases of beer and for loading the three hundred empty cases."

"That's a deal," Chiqui said without hesitation.

Finally, they arrived at two in the morning. Chiqui was starving since his last meal. At the cantina where they were going to drop off the three hundred cases of beer was a small food stand selling rotisserie chicken. Chiqui's mouth watered at the sight of food. "I cannot unload three hundred cases of beer without eating anything. I'm starving. Please buy me half a chicken, otherwise I will not have the strength to do it," Chiqui begged the driver.

He obliged, and Chiqui devoured the chicken, then unloaded the truck and loaded it with three hundred empty cases. Chiqui finished at five in the morning and did not care how exhausted he was. His clothing was beginning to dry but his biggest concern was where he would rest.

A room in a hotel would cost him fifty bolivars. He did not know anyone, and the last thing he was going to do was spend the money he had just made with so much sacrifice.

The only belongings Chiqui carried were a hammock and screen sieve to pan for diamonds. Having fifty bolivars in his pocket gave him some peace of mind. So Chiqui walked around the village looking for a place to hang his hammock in order to be able to rest for a couple hours. It was already five-thirty in the morning.

Chiqui came back to the cantina where he unloaded the cases of beer and noticed that across the street there was another cantina. Next to the building was a room under construction with a zinc roof and no walls.

Chiqui approached the owner, whose nickname was "El Chichero." Chiqui said to him, "Sir, I need a big favor. When you close the cantina can you allow me to hang my hammock at the construction site? I have been traveling for two days, I'm exhausted, I do not know anyone, and the only thing I have in my pocket are fifty bolivars."

"It is alright with me; the only problem is that you are going to have to wait until eight in the morning. That is the time I close," El Chichero replied.

It was only six but Chiqui agreed. He sat quietly on one of the benches. An hour later, the man saw how tired Chiqui was and said, "Go hang the hammock in the next room. It is still under construction and has no walls but at least you can get some rest."

Chiqui thanked him and hung the hammock. But, a half an hour later, he had to get up. The people doing the construction showed up and the village came alive. People walked by to head to the mine, children went to school, and businesses that were not related to cantinas were opening up.

Chiqui unhooked the hammock and with his screen sieve, started wandering around town. Chiqui saw a safe spot where construction was occurring, so he hid the hammock underneath some rocks. Next to the construction site lived the family who owned it so Chiqui was careful not to be seen by them. He continued walking with the sieve in his hands.

He stopped a man in his twenties and asked him, "Where are you going?"

"I'm going to Los Brazileros. It has a high concentration of good material," he replied. That woke Chiqui up. You don't come to live in the jungle, away from civilization, if there is no money to be made.

So Chiqui asked, "Who are you going with?"

"Just myself. If you want, you can come with me," he said. Together, they walked to Los Brazileros for an hour, and on their way, they were surrounded by clay dirt. In Chiqui's ignorance about mining, he asked, "Is there gold in that dirt?"

The man laughed very loud, looked at Chiqui, and said, "No!" Chiqui felt stupid. Once they got to Los Brazileros, they decided to create a partnership. While one was getting the material, the other washed it in the sieve. Whatever they got, they sold and split the profit. Every day, they got up at five and worked until eight at night.

Every night, no matter how tired Chiqui was after a long day of work, he had to wait until eleven for the family who owned the construction site to go to sleep. At five in the morning he had to get up and disappear before they awoke.

What made his sleeping uncomfortable was that the place had no walls and the mosquitoes were having a feast for the eight days he remained there. Depriving himself of a good night's sleep, however, allowed him to put some money together, so that eight days later, he sent Marta enough money to join him.

Chiqui picked her up at the airstrip. Having her gave him the comfort to find strength in the path he chose. He took her to a restaurant where he used to have his meals during the evening. After eating, Chiqui said to the owner, "This is my wife. I understand you need someone to work in the kitchen. Well, she will be happy to do the work."

He accepted her with open arms.

As with every night, they waited until eleven to hang the hammock and at five in the morning Chiqui went to work at the mine while Marta worked in the kitchen. To clean themselves, they went to the river.

To save money, Chiqui did not eat during the day, and by eight at night he went to the restaurant and ate Marta's dinner. While she worked during the day, Marta did enough food picking so by the time he arrived, she would tell the owner that he was eating her dinner. After a month living in these precarious circumstances, they decided to find their own place. They went deep in the jungle and cut some branches to use as poles to hold up a zinc roof. They carried them on their shoulders and cleared a small piece of land. To protect themselves from the cold and mosquitoes, they covered the structure with pieces of cardboard. They went from being homeless to having their own shack.

They made a bed out of branches and used pieces of cardboard as a mattress. As their economic situation started to improve, they could afford buying a mattress and a small kerosene stove. Every day before going to work, they went to the river and, in a small hand-pulled wagon, carried two five-gallon containers to use for showers and cooking at night.

Two months later, Marta quit her job at the restaurant and came with Chiqui to work at the mine. People in town saw them as outsiders and did not trust them because they had no relatives in town. Now that Marta was working with Chiqui, they returned to the village at night and were happy to go to their own place.

Lalo was an average diamond buyer who liked to play chess. One evening Chiqui passed by his office and said to him, "Let's play a game." Chiqui used to play chess when he was younger and had gotten good at it. And, at the mine, Lalo did not have talented contenders, so he was always looking forward to the challenge of a good game.

As time passed, Chiqui asked him for diamonds that he could sell, which Lalo did. This improved Chiqui's economic situation and at the same time gave him the opportunity to learn how to become a diamond buyer. During the evening, he would come back to the village and sell the diamonds and gold he found during the day and play chess with Lalo.

Despite this, Icabaru was not doing well, so Marta and Chiqui decided to go to a mine called, "Uaiparu." They had to walk ten hours and then took a small outboard boat for another two hours. Once there, they would stay for a minimum of eight days. They put four poles in the ground and made a simple roof with plastic on top. This was their home and they hung their hammock, which they shared, and slept with their clothes on.

After five grueling trips to Uaiparu, they decided to return to Icabaru. There, Chiqui joined five workers to work an area that had good potential. When the material was washed, they could not believe how many diamonds they found. They sold them for one-hundred-sixty-thousand bolivars and distributed the money among the six of them.

They said to themselves, "We are rich!"

Chiqui then went to the owner of the construction site where he used to hang his hammock. His nickname was "El Pelado" or, "The Bald" because he had no hair. Chiqui knew that he had some machines so he wanted to make a deal.

"Sir, when I came to Icabaru two years ago, you were building a room next to your house and without you knowing it,

I used it to hang my hammock at night so I could sleep. Five guys and I found an area that is giving out good material. Why don't you bring your machines and we will do our work and provide you with the site. When time comes to wash the material, we all will share the profit," Chiqui offered.

He replied, "No. To move the machines is going to cost me some money and I am not really interested." Chiqui left El Pelado and went to a man whose nickname was "Chorro de humo," or "Raising Smoke. He had his machinery in a place that was not producing material, and not having anything to lose, he decided to take a risk. Chiqui worked hard, trusting that in a couple of months they would wash the material and become successful again.

Chiqui was the whole day standing barefoot in water up to his waist. His body was covered with sores, including his testicles. It was painful, but Marta, with her love and unconditional support, took care of him.

One of the guys washed some material they were accumulating and found a 0.50 stone. They were very excited, thinking the rest of the material would be as rich. They sold the stone, went to the cantina, and got drunk.

Twenty days later, they washed the rest of the material and the biggest stone was 0.10. It was sold for only five-hundred bolivars. The machinery's owner lost, and so did the guys. Chiqui said, "When you grow potatoes, you get potatoes. But you don't grow diamonds and gold. That's why it is an unpredictable business."

That evening, Chiqui went to Lalo's office to play some chess. It was early, and at around nine, the police came to the office, screaming and putting everybody against the wall. They were terrified, not understanding what was going on, begging to know what was happening.

The sergeant in charge was an arrogant nobody whose name was Randy, nicknamed Rambo, because he thought he was from the movies. A real tough guy, so he thought, with an inferiority complex.

Earlier that night, someone went into a diamond buyer's office and robbed him. In the robbery, three guys wore masks and, according to the buyer, one had a Colombian accent. They thought it was Chiqui.

Rambo and his henchman took Chiqui to the detention center, whipped him with a chain, and punched him while he was tied to a chair.

"You did it and you were not alone. Who were the other two?" they accused Chiqui over and over again.

Still in shock, Chiqui replied, "I don't know what you are talking about. I was playing chess at Lalo's office since six in the afternoon. Why don't you ask him and the people that were with us?"

"You are a fucking liar!" Rambo screamed at him. He kept beating Chiqui with the chain while one of his subordinates punched Chiqui in the face. The physical and emotional torture went on until nine in the morning. By seven in the morning, Rambo sent three policemen to Chiqui's shack. Marta was sleeping when they woke her abruptly and began to go through their clothing, expecting to find the diamonds as proof.

Lalo and many others who saw Chiqui playing chess came to the detention center to support his story. However, it did not stop them from torturing him. By ten, because of the lack of evidence, they finally let Chiqui go. His body was bruised and hurting from a night of wrongful punishment.

Working at the mine then became unstable, so Chiqui decided to become a carpenter, which did not require experience, since at the mine, painting and construction was unsophisticated. The Jaramillo's were the wealthiest family in town, and they gave him work. Chiqui painted not only the roof of their house but also their restaurant which, ironically, Chiqui owns now. Marta and Chiqui were still living in the shack.

Now that Chiqui was working as a carpenter and knew how much he was making each day, they did not have to worry about the unpredictability of the mine. They had food on the table every night. Chiqui also kept playing chess with Lalo and when the miners came to his office to sell the diamonds they had found during the day, Chiqui watched the way he classified them. Then, Lalo started going to Ciudad Bolivar during the week and came to the mine on weekends. The rest of the week the office was closed.

"Why don't you let me use your office during the week?" Chiqui said to him one day. He not only agreed, but loaned Chiqui fifteen-thousand bolivars to start. Chiqui left his job as a carpenter and decided to go back to work the mine. Chiqui left early in the morning and came back to the village at two in the afternoon to open the office, which had a small table. Even though Chiqui still did not know much about buying diamonds, he decided to take the risk.

One evening, some miners came to him with large quantities of diamonds. They wanted eighty-thousand bolivars for it. When Chiqui examined them, he knew the real value was one-hundred-thousand bolivars.

So Chiqui said, "I don't have that amount of money with me. I will be back as soon as I can."

It was eight-thirty at night when all the diamond buyers were getting ready to close. Chiqui went looking for the money from people he knew would have it, but nobody wanted to lend to him. His last option was Mr. Marino. During the weekends, the big diamond buyers came to Icabaru from Ciudad Bolivar. He was one of the big ones.

"Mister Marino, I have a good lot of diamonds and I already made a deal with the miners but I don't have the money. Please lend me ninety thousand bolivars for me to pay them, I will bring you the diamonds and you will buy them from me," Chiqui offered him.

"No, bring the diamonds and I will buy them from you," he replied very casually.

Chiqui said, almost in a desperate way, "I can't do that because the miners are at my office and I already made a deal with them. That lot of diamonds has already been bought by me."

Mr. Marino was reluctant. He said, "If you don't bring me the diamonds, I will not give you the money." Time was passing and Chiqui was desperate, going from buyer to buyer looking for the money that would allow him to buy the diamonds and also gain credibility among the miners as an amateur buyer.

Marta had been selling lottery tickets on the street with nothing more than a chair and a table. Chiqui went to Marta and asked her, "Can you please give me the money you have? I promise you will have it back before you cash out."

Fortunately, Chiqui could get the rest of the money from the Jaramillo family. It took him approximately two hours to put the money together, but then, Chiqui bought the diamonds and resold them for the same price.

Chiqui did not have the reputation as a diamond buyer because he was just beginning and his direction was uncertain. The diamond buyers closed their offices at about eight at night and Chiqui stayed open until ten or eleven. He did not care if the miners showed up or not. If Chiqui made enough money to buy a Coke, he was satisfied. The goal he set at that moment was to be among the twenty most successful buyers in Icabaru. The competition was that of sixty buyers.

Almost everybody went to the big buyers. Meanwhile, Chiqui waited patiently every night for a poor, hungry miner to stop by the office and sell his diamonds. Chiqui paid Lalo back the fifteen-thousand he loaned him and began working with his own money. Every penny that Chiqui made, he invested in jewelry for Marta. He saved the gold as a reserve.

They bought a small house. This time it was made of zinc, had a cement floor, and they already had the bed and kerosene stove. Two months after they moved to the new house, somebody knocked on the door in the morning.

Chiqui was not too pleased with the news he was delivered. "Cono Chiqui! Get up. Somebody broke into your office," the person yelled. All the money Chiqui was saving was gone. He managed to save twenty-five-thousand bolivars in a small jar. The only one who knew where the money was happened to be a photographer he trusted. Even though Chiqui always knew it was him, he chose not to confront the thief.

When Chiqui told our father about the robbery over the phone, he said to Chiqui, "What people steal from you, God gives it back to you in double."

Chiqui had to take Marta's jewelry to a pawnshop and use that money to start over again. This time, at least some miners knew Chiqui as a buyer. He kept working and put together eighty-thousand bolivars when Marta came down with yellow fever.

Her condition was so bad that she would get better, then relapse, seventeen times in one year. She had high fevers, chills, headache, muscle aches, and vomiting. Her yellow fever was jungle yellow fever, transmitted by mosquitoes that were infected by monkeys. It was a common disease among miners and many people died from it.

Chiqui took her to Santa Elena for treatment because in Icabaru, the doctors said that she would die. Chiqui stayed with her in Santa Elena and as time went on, their savings went down to nothing. Chiqui had no choice but to stay at the hospital. During the day, he shared the hospital food with Marta and at night, they slept in the same bed.

Marta required intravenous care for one month and once she felt stronger, they went back to the mine to start over again. As soon as Chiqui got back in Icabaru, he went to a buyer he knew named Pedro Hungaro and asked him for a loan of 50,000 bolivars to get him going again.

In Icabaru, there is a government branch in charge of taxing the mining industry. Since Chiqui had no license to legally operate as a buyer, they came and closed his doors, putting him out of business. At this point, Chiqui was getting used to having nothing and starting over again, so to him, this was just another inconvenience to work around. Giving up was never in mind.

Chiqui decided to go with Marta to Ciudad Bolivar to get the paperwork required by the taxation department to operate legally as a diamond and gold buyer. This would take two months. Before Chiqui left, he offered the office that he had subletted from Lalo to another buyer nicknamed, "Bolsillo Loco," or "Crazy Packet." He was thankful for the opportunity to have a proper office and location. Chiqui did not charge him because his intention was to help the man, since he already knew how hard it was to start from the bottom.

When Chiqui returned two months later, he went to the office and said to Crazy Packet, "I'm looking forward to working again now that my papers are in order. I would thank you if I can have my office back tomorrow." His answer left Chiqui speechless.

"Down the street is another office for rent. You better go and find out because I'm not going anywhere," he replied.

Chiqui had been subletting the office from Lalo, but the real owner was Manuel Garcia, who lived in Ciudad Bolivar. His brother, Pedro, was an alcoholic who managed to get three months in advance of rent from Crazy Packet. So, Chiqui flew to Ciudad Bolivar and explained the situation to Manuel Garcia. He was disappointed at his brother's abusive behavior and said to Chiqui, "We are going to the mine together tomorrow."

Manuel Garcia was a wealthy diamond buyer who owned a small plane. He was one of the best pilots Chiqui ever flew with. However, he never did maintenance on his plane. The door latch would not keep closed, so Chiqui had to hold the door closed for the duration of the flight which was a two-and-a- half hour trip. The starter motor did not work either, so with the ignition on, he would go out and spin the propeller by hand. The whole plane was nothing less than a mechanic's nightmare, yet it still worked.

Manuel and Chiqui cleared everything up and got the office back. A month later, Chiqui offered to buy the office from Manuel for fifteen-thousand bolivars. The office was big enough for Marta and Chiqui to live in the back, so they moved in. Marta became pregnant and on October 19, 1993, their daughter, Joanna Paola, was born. Joanna Paola was two months old when they were invited to Jairo's house, a good friend of Chiqui, to celebrate his niece Clara's twenty-second birthday. She lived in Barquicimeto and came to the mine for two weeks to visit his uncle's family.

On the day of the party, Clara was thinking of going back to Barquicimeto but Jairo insisted she stay to celebrate her birthday. When Chiqui showed up at Jairo's house, Carlos Medina and Jose Ruiz were already there and had been drinking since the early afternoon. By eight at night, they were drinking scotch and playing chess. Jose Ruiz began acting like he was possessed by the devil. He took his gun and pointed it right at Chiqui.

In his drunken stupor, he said, "What would happen if I kill you right now? I just have to pull the trigger and you are dead." This situation went on for two hours, making everyone nervous. Carlos and Chiqui tried to calm him and distract him from waving the gun but had little success. At one point, Jose pointed the gun at Carlos and pulled the trigger. Fortunately, the gun did not fire. It was not his day.

At that moment, Clara came into the room and aware of what was happening, brought a bowl of food to Jose Ruiz, hoping to distract him from the gun.

"Jose, please eat. Just calm down and eat. I can bet you that if you put something in your stomach, it is going to help you feel better," she said to him. Now, all his anger was directed towards her.

"You are going to sit here with us and eat it," he taunted. Clara got up and walked toward the door to leave the room. Jose yelled, "Sit down! I am talking to you!"

When she turned around to look at him, he shot her in the neck, right in the aorta. Everyone got up and ran outside in fear that more people would be shot.

Clara saved Chiqui's life. If Jose had not killed her, he would have killed Chiqui, since that was his intention the entire night. Chiqui was in shock for many days after. To this day, he still cannot believe what happened that night.

Jose was caught and went to jail for only three months. Now he is a free man living at the mine. He does not remember what happened that night.

Things started to improve for Marta and Chiqui. Now that Chiqui accomplished his goal of being in the top twenty buyers, it was time to set a new goal: to be among the best. Being one of the top meant that he would have a large flow of business. This flow came at a price which he paid a long time ago when he was getting started.

There were times when Chiqui made a deal even if he would lose money, simply to establish trust and movement in his business. Over time, these miners brought other miners, thus growing the business. The miners found him easy to deal with and trustworthy. They knew that if they needed help, they could come to Chiqui. Many buyers came and went. The reason he remained in business in the same office was because Chiqui never gave up and made many sacrifices to stay in business. He denied himself little pleasures and put the business first.

Many times, Chiqui wanted a can of soda but decided to save the money. Staying open until ten and eleven at night brought him a miner or two who also worked late. What got him where he is right now is perseverance. He said, "No guts, no glory." By 1996, Chiqui was an established diamond and gold buyer when Cesar Gomez, the richest diamond buyer in Venezuela, came to the mine and asked Chiqui to work for him. He was nicknamed, "the King of Diamonds." Carlos Gomez, his brother, was the only competition Chiqui had, and he had his powerful brother to back him up.

In the beginning, Cesar gave Chiqui one-hundred-thousand dollars to buy diamonds and gold. Chiqui always sent to him the production from the mine in sealed packages with a pilot. In return, Cesar would send Chiqui cash through the pilot. Most deals were verbal, and many times were done through other people because Chiqui was at the mine and Cesar was in Ciudad Bolivar.

Two years after working together, Chiqui went to Ciudad Bolivar to take a break from the mine and visit Cesar to talk about business. When Chiqui showed up at his office, he said, "I sent you one-hundred-thousand dollars a month ago, and you owe that to me in production."

Everything in Chiqui's brain started moving in slow motion. Chiqui was saying to himself, "Maybe I am sleeping and very soon I am going to wake up. This cannot be real."

Chiqui looked at him in disbelief. "I don't know what are you talking about," Chiqui replied, very honestly.

Meanwhile, Chiqui was trying to pull himself together, so he asked, "Who did you send that money with?"

He did not have an answer since he had so many people working for him. Since there was no explanation to back up his story, he said his accountant wrote a check to Chiqui and sent it to the mine with a pilot. Chiqui asked him to speak to his accountant because Chiqui wanted to have the canceled check that was supposedly made out to him. Chiqui never received it, which meant it couldn't have existed.

Some people say that it was the accountant who was fraudulent, but others say that it was Cesar himself who tried to get Chiqui out of the mine so his brother Carlos could become the biggest buyer of Icabaru. Although Chiqui did not owe him that money, Chiqui knew it was time to play his cards the right and careful way. So Chiqui agreed to pay him what he claimed he owed.

Chiqui knew the dollar was going up which would make it easier for him to pay his so-called debt, so Chiqui asked for the opportunity to keep working for him.

"No," he replied, very simply and bluntly.

Once Chiqui realized that he was out with Cesar, he had to regroup because he did not want to start again at zero. Luckily, Chiqui had some savings that allowed him to stand on his own. Now it was time to prove himself, and Chiqui had nothing to lose since he already had lost everything.

Every lot of diamonds that was taken to Carlos's office was also brought to Chiqui for appraisal. If Carlos offered one million, Chiqui would automatically offer more just to make the deal. Chiqui didn't even inspect the lots before making the deal.

Now his goal had become to get Carlos out of the mine and to remain as the number one buyer in Icabaru. It took him six months to accomplish this goal. Carlos left the mine and Chiqui became the number one. During that time, Chiqui did not have a friend willing to give him a hand, so he had to do it on his own.

At the end of six months, Chiqui had given Cesar eighty-thousand dollars. Marta was in Ciudad Bolivar with the children when she got a phone call from a very close friend.

"Tell Chiqui to come immediately to Ciudad Bolivar," the friend prompted Marta.

When Chiqui began working for Cesar, he asked Chiqui to sign a blank note. It was supposed to serve as an agreement between them, since Cesar was the one using his money to put Chiqui in business. This is a common thing between buyers; and usually after business is going well, it is ripped up and thrown away. Chiqui was surprised to find that Cesar falsely filled out the note for an additional hundred-thousand dollars and was thinking of taking Chiqui to court to press charges. This time, Chiqui was furious.

Chiqui went straight from the airport to his office.

"What the hell do you think you are doing? I have not done any harm to you and you know very well that you did not send those first hundred-thousand dollars to me. You know what? Here is the twenty thousand remaining of the money you claim I owe and I want that blank letter with my signature. How can you dare to write in that blank letter another hundred-thousand dollars that I don't owe you in the first place?" Chiqui confronted him.

He actually obliged with Chiqui's demands. Chiqui got the letter back, and for four years, remained at the mine without going to Ciudad Bolivar. Chiqui got the strength back, and eight days before Cesar was killed in a car accident, they spoke about working together again.

Cesar was leaving for Belgium on January 30, 2002. Early in the morning, before Cesar left to Puerto Ordaz, his brother Alfonso showed up to say hello. Cesar asked him to join him during the trip. In the car were Cesar, his brother Carlos, who was driving, Alfonso, and a twenty-two-year-old friend whom Cesar invited many times to go to Belgium. They were driving fast to catch the plane. Five minutes before getting to the airport one tire blew out. Because of the high speed, the car went out of control. It flew over the divider and over the oncoming lane into the hillside. Cesar, Alfonso, his brother, and his friend were killed. Carlos was the only survivor.

Cesar was only forty-two years old. He accomplished so much in his short life. He was basically in control of the diamond market in Venezuela.

There may never be another king of the diamonds because this reputation can be dangerous. Now, it is safer to be small. Many buyers have been robbed and killed because of the large economic gap amongst people living here.

Another problem Chiqui was confronted with in this business was people coming from other countries and carefully gaining their trust. In the beginning, they dealt with him on a small level to prove their worth. As time passed, and more deals were made, larger deals were proposed and latter paid off to maintain their status.

Once they came with an incredibly large deal, and asked Chiqui to supply them with ten times the amount of diamonds or gold of previous deals. Since they were trusted in the past and their word was honorable, Chiqui trusted them. These friendly foreigners disappeared with the gold and diamonds that weren't paid for and never heard from again.

For fifteen years, Chiqui went through hard times but always remained optimistic. Perseverance is the key to success. In the jungle, where life is lived in the wild, small planes offer transportation to and from the jungle. This is risky for reasons like rapidly changing weather conditions and unregulated aircraft maintenance. As a result, there are more than four or five plane crushes annually. The survival rate for these crashes is ten to twenty percent. Pilots generally fly with dead reckoning and no real sophisticated navigational aids. Once the planes are in the clouds or fog, they are as lost as anyone walking in the dark.

The airstrips are short, from two hundred to three hundred meters. There are other obstructions, such as tree lines at the end of the runway, or sometimes a hillside which make takeoff and landing dangerous, even on a good day. Risks such as these are what make this kind of job and lifestyle exciting to Chiqui. You become addicted to the unpredictability of outcomes, which is the same adrenaline rush you get from gambling.

Chiqui does not regret the life and hardships he chose.

CHAPTER 30: A Garden of Emotions

Sandra Bonilla Lopez was born in Cali on April 7, 1965. She is the oldest and only daughter of three children. Her mother, Libia Lopez Gonzales, inherited from her mother the dedication and service to the underprivileged, as well as a fondness for praying and going to church. In her younger years she was a beautiful woman with white skin and pretty features, especially her brown, vibrant eyes. Her hair was black and she had a gracious, proportioned figure. Even though she was a beautiful woman, she always had the idea to become a nun but was rejected in her first attempt because she was an only daughter.

The rejection from church did not change her inner qualities. Her kindness, generosity, and beauty made her very attractive to men her age. Sandra's mother studied to be a commercial secretary and worked in that profession for many years. She got married for the first and only time when she was twenty-seven years old to a young man from Flandes, six years older than she.

Sandra's father, Alfonso Bonilla Cuellar, was born on June 27, 1932. He was tall, elegant, and so handsome that Sandra's mother could not resist falling in love with him. He took everything very seriously and was strict, demanding, and responsible. He was the oldest son of four from a very old-fashioned family. He studied technical accounting and worked as an assistant of purchase in a multinational organization in Cali for most of his life.

As a couple, Sandra's parents were envied by many people and after many years of marriage, they still love and respect each other. As parents, they had been the best. When Sandra and her brothers were growing up, their father did not sleep if one of them got sick. It did not bother him to get up at any time of the night to give them medication.

When Sandra's father came home from work, he would bring a new toy to whomever was convalescent. He would get a chair, sit close to the bed, and read out loud. After the children fell asleep, he would check on them to make sure that they were alright and that no mosquitoes bothered them. He covered their bodies with a blanket, turned off the light, and prayed for them very softly. He did not like them to know he was there.

During the children's school years, both parents were their private teachers. They were good students and learned from their mother to be organized and methodical. Their father emphasized acting honestly and never lying. When the kids were growing up, he did not punish them as long as they told the truth.

In August 1992, Sandra was in her last semester at the "Universidad del Valle" taking final exams to complete her master's degree in finance, when she met Jose Carlos. He just finished his master's degree in soil and water at the Universidad Nacional in Palmira. They had many things in common and enjoyed the simple things in life, like going to the movies or spending an afternoon watching a bullfight.

Even though Sandra and Jose Carlos went to a disco once in a while, it was not their best way to spend time. They had been raised with the same values and were an old-fashioned young couple with a good sense of responsibility and maturity. All of these qualities made Sandra realize he was the man she wanted to spend the rest of her life with. On March 18, 1995, they were married.

They had the wedding reception at Club La Rivera in Cali. Me, being Jose Carlos' sister, and Mama came from New York. Coworkers, friends, and members of both sides of the family were present. The night ended splendidly with a serenade arranged by Sandra's brother. They played a beautiful song that touched everyone. We could not hold our tears back.

Two days after the wedding, Sandra and Jose Carlos went on a honeymoon to San Andres Island. The second day, Jose Carlos rented a motorcycle and they traveled around the island. Carlos was so excited to see the ocean that he steered the motorcycle down a road he thought would be as smooth as the others. This road was very bumpy with rocks and soft sand, making it quite a challenge. They went down and Sandra banged her nose painfully on the sand and cut open her knee. Slowly, her breath came back as the tears poured down her face. Despite her situation, Jose Carlos was laughing.

After the honeymoon, Sandra and Jose Carlos returned to their apartment which Jose Carlos bought before they got married. They had no furniture and were sleeping on an inflatable mattress on the floor. It was near five in the morning when Sandra whispered into Jose Carlos' ear, "I am pregnant."

Jose Carlos was so excited that he could not even talk straight or go back to sleep. "That's good! At least we are not sterile," he blurted out. Sandra hit him in the head with a pillow. That cured his speech problem and really woke him up. They looked at each other and he could see how angry Sandra was over his comment and she accused him of being insensitive. They were going to be parents—this was a big deal and very serious.

It was not easy when Jose Carlos' friends joked with them about how quickly Sandra became pregnant. They made fun of the couple by comparing the whole pregnancy to the gestation of a chicken's egg. Sandra guessed they meant since she got pregnant so quickly, the child would also be born in no time.

Jose Carlos understood his friends' sense of humor and laughed with them, but Sandra saw nothing funny and tried hard with a smile to conceal her disappointment and humiliation. She could not understand why educated people would compare the conception of a baby to a chicken.

It was not difficult to choose the name of their son. It would be Juan Camilo, which they chose even before getting married. The pregnancy was what so-called "normal" is. Sandra was throwing up in the morning and disliked eating rice. While Jose Carlos was working, Sandra spent the days at her parents' house and after work, Jose Carlos would pick her up.

On their way to the apartment, they passed a large outdoor meat market. Fresh killed cows and pigs hung on hooks in open refrigerator trucks and men moved large pieces of raw meat on their shoulders. The smell of blood and fresh meat was everywhere. Sandra could not bear the sight of it and the smell made her sick to her stomach. Her likes and dislikes became so predictable that they carried plastic bags for the occasional vomiting. Sandra preferred the long way home with plenty of fresh air and the lights of the highway rather than the shortcut through the meat market.

Juan Camilo was born on December 4, 1995. His features were a carbon copy of his father's, especially the Arbelaez nose. It was big and flat for his little face and was the only thing you could see when he was wrapped in a blanket.

He was a very peculiar boy with a strong frown and a deep stare. He did not like to drink water and would only drink maternal milk for the first four months. On one occasion, the family went to my sister, Maria Luisa, and her children in Ibague. Once there, Sandra and Jose Carlos decided to go for a ride to a nearby town called Corregimiento de Guayabal in Armero. The heat was so intense and they could not believe that Juan Camilo was actually drinking cold water for the first time. He kept growing as a healthy boy, even though he refused to try new foods.

Since a very early age, he showed great interest and ability for tennis. It is his favorite sport to this day. His leadership and power of conviction was noticeable since he was three years old.

One day, Sandra's parents were busy receiving a delivery when Juan Camilo took his cousin's hand and walked out of the house to the corner where his grandmother took him on many occasions to buy candy. As soon as Sandra's parents noticed the boys disappeared, they began looking everywhere, thinking the worst. Friends and neighbors joined in this frantic search. About a half an hour later, the boys showed up holding hands with their guardian angel. They did not understand the commotion the adults were creating over them.

Juan Camilo got bored with his toys very quickly and was always looking for something new to do. Sometimes, he liked to climb onto the hood of my father's car and then up the windshield onto the roof while holding the radio antenna. They do not know how many times he did this, but he became very good at it and fast.

When Sandra and Jose Carlos bought clothing for Juan Camilo, he loved to have them next to him before he went to sleep. He was afraid of clowns, as he was of the clock when it announced it was one in the afternoon, time to go to school. It was also the hour that required more creativity from Sandra to get him from underneath the bed where he used to hide and cry. It was a hard task to make him wear his blue and white uniform, white socks, and black moccasins.

He cried the three blocks it took to get to school and jumped with happiness when he was picked up, especially if it was Sandra's father, Alfonso. His excellent sense of observation and his uniqueness made him Sandra's parents' favorite grandson.

In April 1999, my sister, Maria del Pilar, called Jose Carlos from New York. She was aware of the economic situation he and Sandra were going through and asked them to come to the United States. She was dating Joseph Seviroli at the time, who owned a pasta factory in Garden City. He offered Jose Carlos a job. Sandra had been unemployed for almost two years and even though she had occasional work, it was not enough to contribute to the monthly expenses, and above all, to come up with the money to pay the four months they were behind in apartment payments.

It was a decision that did not take long to make. Sandra and Jose Carlos had no other option. The three of them got visas and made the trip immediately. Jose Carlos left, and the following month, Juan Camilo and Sandra joined him. Sandra had to sell the furniture, electric appliances, and make sure the apartment was rented out.

Those days were very difficult for Sandra, especially since Jose Carlos was not with her to provide emotional support. They did not have a lot of furniture because their objective in the beginning had been to buy little by little but good quality.

Sandra made a list of the things she could sell, such as the washing machine, microwave, refrigerator, television, stereo, computer, and bedroom and dining room sets. She had no time to be sentimental since she was very busy paying the bills and interviewing people who wanted to rent the apartment.

When Sandra gave people the things she bought with so much love, she suddenly felt the emptiness. She was nostalgic because she was cutting from the root the dreams she looked forward to for all of her life. Sandra could not resist taking pictures and videotaping the little things that were left. She knew that these would be the last memories of her first home.

Sandra videotaped the balcony of the apartment. It was her favorite place. It was unavoidable to hold back the tears while saying goodbye. Sandra thinks the balcony was more beautiful than any other part of the building. It had a moon shape that displayed a beautiful helecho plant from Miami. As the plant grew, it wrapped itself around the cement column and went up to the next floor. Next to it, were two veraneras. One was vibrant yellow and flowered twice a year. Its arms became intertwined with another veranera, which had a bright red flower. To the right, there was a fuchsia azalea that Jose Carlos gave to Sandra when they were dating. At the end, Sandra had a full red biflora, a gift from her grandmother.

Gardening had become such an important part of Sandra's life that during those sad days, it was her only refuge. Her grandmother used to say, "Plants can feel the mood change of the person who takes care of them. For a plant to be beautiful and healthy, it is important the plant is given to you with good intention and there must be a feeling of sincerity and affection from both sides—the giver and receiver. Otherwise, no matter how much you try, its growth is stunted."

Maybe it was the strong bond Sandra had with her grandmother that led her to believe the biflorea started to decline as she prepared to leave. It was like a message of sadness from her grandmother in heaven.

The days leading up to their departure for America came quickly. Sandra rented the apartment and spent the last week at her parents' house with her son. Sandra thought that saying goodbye for a long time was going to be very hard, especially for Juan Camilo, whom her father adored.

Despite the feelings, Sandra and her parents got the strength to hide the pain. A little inconvenience at the airport when they were registering the bags distracted them from a long, emotional goodbye. Immigration was questioning the date of the authorization letter for Juan Camilo that would allow him to leave the country.

Sandra had to go to another window to be approved. From there, Immigration sent her to the supervisor who gave her a green light. Solving the issue took longer than anticipated and the departure time for the flight was getting closer.

Finally, when Sandra thought they would miss the flight, she got the seal of approval for Juan Camilo. She put a mask of happiness over her sadness and hugged her parents, brothers, and little nephew, Julian Andres.

"Goodbye. We will see each other soon. I promise," Sandra said very simply but with a heavy heart. Once on the airplane, it was different. Juan Camilo fell asleep almost immediately and Sandra could not avoid crying. A new and unpredictable life was waiting for them in an unknown country. This new life was taking them very far from their loved ones.

Sandra and Juan Camilo arrived at JFK airport in New York on June 30, 1999. Juan Camilo was very happy to see his father again. That made Sandra forget the sadness she felt for leaving her family behind. Together, next to four bags full of memories, they waited for the destiny waiting ahead.

It was not easy to get adjusted to the changes of this new life. Jose Carlos was with our family and little by little, Sandra accepted the idea that leaving Colombia was the smartest decision she made. She and Jose Carlos helped her parents pay the bills and apartment in Colombia. At the same time, their son learned the English language and got the flavor of the culture he would embrace as a grown man.

In October 2004, Sandra and Jose Carlos received their green cards. It was the happiest day of their lives. Life in America could not have gotten any better for our family.

CHAPTER 31: A Love Story and Bob

The Tavern on the Plaza was a pub-style bar in Locust Valley, New York built in 1965. It had English/Irish décor and was a very popular place. There was a unique clientele that frequented the Tavern: lunch time would attract retired and wealthy locals, and happy hour was a combination of semi-retired and established working-class people. Weekends and nights attracted kids new to the legal drinking age and anyone who loved to party and listen to loud music or swing from chandeliers.

Weeknights, the Tavern was relatively quiet, with the television playing sports. It was a Tuesday night, February 2, 1996, when I met Jeffrey for the first time. He went to have a few beers alone and watch "Magic" Johnson, the famed basketball player who had been let back into the professional league. Jeffrey was not a basketball fan, to say the least, but decided this particular evening was special to watch Magic Johnson rejoin his team. Jeffrey also thought it would be a quiet night at the bar. That was true until I showed up with four sisters and Bob, from whom I was already separated for six months.

Jeffrey was sitting at the L-shape end of the bar minding his own business and he immediately looked up when the five of us walked through the door, followed by Bob. He kept watching us as we moved to the bar, and while we ordered drinks, Jeffrey was trying to figure out the best way to approach me. He noticed Bob went to the jukebox and began playing Frank Sinatra. Jeffrey, being a Frank Sinatra fan, figured that this would be his opportunity to speak to Bob. He knew that the only way to me was through Bob. So Jeffrey approached Bob while he was selecting a song and said, "Did you play the last song?"

Bob looked up at the stranger and smiled. "Yeah, did you like it?"

To that Jeffrey replied, "I love Frank Sinatra's music." They immediately began talking about all kinds of music. Finally, Bob asked Jeffrey, "What kind of work do you do?"

Jeffrey said, "I work with Vintage Race Cars." Once Bob heard that, he could not leave Jeffrey's side. Bob was tremendously enthusiastic and began telling Jeffrey a story of a 1966 Shelby Hertz car he rented and drove as if he were a racecar driver. Bob could not talk fast enough about that lifetime experience. Jeffrey told him that he built an engine similar to the Shelby's and had put it in his grandfather's 280 SL Mercedes. Then, he pointed out the window to the parking lot. "The Mercedes is right out there if you want to check it out later."

Bob and Jeffrey hit it off so quickly that Bob invited Jeffrey to meet my sisters and I. He specifically turned to me and said, "I want to introduce you to a very interesting man." All of us have the first name Maria and when Bob introduced each one of us to Jeffrey and we said our names, he thought that we were joking with him.

He stayed and chatted with us for the rest of the night. Before Jeffrey left the Tavern, he made sure that I had his phone number. I called him five days later and we agreed to meet at the Main Maid Inn in Jericho New York. Built in 1789, it had been a temporary hiding place and a safe house for slaves heading north to freedom after the Civil War.

When Jeffrey was heading to the Main Maid Inn to meet me for lunch, he had a strong feeling that a life-changing event was about to happen. He confided in his friend John, "I don't know what is going to take place, but I'm about to find out—I feel it in my bones." He was kind of staring off into space while saying, "I can picture the beautiful woman in my mind with no apprehension. I know my life is about to change. I'm going to meet the girl of my life."

When I arrived, Jeffrey was already waiting for me. He told me that when we made eye contact the first time we met at the Tavern he said to himself, "Oh my God, what just happened to me? I wonder who the girls are with her, and the older man in the blue blazer. Obviously, he plays an important role in their lives." And that's why he tried to figure out how to speak to me.

Jeffrey said, "I never expected Bob to take me to you, the beautiful girl I was interested in. He virtually took me by the hand and brought me right to you. Sometimes you can hope for things but this worked like magic, and there I was, face to face with you, the girl I was aching to meet. Saying hello to you for the first time was a very attractive and moving feeling and judging from the way you greeted me, I felt like it was mutual. It was the first time in my life I felt like I was hit by a ton of bricks. And that's how I felt when I met you. I was so happy to stand next to you and look at you enjoying our conversation."

And for three months after that first lunch date, we met at the Main Maid Inn. We shared stories with each other and took our time getting to know each other. It was a romantic courtship.

Meanwhile, Bob refused to leave Mama's house where he felt loved and most importantly, he was not alone. He became my best friend and when we got divorced I did not ask for anything. Bob was adored by the whole family and the Arbelaez family was the only one he had. His three children lived in other cities and he saw them very infrequently. For that reason, he clung desperately to the family that received him with unconditional love, and that was my family.

One night I got a phone call from Jeffrey inviting me to go out. Near the telephone was a closet, and while I was talking on the phone, I heard a noise. I opened the closet door and there was Bob, hiding with a cordless telephone, listening to my conversation. I was furious and yelled at him, "Bob, this time you crossed the line. You are forgetting that you were the one who allowed your son to kick me out of the house, not once, but *twice*. You helped put my clothing into the back of your car as if you were going to drop me off on someone else's doorstep. Do you know what a mirror is? When was the last time you looked in one and actually saw yourself?" He had no response. He looked at me like he was a complete fool and it made me feel bad.

The relationship between Jeffrey and I had enough strength to wait six years for Bob to accept the fact that he and I were at a point of no return. What kept Jeffrey and I together was the love he felt towards me. He did not just love me, he adored me, and that allowed him to wait patiently for the day I would get rid of the feelings of guilt and responsibility that I had for Bob.

Our wedding was set for February 2, 2002. By that time, Bob left Mama's house and found an apartment in Old Westbury, New York, five minutes away from so he could still see the family. For the wedding, Jeffrey found a 1928 Daimler Limousine which was not only in disrepair but needed new tires and a paint job. It had been in somebody's garage, unused for twenty-five years. It was an elegant and prestigious car in1928 and Daimler was used by the royal family of England.

For Jeffrey to know I would ride in a beautiful enclosed car gave him a great enthusiasm to move forward with the repair work. He worked every night to get it ready. He stripped the old paint, fixed the dents on the body, primed it a few times, and painted it dark blue.

I told Jeffrey that it had to have a red stripe down the side from front to back. I was constantly asking him, "Is the red stripe on the car?" and Jeffrey would respond, "I'm not at that point yet." Finally, one day I asked him if the red stripe was on the car and he replied, "Yes, dear, the red stripe is on the car."

"Good. Now we can get married," I told him. The car was finished a week before the wedding. Felipe drove me to the Episcopal Church in Westbury, Long Island and we held the reception at the Main Maid Inn-a place that had much significant meaning to our love life and future together.

The day before the wedding, Felipe took Bob out to dinner and told him, "Bob, after six years, you need to let go. You need to go and live your own life. You are not losing us. You will always be a part of our lives." Felipe had a good reason to have great admiration for Bob. After all, he was the father figure since Felipe was fifteen. He always harbored unconditional love toward Felipe to the point of seeing him as if he were his own son. Bob and Felipe would keep their relationship, even though I was marrying another man, and Bob would remain a loving and welcome figure in our family,

From Felipe to me before the wedding:

To Mary

Thank you for giving me life, thank you for watching for me, thank you for giving me school, thank you for buying me clothes and toys and for taking me out to eat ice cream and lasagna, and for taking me to the movies and to the pool.

Thank you for bringing me here to this country and for giving me college and for giving me a car and for giving me respect. Thank you for being so honest, filled with good advice and understanding.

Thank you for pushing me to travel and being supportive and for always putting me in first place. Thank you for being so good and pure and if I am ever criticized of giving too much of myself or helping someone too much or being stupid for letting others take advantage of me or being too nice, I can only blame it on your example with everybody around you. I know that I can be distant sometimes, but I really don't mean it.

I wish I was a little more expressive with you and be able to pay you for everything you have done for me, but the debt is too big. My heart thanks you for saving my life during my hepatitis and my appendicitis and my head surgery and my hand surgery, and for making my ulcer better and for being with me during my knee surgery.

Thank you for the trip to France and the trip to Hawaii (I had the best time). Thank you for helping me move out not once but twice, and for pushing me harder than me. Thank you for being supportive about my career decision and trusting me.

Thank you for respecting my relationships and coming up with the most precise advice at the most needed time. My thanks got to you for not only being my mother but my guardian angel as well.

My love always, Felipe.

I wish you nothing but the happiest life any mortal could have during marriage.

CHAPTER 32: Tragedy on The Mountain

Pilly and her husband Joe were on the top of the mountain on a ski trip when the unexpected happened. Joe stood up slowly, feeling as if his chest was going to explode. He said to Pilly, "I'm dizzy" and fell right back down. He tried to get up again and looked at Pilly with sadness; his face was as pale as if blood had stopped flowing. He fell again. Pilly began to shout for help to everyone who was skiing near them, "Someone please help me! My husband needs help, is there anyone who can help me please?! He may be having a heart attack!" Two people who were going down the mountain stopped and began to give him mouth to mouth resuscitation. Unfortunately, there was nothing that could be done.

In her heart, Pilly knew Joe had died. She felt it was the end of the world not only for him, but for her as well. She had been waiting for so long to find the love of her life, the man who fulfilled her completely. Pilly not only loved Joe, she was infatuated with him. She admired him, respected him, and now could not even hope for a miracle. This was it. She said to herself, "Oh my God, how am I going to live without him? From where am I going to draw the strength to overcome this loss?"

Five minutes before, a paramedic came by and asked Joe, "You don't seem okay, would you like to go down on a sled?" He stubbornly said no. He was too proud to let anyone know he needed help. The same paramedic came back and put Joe on a sled and Pilly on another to lower them from the mountain. Mama, who was down at the lodge with John Joseph, saw Pilly while they lowered her. She was covering her face. The first thing Mama thought was that she had an accident and hurt her face. The fact that Joe was gone was the last thing Mama would have expected.

Three days before, on February 18th, Joe planned a trip to Aspen, Colorado with his entire family, including his son Joseph, his daughter Maria, his grandchildren, John Joseph who was only nine months old, Pilly, and Mama.

Joe suffered from diabetes and high cholesterol, and before the trip, he told to Pilly, "I have been having this strong pain in my chest and it goes all the way to my back. I think I should see the doctor before we leave for Aspen." Joe went to see a doctor who said, "I think the most prudent thing to do is to cancel the trip and go to the hospital; you are having all the symptoms that indicate a possible heart attack." But Joe decided that he was going to take care of his health issue when he returned from Aspen.

Before leaving the apartment, Joe came to the door and without having stepped outside the threshold, he returned. He went into each room looking at each picture, each vase, and all the art he proudly chose when he decorated the apartment. Many times in life we walk right pass the things that once were important without looking at them. That day, Joe looked at everything as if it were the first time, with nostalgia, as if he was saying goodbye.

When they arrived at the airport, Joe was very quiet, which made Pilly concerned. She knew that he was not well, but Joe did not want to ruin the vacation he planned with such enthusiasm.

"Joe, tell me the truth, how do you feel?" Pilly looked at him, distressed and afraid of his response. He said, "Don't worry, I'm fine," while making a great effort to make his voice sound spontaneous.

The next day they went skiing and he remained silent and cranky during the day. That night, Pilly had a dream with two hundred brides dressed in white. When she opened her eyes, she said with tears in her eyes "Somebody is going to die. It's going to be Joe or John Joseph."

The following morning everybody went to have breakfast at Joe's daughter, Maria's, suite. Joe ate two eggs and when he finished, he asked for two more. Pilly said, "Joe, don't you think you had enough?" His answer was "This is what I want to eat today."

At around ten in the morning, Joe and Pilly went skiing and Mama stayed with John Joseph at the Lodge. Joe was an excellent skier but that day he fell three times. When they were down the mountain after the first climb, Joe said to Pilly, "What a nice day. You have given me the best six years of my life and you have made me immensely happy." On previous occasions, Pilly asked Joe, "What is the most important thing for you in life?" And he always answered "money," to which she replied, "Joe, money is not the most important thing in life. We should not take for granted that we are healthy, have a beautiful son, and are alive."

Later that day when they were going up the chair lift, Joe asked Pilly, "What is the most important thing for you in life?" Pilly said, "Joe, I know what the answer is for you and it will always be money." He said to her, "Today I realized the most important thing is not money." There was a sense of loneliness and foreboding in his voice. They got to the top and skied down the mountain and met with Mama and John Joseph for lunch. When they finished lunch, they were saying goodbye to Mama when Joe decided to wake up John Joseph who was asleep. Joe lifted John Joseph with one hand high above his head and balanced him there while Mama took a great photo of a father proud of his new son.

Pilly and Joe went to ski again. When they were getting on the lift Joe said, "I should not have gone up." Pilly, listening to him with anguish, begged him to go down but he insisted that he wanted to ski one more time. "I want you to know that I have five thusand dollars in my pocket in case something happens to me," Joe said to Pilly when they reached the top of the mountain.

They got off the lift, and he fell at the first bend. They both took off their skis and sat on the snow waiting for Joe to feel better. It was there at the top of the mountain where Pilly saw her husband, the man she adored, take his last breath while she hugged him and begged him not to leave her. It was February 21, 2002.

In 1996, I was separated from Bob. He did not have a place to live and asked Mama if he could stay at her house while he found an apartment. At the house, everybody loved him and he became my best and unconditional friend. One day, like many others, Bob invited my sisters Pilly, Maria Alejandra and I to a restaurant called Piping Rock, which was located on Post Avenue in Westbury, New York.

While we were getting ready to go out, Pilly was taking a bath when her body began to tremble uncontrollably. It was as if the other world was sending her a telepathic message and inadvertently she heard herself saying, "Today I will meet the man I'm going to marry." When we got to the restaurant with Bob, there were only two men in the bar with us.

When Pilly saw Joe, she felt a slight chill in her body. At the restaurant they were playing music and Joe asked Pilly to dance with him. They danced the whole night and when it was time to leave, Joe asked Pilly, "Are you married?" She replied, "No, I have been waiting for you all my life."

After two years of dating, Pilly went to clean Joe's apartment and while she was in the bathroom, she saw a black hair in the drain. She felt like she wanted to throw up. Her hands trembled as she said to herself, "How could he do this to me after I gave him all my love?" After the first moments of confusion, she realized that despite how much she loved him, she had to end their relationship.

Three months later, Joe came back asking for forgiveness. Pilly said to him, "I would prefer to live with you the best six years of my life and not thirty with someone I would not love."

Pilly and Joseph John Seviroli got married in October 2000 and John Joseph was born in April 2001. They were as Pilly predicted, the best six years of her life.

After the funeral, Pilly came to the realization that the man who made her happy was gone forever. She thought that her life no longer had purpose, so she began to smoke. It was as if the smoke of the cigarettes clouded her brain and helped her somehow reduce the pain.

Three years later, Pilly spent the night with John Joseph at Mama's house. It was December 31st, in the morning, and with tears in her eyes she asked Joe, "If it is true that you ever loved me, I want you to let me know by showing me the biggest heart I have ever seen in my life." When John Joseph woke up, Pilly put a video of Barney on television. She was lying on the bed next to John with her eyes closed when she heard Barney say, 'I'm going to show you the biggest heart you ever saw in your life." When Pilly opened her eyes, Barney was showing a huge heart that covered almost the entire screen. Pilly got up immediately and rewound Barney's video. The heart was there but not the phrase she heard so clearly.

For eight years, Pilly's heart was in mourning. Somehow she found it difficult to accept the idea of living without Joe. Mama took care of John Joseph while Pilly went through those difficult years. When she finally learned to live with the memory of Joe, she began to take care of John and started regaining the time with him from when she had died with Joe.

Chapter 33: The Rooster

My husband works with Vintage Race Cars and part of his job is to go to racetracks in different parts of the country. On these occasions, I would take advantage of staying at Mama's house. The house has a room with a fireplace and a private bathroom which was annexed more than one hundred years ago. It is wallpapered papered with the minute men of the Civil War. This is where I like to stay.

At four in the morning, Sandra is in the kitchen preparing breakfast for Carlos, who goes to work early in the morning. They had been living at Mama's house with their son, Juan Camilo, since they came to this country in 1999. Carlos has been a father figure for Luisa's children, including John Joseph. Unfortunately, they lost their father when they were very young.

At five in the morning, Pepe, a Venezuelan troupial bird, starts whistling. I like to get up late, but at Mama's house there is so much activity in the morning that it forces me to rise early. By seven a.m. the smell of hot chocolate is all over the house. Mama is in the kitchen making arepas, which are Colombian tortillas that she grilles on a small electric burner next to the stove.

Maria Alejandra comes downstairs to get ready for work; Felipe arrives with his dog Izzi, a Staffordshire bull terrier, who then gets to play with Mama's dogs Sacha, a Border Collie, and Muneca, a Maltese. Meanwhile, one by one the rest of the family, who are also getting ready for work, congregate and greet one another in the kitchen.

Monica lives nearby with Carlos Mario. Every day at eight in the morning she shows up at Mama's to say hello and to have a cup of coffee before she goes to the office that is only a few blocks from Mama's house.

In the kitchen, Mama placed a television on the counter which is on all the time. By this time, the birds are also waking up and talking. Tonyo, an African grey parrot, two Amazon parrots, and J.J., a Blue Macau, who have been in the family for many years.

Typically it is a harmonious morning which evolves into discussions of various types. The subjects can be social, political, or personal. Sometimes the conversation escalates into a political debate because one disagrees with the other while everyone adds their opinion to the discussion at hand.

This can appear to be somewhat argumentative, but all is forgiven and each has learned from the subject. Toyo becomes part of the debates and we can hear him in the background saying, "Que paso?" "What happened?" He barks exactly like Muneca the Maltese and repeats everything he was taught by each one at the house.

The most exciting moment is when the rooster is let out of the cage. His feathers are bright and have vibrant colors. He is big and has arrogance written all over his body. Once out of the cage, he runs into the kitchen. He is used to the family gathering in the morning and likes to be fed by everyone while they are having breakfast.

The rooster came into our lives three years ago. Isabella was five years old, and Felipe and Natalia had just learned that their next child was coming into this world. Everyone was happy about it, but Felipe was concerned about the five years difference between Isabella and Camilla.

Natalia was three months pregnant when Felipe said to Isabella, "I'm going to teach you how to hatch a chicken egg." Felipe's intention was to have Isabella understand what a new life was about and for her to have the understanding and the acceptance of the new freshly hatched animal into life. Felipe wanted Isabella to love her new sister rather than feel that she may have somehow been preempted or had taken her place.

I live on a farm where there are chickens and fresh eggs every day. Felipe asked Jane Armstrong who raises chickens at the Dairy in Lattingtown, New York, "Jane, can you give me four fresh eggs? My wife Natalia is pregnant and it's very important that my daughter Isabella understands the importance and responsibility that involves creating a new life."

Felipe did his research with Isabella on how to hatch an egg and then got everything together: the Styrofoam box, the heat lamp, the temperature and humidity sensors, and the glass top, along with a light dimmer to create a daytime to nighttime light cycle.

Every day the two of them rotated the eggs periodically. This prevented the yolk from sinking down and pressing the chick against the shell. Felipe marked each egg with a marker so he could turn them every eight hours as a mother hen would do with her beak. This was taking place in a two-bedroom apartment on a third floor in Williston Park, Long Island in New York.

The incubation of the chicken eggs took twenty-one days, and Isabella and Felipe watched with great enthusiasm, waiting for the moment to see the egg shells crack open and the chicks arrive to their new life.

Seventeen days later, Felipe was observing each egg, holding them up to the light to see if there was movement and he only found one that was in fact alive and moving. He said to Isabella, "From the four eggs we incubated, only one survived. Let's make sure this egg gives us a chick."

On the twenty-first day, the chick began to break the shell. Isabella had just arrived from school and was changing her clothing when she heard Felipe calling, "Isabella hurry up! The chick is starting to break the shell. Love, it's very important you understand that you should not help the chick break the shell. This is a strengthening moment and experience for all animals that hatch from eggs. It also adds tenacity to their survival."

At five in the morning, Felipe woke Natalia and Isabella. "I want the two of you to witness this magical moment we have been waiting for."

In the afternoon, the chick pecked holes in the shell and the process took so long that the poor chick had to take breaks to rest. This went on for seventeen hours. Isabella was frightened thinking that the chick was dead, when it finally got out of the shell and did not move right away.

Almost crying, Isabella asked Felipe, "Papi, is the chick dead?" He said, "No my love. You have witnessed how long it takes for the chick to break free from the shell and it is obvious that he is exhausted and does not want to get up or move right away."

Felipe suddenly realized that the chick was relying on him, as if he was his mother. In the morning, Felipe had to go to the office and realized that he had no choice but to take the newly born chick with him. His office is at a travel agency owned by the family. The office is run by my sisters Pilly and Monica, as well as my sister-in-law Sandra. When Felipe arrived at the office, they got very excited to see this little chick, which they had all heard about.

Every movement Felipe made, the chick would follow him. If he went to another room and left it alone, the chick knew Felipe was out of sight and began to cry, "Pio, pio, pio…" This made everybody laugh because the chick thought Felipe was his mother and Felipe thought it was wonderful too. But now he had this new responsibility.

During the evening, Felipe got home with the chick and Natalia and Isabella were delighted to see the little thing and marvel over it. When it was time to go to sleep, the chick would not be quiet unless Felipe was next to him. The morning of the second day, Felipe realized that he must find a solution for the situation, and while having breakfast, said to Isabella, "This afternoon as soon as you get back from school, we are going to a farm out east that raises chickens." Isabella said, "It's going to be a long morning. He is so cute that it will make me very happy to have more of them."

It was summer, Felipe's air conditioning was not working, and it was a hot day. It took them one hour to get to the farm. When they got to there, the owner said to Felipe, "Listen, if the chicks are going to be raised for consumption, I would not sell them to you." Felipe replied, "I hatched four eggs hoping that all were going to make it. Unfortunately, this is the only chick that survived and he needs company." The farmer said to Felipe, "You need to buy two chicks. In the event one dies, the new chick will still have company and can also learn normal habits from them."

Felipe got the two chicks from the farmer and drove one hour back home. As soon as he got home, Felipe realized the chicks were dehydrated so he gave them Gatorade and they were doing well in no time.

Felipe and Isabella's new chick did not know how to eat on its own and quickly learned by watching its two new friends. He put them in a big cardboard box. They grew very quickly and the cardboard box became too small in just a few days, as they were able to jump out in no time. Felipe went to Mama's house and said to her, "Mama, now I don't have one chick, but three. Can I bring them here? You have a big backyard and I can build a coop for them." Mama, who loves animals, immediately agreed.

Felipe built a big and strong coop in Mama's backyard. It turned out that the egg that Felipe hatched was a beautiful, colorful rooster and the two chicks were hens. As they grew, the hens followed the rooster around. The problem was that the rooster did not have a role model and started singing at three or four in the morning, waking up the neighbors. Afraid of the neighbors complaining to the Village, Mama put the rooster in a cage at night inside the house and the hens remained in the coop.

In the morning when Mama let the rooster out of the cage, he went straight into the kitchen and became part of the early gathering. He was fed by everyone while they were having coffee and the rooster quickly became part of the family. He still did not know when to crow or when not to crow, and so unexpectedly throughout the night, he decided to crow and wake everybody.

Things got complicated when the chickens started laying eggs every day. There were only two eggs and to have a Solomonic decision at Mama's house with so many people, it was decided that every day in the morning was going to be a raffle.

One day a friend of the family with a high position in the police department stopped at Mama's to say hello. Mama was very happy to show him the fruit trees and other exotic plants she planted around the house. They were enjoying their walk when suddenly the rooster felt his domain invaded and ran up behind our friend and began to peck him on his butt. It was so unexpected that our friend got so scared he began to run, only to find that the rooster was behind him, nipping at his butt, again and again. It is not every day you see a man well-versed in combat being chased by a rooster.

One day Mama received a letter from the Town Hall asking her to get rid of the rooster and the hens. On the following morning when the rooster did not show up asking for food in the kitchen, we all knew that the rooster and the hens were gone forever. We mourned them for many mornings and missed the eggs raffle.

Forty years earlier, the whole family still living in Colombia, we would have been faced with the possibility of Mama cooking the rooster and the hens and offering them to us for dinner. Fortunately this time, Mama gave the rooster and the hens to the man who cut the grass at her house. His wife was pregnant and craved chicken soup.

CHAPTER 34: It Takes a Village to Catch a Bird

It was winter and starting to get dark when Mama realized she had not heard Tonyo's voice while she was cooking in the kitchen. All the bird cages are close to the front door. It is common for Mama to take Tonyo out of the cage a couple of times during the day where he sits on his perch in Mama's view from the kitchen. Mama talks to the bird and the bird talks back. Tonyo's ability to repeat and talk back is fascinating to the entire family. When Mama realized she had not heard anything from the bird for a while, she began to walk out of the kitchen and look for him in the dining room. He was not there, so she went to the living room and he was not there either.

She began to call him, "Tonyo, hello Tonyo. Where are you?" Mama's heart wanted to leave her body when she realized the bird was not in the house.

At about four in the afternoon, my sister Claudia came to Mama's house. Later, when Claudia was leaving, she left the door open just enough and Tonyo flew out of the house without her knowing.

Mama began to search outside in the dark with a flashlight. The bird knows Mama very well and would come to her under normal circumstances, but now the bird is outside, it is cold, and he is not familiar with every place. Mama bought Tonyo four years ago when the bird was only five months old and he did not have a clue about being outside on his own. He was not familiar with flying since he lived in a bird cage. For him to fly for three seconds in the house would have been his maximum distance.

Mama continued searching for him outside the house and around the house calling, "Tonyo, come to Mama Tonyo!" It was getting colder and this made her panic even more. While she was walking around the block looking for him, she was so distressed that she said to herself, "What am I going to tell everyone at the house if I don't find him?" She kept searching with the flashlight and thought, "Why did I not pay more attention? I should have clipped his wings; if I had done it, this would not be happening." She was getting tired, frustrated, and cold. "God, I promise you that if I find Tonyo, the first thing I'm going to do is clip his wings." Her biggest concern was that he would be eaten by a cat.

Mama decided not to alarm anyone. After three hours of searching, she decided to come back to the house, set a candlelight for the Holy Host and the Blessed Chalice, offered to go to Mass that coming Sunday, and went to bed.

She knew it was going to be a long night. That night while she was crying against her pillow, she looked at the clock and wished the clock handles could move faster so her agony would end sooner. The only thing Mama wanted was that it should become dawn as soon as possible in order to resume her search.

At five in the morning, Mama got in her car and drove one mile per hour, street by street, looking at every tree. By six-thirty, she found Tonyo at the park across the street from Westbury Middle School, five-hundred feet from her house. Mama was bursting with happiness. The joy did not fit in her body and she thought she was going to explode; all she wanted to do was to scream for anyone to hear that she had found Tonyo.

She immediately came back to the house, climbed the stairs as fast as she could, and knocked hard on Julio Cesar's bedroom door, as if wanting to knock it down to wake him up. Mama was screaming, "I found Tonyo! I found Tonyo!"

At seven in the morning, my phone rang. It was Julio Cesar, "Mary, you have to come immediately. Tonyo got lost yesterday and Mama just found him in a tree." I could hear the excitement in his voice. In half an hour the whole family received a phone call. Everybody showed up at the park where

Tonyo was still sitting on a branch in the tree where Mama found him.

We got out of the cars and were smiling. The question now was how to get the bird to come down from the tree. This was the time of day when most people were getting ready to leave their homes to go to work. This made it much easier for us to track Tonyo as he began to move east through the neighborhood. Fortunately, there was no one at home to ask permission when Tonyo started to fly from yard to yard.

We were twelve people coming onto private property, sometimes over fences into the next backyard just so one of us could keep an eye on where Tonyo landed next. Felipe said, "Let's throw sticks at him. Maybe we can get him to fly down from the tree." Meanwhile, John Joseph was throwing his football accurately at him, but all this did was make Tonyo fly five to ten seconds to the next tree of his choice.

For us on the ground this meant jumping in our cars and drive to the next block or street in the direction Tonyo was last seen flying. Communication with everyone involved was shouting over a backyard fence to someone that might be on the next street to guide to where Tonyo flew. This went on for hours and it was still very cold out.

That morning I made a phone call to an animal rescue association. A woman with a friendly voice answered the phone, "Hi, this is Kathy, how can I help you?" I said, "Kathy we need your help. Our African grey parrot, Tonyo, is up in the trees and we have been unable to get him down." I was drowning in tears. She answered with the certainty of someone who knew what they were talking about. "I'm familiar with recovering birds. I have to drop off my kids at school and I will be there as soon as possible."

When Kathy showed up, she brought with her a big cage, with a big white cockatoo, and a net. We gathered around her while she described the many ways to recapture a bird in this situation. She said, "It's important to get the bird wet, that way he would not be able to fly." That sounded like the last thing we wanted to try to do because of the cold weather and not knowing if Tonyo was going to survive.

Many times we were close to Tonyo. He was sometimes eight or ten feet high and John Joseph, very good with the football, could hit or spook the bird from the branch he was on. This only led to the next fifteen minutes of confusion about which backyard had he flown to next. By this time we had been in at least fifteen backyards, driveways, and front yards.

Frustrated and not getting anywhere, Jeffrey said, "The idea of getting the bird wet makes sense. I'm going to Carlos Mario's house to get his pressure washer." By the time Jeffrey came back with the pressure washer, the recovery of Tonyo had become an attraction in the neighborhood. Once people learned what was taking place, they were all willing to help in any way they could.

In a moment of disbelief, a red tail hawk spotted Tonyo and began to circle. The hawk got closer and closer while Tonyo was perched on top of a telephone pole. Finally the hawk came in and made contact just for a moment with Tonyo. We shouted at John Joseph, "John, throw the football." John Joseph threw the football at Tonyo and the bird flew from the telephone pole to a tall pine tree in someone's backyard.

There was a section way up high in the pine tree that looked as if a part of the tree was missing. That was where Tonyo chose to land. The hawk was in a nearby tree watching Tonyo when suddenly he made his move and again flew towards Tonyo. We began to scream as we feared the worst. We shouted so loud that it was enough to spook the hawk and he flew away. Tonyo stayed on the branch; the hawk came back one more time, and we screamed him away again.

We were very lucky. There was a garden hose and an elevated deck in the backyard where Tonyo was. Felipe moved the pressure washer to the deck yard, made the connection, and made it ready for use. Felipe tried to spray Tonyo to get him wet, but it did not spray high enough, so we got up on the deck. Still it was not high enough. Jeffrey got on top of the railing surrounding the deck and carefully stood as tall as he could with the pressure washer in his hands.

There were at least four or five people steading his legs and feet on the railing so he could focus only on being sure he would hit Tonyo with the water from the pressure washer. The spray finally reached Tonyo only for a moment, which seemed not enough and Tonyo flew. We noticed immediately his flying brought him lower and lower very quickly to the point where he was so much lower in the nearby trees than we had seen him in the beginning. He was easy to spook and came down again, finally to land in a low level pine tree, six feet high. This was our chance.

Jeffrey said to John, "Get the net now and don't worry about the bird." In the corner of a fence in the backyard was this pine tree that Tonyo finally landed in, at our level.

Jeffrey told John, "Just go after him with the net, you will get him!" And he did. Tonyo screeched and screeched while John had him tangled in the net and Jeffrey said, "Don't worry about him, and just stay with the net." Felipe came and handled the bird carefully with his hands, getting him out of the net.

We all shouted, no longer with fear but with euphoria and happiness.

The feathers of the poor Tonyo were dripping water and he was shaking. He had been exposed to the cold weather for so many hours and in an environment completely unknown to him.

Felipe wrapped him in his jacket and we went to Mama's house. Kathy followed us and kept saying, "I have never seen so many people trying to save a bird. I'm impressed by the tenacity and persistence you had to get him back."

Immediately after, we took Tonyo to the veterinarian to make sure that he had not been hurt by the hawk.

We could not believe that twenty-one hours later, we had Tonyo back in the family. There is a special reason to understand why this situation ended the way it did. Mama always instilled in us the importance of being together in any circumstance, in good as well as the bad times. A single phone call was made and it did not take more than five minutes for people to show up to help physically and mentally. What a blessing.

EPILOGUE

Sometimes, life is filled with challenges that we do not have control over. When life throws these obstacles in our path, it is up to us, as individuals, to jump over them or let them deter us from moving forward.

My family and I were in many situations that constantly made us question if we were making the right decisions. But as you can see, we persevered, and none of it would have been possible if it weren't for Mama.

Mama taught us to push past all roadblocks, to always look toward the positive things in life, and to create our own opportunities when they weren't served on a silver platter before us. My brothers took control of their lives when they decided to work in the mines and become successful diamond buyers. I took risks when I tried to find myself and where I belonged in the world. I realized that I did not belong anywhere but in America. And what led me to America was my dear mother. She was the first to leave us, but the first to reunite us. She knew that, no matter what, we would all find our way to her—like chicks following a mother duck.

We all live a better life now that we took the risk of making it to America. Whether it was illegally or legally, we took the risk for love and for our family. In the face of pain, starvation, animosity, and loss, we persevered. And here we are today: a reunited, happy, loving family that grows by the day with laughing grandchildren and smiling relatives and friends. We couldn't be happier.

When life gives you lemons, make some lemonade. My life has been blessed with the gift of family and strong bonds between us. Had it not been for these blessings, I do not think I, nor anyone else in my family, would have found our rightful places in the world.

Thank you, Mama, for being the beacon of light and symbol for hope in our family. I hope that many others experience the same love, devotion, and commitment as we have. We all need that strong figure in our lives to make us see through the fog, past the obstacles, and into the light. I followed Mama's light to the end, and so did my brothers and sisters.

America has been good to us; it is the land where dreams really do come true.

ACKNOWLEDGEMENTS

Mama is the one that I will never be able to thank enough. She started raising her family at age fourteen and through good and bad times, she never once thought of abandoning any of her nine children. To her, it was not an option. Where her stamina, strength, and drive came from, I cannot imagine. It seemed as though she never stopped working to take care of the family, along with her birds and dogs, which she viewed as part of the family. I love her dearly; she is the center of all our hearts. I thank my Mama as the heroine in this book for everything she has done for the entire family.

Felipe is my son, my only child, and my inspiration. There is no doubt in my mind that God blessed me with a truly wonderful person. He has never once been a burden to me. He was born with wisdom, almost as if he had been here before. I have always been taken aback by Felipe's way of kindness, consideration, and the true gentleman that he is. There were many times while raising Felipe when I felt like he was raising me. He has tremendous patience and is a great listener which allows him to help people find solutions to their problems.

Learning and reading have been his passion, including Shakespeare and the classics along with history. He has been this way from the time he was a child and now he is feeding this to his two children, Isabella (11) and Camilla (5). Natalia Parra Jaramillo is the woman who came into his life as his bride. Together they are raising their daughters whose manners are impeccable. Natalia and Felipe make sure of this. Isabella and Camilla are my two queens.

I want to thank my brothers: Julio Cesar, Jesus Fernando, Jose Carlos Augusto, and my sisters: Maria del Pilar, Maria Luisa Fernanda, Maria Claudia Mercedes, Maria Alejandra, and Monica Patricia, as well as my nephews and nieces for the wonderful times we have shared, good and bad altogether. You give life to the chapters of this book.

My special thanks to my oldest brother, Julio Cesar. You showed me that there was a world out there beyond my small thinking. I learned many things from you: you taught me how to be strong, wise, and fearless, which empowers my ability and desire to go places and experience life. You are the one who opened my eyes and showed me that I was the only one that could put limitations on myself.

My Aunt Maria Belisa is my mother's sister. She has been living in the United States since 1966. She would frequently travel back to Colombia and visit Mama. She could see the hardship in Mama's day-to-day life and encouraged her to come and live in America. Mama seemed to be interested but would not make the journey, until the youngest child, Monica, would be fourteen and taken care of by the older siblings. Maria Belisa finally convinced Mama, and in 1986 she came to the United States. We are all grateful to Maria Belisa who got the ball rolling for the family to be reunited in America. Had it not been for her, I'm quite sure life would have been very different and nowhere near as good as it has become. The tremendous ripple effect of her influence cannot be put in words. She is responsible for new families of ours being raised in this wonderful country.

Thank you to Steven Bergano, photographer from Creative Compositions Fine Photography, for photographing me for the cover. Also, many thanks to Charles Kruvand who allowed me to use his photo for the background of the cover. That photo holds a lot of significance to my family. The photo is of Mariscal Canyon Rio Grande River in Big Bend National Park. Charles is from Austin, Texas and his photos appear in many museums. I am so thankful for him to share his beautiful artwork with me in support of this project.

I needed a special person who could guide me to finish this book the right way. Dr. Joan Digby, Professor of English at LIU Post, you have been an angel to me. Thank you for everything, including the countless hours you spent piecing together the artwork of Steven and Charles to create the front and back covers of this book. I know it would not look as amazing as it does now if it weren't for your hard work and dedication.

Thank you Chloe Margulis, with your experience in writing books, for helping me throughout this process with synthesizing, editing, and creating the final version. I enjoyed working with you to piece together the stories of my family and breathe even more life into the pages of this book.

ABOUT THE AUTHOR

My name is Maria I. Norton. I was born in Colombia and have resided in the United States since 1987. I went to Nassau Community College and studied surgical technology. Did not graduate. I graduated from Queens College with a major in Anthropology and a minor in Psychology. I have a Master's degree in Gerontology from Hofstra University. I was trained by the well-renowned hypnotist, Gerald (Jerry) Kein, in Hypnosis at the OMNI Hypnosis Training Center in DeLand, Florida, and I'm a Reiki Master.